Autobiography: A Reader for Writers

AUTOBIOGRAPHY
A READER FOR WRITERS

~~~~~~

Robert Lyons

Queens College
of the City University of New York

NEW YORK

OXFORD UNIVERSITY PRESS

1977

Third printing, 1978.

Copyright © 1977 by Oxford University Press, Inc.

Library of Congress Catalogue Card Number: 76-42671

Printed in the United States of America

PREFACE

The purpose of this book is to help students gain confidence and control as writers by using their own experience as a starting point for their writing. Students writing autobiographically can approach their subject with less anxiety, since knowledge of that subject is already theirs, possessed in a way that could only be approximated with an academic topic. As a result, students are better able to concentrate on exploring the many different ways to communicate their experiences to an audience. Autobiography, then, makes the writer an authority, at least about his subject, and that initial security can serve as a powerful incentive to create an authoritative style.

The anthology is organized so that students may begin with informal and loosely structured forms of expression and then move on to more organized forms, such as narration and description, before concluding with autobiographical selections relying on a considerable degree of generalization and abstraction. The first chapter focuses attention on relatively spontaneous recollections (interviews and oral narratives, diaries and journals). Chapter Two includes a series of opening paragraphs from full-length autobiographies, illustrating how writers choose to introduce themselves to their readers. Chapters Three and Four deal with familiar occasions for memory (events and places) in which the writer must be concerned with selecting specific details and controlling them through point of view. Chapters Five and Six form a gradual transition to ways of generalizing from specific recollections, with the selections in the last chapter all being efforts at summaries and evaluations of experience. Chapters Three and Four, then, can be particularly useful in discussions of specificity and of structure in writing, while Chapters Five and Six provide an introduction to modes of generalization and abstraction.

Many teachers who include autobiographical writing in their courses agree that one of the greatest difficulties for students lies in making the transition from personal writing to the analytical and expository modes that customarily predominate in composition courses. When students are finally asked to write an academic essay, at whatever point in the semester, many of them fail to recognize the requirements of this specialized form and fail to adapt their writing to it. Their confidence vanishes, and with it their competence. This anthology tries to surmount the problem by implicitly offering a bridge to less personal and immediate forms of expression. The last two chapters emphasize how generalization and abstraction mix with the particulars of concrete experience within autobiography itself, so that a student, while still recollecting his own life, can become familiar with the kinds of language appropriate to academic writing. Because this book concentrates on writing about personal experience while anticipating that academic writing will be a necessary accomplishment for the college student, the anthology is perhaps best suited for the first half of a semester course in composition.

All the selections in the anthology were written in English, and most are by contemporary writers. Brief headnotes with biographical information about the author accompany each selection. An effort has been made to include several younger writers exploring their immediate pasts, and to include in Chapters Three through Five some selections that have a common subject matter (school experiences, descriptions of New York City, characterizations of fathers and other close relatives), topics that could easily be adapted and used by students in their own writing. In addition, one writer, George Orwell, is represented by a selection in each chapter of the book, so that students can trace one person's autobiographical impulse expressing itself through different subjects.

An introduction to each chapter defines some rhetorical issues that are particularly important for the selections in that chapter. Each of the selections is followed by questions for class discussion; most of these questions focus on the connections between rhetorical techniques and self-expression. The suggestions for writing by students offered at the end of each chapter often parallel the subjects and methods represented in the chapter's selections, so that some useful comparisons between student writing and published writing can be made. The suggested topics also follow the book's movement toward more analytical writing, and therefore topics involving the analysis of autobiographical writing itself are introduced only in the final two chapters.

Some brief comment needs to be made about how the readings in this book can supplement the writing the students themselves are doing. The selections are intended to represent a range of possibilities rather than an established set of models. Students should approach these selections not as sources of information from indisputable authorities, but as examples of autobiography written by people who, like themselves, are attempting to define for others something that they have experienced. If students can begin to think of these published writers as in some sense their peers, they can look at the excerpts as they might consult another classmate writing on a similar topic. In that frame of mind, they can examine the selections with a new kind of attention, seeing them as potential sources for anything from an evocative phrase or a dramatically compelling form of organization, to a general stance before the world. What can and should bring both "professional" and "unprofessional" writing fruitfully together for students is their growing sense of themselves as writers, to whom words and their placement on a page mean a great deal.

CONTENTS

CONTENTS

VI. Perspectives on Experience   329

Autobiography: A Reader for Writers

Introduction

Everyone who is going to write autobiographically has to get beyond the first awkward moment when he may think, "I have nothing to write about." A writer seldom recognizes how common that moment is, and is only uncomfortably aware that he has nothing to say about the one subject he should know best of all. The purpose of this anthology is to help writers learn how to regard themselves as a subject for their own writing, and how to write about that subject with authority.

We have all had the experience of meeting an old friend we have not seen for a long time, and of having the friend ask "What's new?" or "What have you been doing?"—in other words, tell me something autobiographical. Usually we shrug and say "Nothing much" or "Everything's fine." Obviously many things have happened to us, but it is difficult in a moment to isolate an event and to explain why and how it was important in our lives. We hesitate because, in effect, we are being asked to choose the autobiographical subject that best sums up the quality of our life since we last saw our friend. We are always relieved if there has been some publicly significant event that could serve to answer the friend's question—I got married, I changed jobs, I'm going to a new school—the kind of information that the local newspaper might print as part of the neighborhood news. Only after we have reestablished some intimacy with our friend do we relax, express ourselves more fully, and begin to create a more personal portrait of our life for him. The sources for this portrait are varied; they may be responses to specific questions by the friend, sudden random associations, or memories of shared interests in the past. Whatever they are they lead to specific recollections which, fragment by fragment, begin to compose an autobiographical sketch.

Our feeling of having nothing to say about ourselves is actually based on the enormous number of potential subjects (one could say that every moment in our past life is a potential subject) that momentarily paralyze our powers to choose and discriminate. In addition, we may not be used to seeing our own behavior from the outside rather than the inside. Unless we are in the habit of cultivating a certain amount of detachment toward ourselves, we may never have interpreted our own experiences or established links between the present moment and what has shaped it in the past or what it portends for the future. Of course, our lives are lived in the first person, not the third, and too much objectivity about ourselves can be dehumanizing, but some is necessary for self-understanding. If we have not thought about our actions, feelings, and motives, we have no way of verbalizing an answer to our friend's question.

One advantage we would have in talking about ourselves to a friend rather than a stranger is that we could call upon whatever shared experiences, interests, and values created the friendship to begin with. Many things could be left unsaid or explained by referring to some common memory ("It was a day like the one when we went sailing on Long Island Sound"). Consider instead another autobiographical moment, when we are being asked about ourselves by a job interviewer. In one sense, it may be easier for us to find something interesting to say, because we are likely to be asked specific questions about our background and experience, and we will have some clear expectations about the kinds of experiences we should be prepared to talk about. To a job interviewer, for example, we would probably present moments in our lives when we showed a great deal of initiative and responsibility and we would not tell the story of a balmy day of sunning and sailing on Long Island Sound. However, the main difference in this second autobiographical situation is that we are dealing with a stranger. Some of the same problems we had with our friend would still exist—choosing what to select and how to present

4

it—but we now would have to be much more conscious of an audience uninformed about our life and its context. We would have to include many more details in our story and we would have to make firmer and more conscious decisions about how we wanted to present ourselves. We could no longer rely on those casual kinds of shorthand communication that friendship and familiarity make available to us.

Whichever audience we have in mind, being autobiographical always forces us to select from the multitude of our minute-by-minute, day-by-day experiences, to give shape and order to our selections, and to convey to our audience some sense of why we have chosen to emphasize this particular aspect of our lives. Written autobiography follows this same process, whether it deals with private experience or public accomplishment. Moreover, written autobiography addresses an unknown audience, one that we can imagine to be as well disposed toward us as our friend, but one that we must remember has as little information about us as does the job interviewer.

The audience for autobiography in a writing class occupies a middle ground between friend and stranger. Although most of you, as students of writing, may not know one another personally at the beginning, you will share some common traits and some common experiences (the life at the school, if nothing else). Furthermore, you will become more familiar with one another through the meetings of the class itself and, most important, you will share a common interest in the craft of writing.

Autobiography involves a different kind of writing situation from that imposed by academic subjects, since you know your own experiences differently from the way you know the material in a history course. Writing about yourself, you are usually aware of the innumerable threads of thought and feeling that connect any one experience with other experiences in your life. For that reason there is invariably some sense of frustration when you try to catch your past in words. You may be among the many students who find that a less personal subject may prove less demanding, at least to their sense of what they can achieve as writers. For example, a college freshman can approach a vast historical topic, such as the American Civil War, and, after doing some research, can develop an ordered account of the main causes of this immensely complicated series of events. The student finishes such a paper with a sense of control, based in part on the fact that a good deal of the preliminary work of organizing his subject has already been done for him. Each historian he has read while researching the topic has offered him some pattern of causation for the war, so that the student begins writing with some coherent outlines for his subject already in mind. When the same student writes about a single moment in his own life, he finds himself uneasily trying to decide what details are important and what pattern of significance he can create for them.

On the other hand, there is one great satisfaction for the autobiographical writer; he is clearly in command, the best and indeed the only authority on his subject. If we sometimes feel inadequate to deal with our experiences in words, we should remember that no one else can make the attempt with anything like our chances for success. Especially for students who have to write in college courses, where the instructor is more knowledgeable about most essay topics than they are, writing about oneself should be a potentially liberating experience. Furthermore, the very difficulties of the autobiographical process that we have been discussing do have their own rewards, for the difficulties create pressure to clarify and interpret one's past in order to present it convincingly to a reader. Through the effort to find words to communicate transient experiences, a writer starts to formulate answers to such permanent questions as who he is and what he has accomplished. In fact, the motivation for many writers of published autobiographies is as much a desire for self-definition as it is a desire to create a public record of a life.

CHAPTER ONE

TALKING ABOUT OURSELVES

Part One – Recollections and Interviews

Introduction: From Speech to Writing

*This first chapter is intended as an introduction to the auto-*biographical process, offering some informal ways to experiment with being autobiographical. The first section of the chapter is devoted to spoken recollections directed to a listener, usually an interviewer, who with his questions prompts the speaker to remember more. Talking about ourselves is obviously less demanding than writing about ourselves, basically because we are so much more accustomed to talking than to writing. Although we may know someone whose particular form of eloquence is close to written prose, someone who we say "speaks in paragraphs," most of us feel more comfortable with speech because it is a less constrained, more improvised form of expression.

There are many reasons for this lack of constraint. First of all, speech seems a matter of the moment; in most situations, it does not involve the same kind of commitment on the part of the speaker as do words on a page for a writer. This impermanence gives us a sense of freedom, because we can elaborate upon, redirect, even contradict what we say as the flow of talk continues. Secondly, speech can always be assisted or complemented by the tone of our voice, the look on our face, the gestures of our hands, the position of our body—all additional and compelling features of our language. In addition, we have an audience present before us, who confirm or deny what we say with their reactions and who motivate our speech with their words in the give and take of conversation. Finally, because speech usually involves a far greater element of improvisation than does writing, we take pleasure in its spontaneity as a mark of its deeply personal quality, its capacity to reflect what is unique about each one of us.

This is not to say that everyone's speech has these qualities or that every situation in which we use speech calls them forth. However, when we read the record of Nate Shaw's spoken recollections, we hear the compelling speech of an immensely gifted storyteller raised in a society where an oral tradition still survives. Shaw's speech has the colloquial richness, the ease and directness, the narrative energy of a lively human voice. It also makes positive use of repetitions of words, phrases, and grammatical structures, as well as sentence fragments and run-ons; all of these devices would be inappropriate in most kinds of writing, but they have a powerful expressive force here. The most striking characteristic of all the spoken recollections included in this section is the sense of an individual voice that in each case still exists on the page.

It may seem odd to begin work on writing by concentrating on speaking, but on the other hand it would be difficult to write convincing autobiography without having a sense of what one's own voice sounds like and how and to what degree it can be transferred to the printed page. Writing and speaking are unquestionably separate activities, rather than different versions of the same process; writing, however, is learned later and more formally than speech, so it should, as our "second language," draw as much as possible on what we have mastered of the first. Grounding our writing on the characteristic cadences and patterns of our own speech is a way of making sure that the writing will never become completely cut off from its human source, and therefore will not disappear entirely into the faceless, voiceless world of cliché and jargon.

Speaking can also lead us to writing in another way, since speaking is a more familiar and less inhibiting form of communication. When we need a starting point for our written work we should take advantage of our ability to produce words quickly and easily in speech. Our beginning forays into our past life ought to rely on the freedom of association, the opportunities for sudden digression, and the lack of formality that we associate with oral expression. In addition, the interview, a familiar source for oral autobiography today, can be a great help in making us see what kinds of questions we need to ask ourselves as we start to become autobiographical. In fact, a very useful way for students to begin working with autobiography is to trade off the roles of interviewer and interviewee with other classmates, learning both to formulate and to answer questions about personal experience. Ultimately, the procedure becomes internalized, and the writer is able to explore his own experience by interrogating himself.

A valuable first step for the writer, therefore, is to use self-questioning in order to re-create as many facets of an autobiographical event as he can. Sense impressions, feelings, actions, relationships with other persons (if others are involved in the event), causes, and results—all these elements contribute to the event and any one might prove central to an understanding of it. For example, a student knows that attending his high school graduation was somehow a memorable event in his life, but he cannot think of any way to talk about it and make it personal until he starts to re-create the event out of its many details by asking himself about those details. What did the hall look like? How did I feel as I entered the hall? Who was on the speaker's platform? How did each speaker behave and what did he say? If I can't remember those details, why not? Was I thinking of other things during the ceremony? What were they? Why did they come to my mind just at that time? In fact, questions often tend to produce other questions, or one mental image of the past will lead to another, so that if we begin actively to explore some past moment, the process itself rapidly becomes more comfortable and more rewarding.

This same process of exploration is often even more important when a writer feels that he can communicate his experience without any kind of self-questioning. Sometimes, of course, that may be true, but often the result is surprisingly trite and impersonal. For example, we all have some sense of what a high school graduation would be like, even apart from whatever we experienced ourselves, because we have often read accounts in newspapers or watched television coverage of such events. It then becomes very easy for a writer to rely on what he knows about the standard form of such an event in any school—walking into the auditorium, singing the school song, listening to the valedictory speech, receiving the diploma from the principal—and to transpose it into the first person. He can go ahead and write because he feels he has enough to say, but in fact he introduces virtually nothing that would represent the distinctive nature or quality of his own experience of the event. Actually exploring his memory will certainly help the writer who is unable to get started, the writer who has difficulty getting beyond conventional summaries of his experience, and even the resourceful and talented writer who may find in some previously ignored detail a new dimension to an event that he then may want to develop. A writer may produce material at this stage as simple lists of words or phrases that trigger his imagination, as ordered notecards, as paragraphs of random fragments of recollection, or as stretches of free-form associative writing. The method chosen depends on the individual's preference and on simple experiments to find out what works best and proves most congenial to his creative energies.

∽ Harry S. Truman ∽

(1884-1972)

Harry S. Truman was born in Missouri. He became involved in politics after his failure in business during the Depression. He was U.S. Senator from Missouri (1934–44) and then became Vice-President under Franklin D. Roosevelt. When Roosevelt died in 1945, Truman became the thirty-third President of the United States and won election to a full term in 1948. Merle Miller, novelist and journalist, conducted a lengthy series of interviews with Truman at his home in Independence, Missouri, in 1961 and 1962 and later published them under the title Plain Speaking *(1973).*

THE HAPPIEST CHILDHOOD

[HARRY TRUMAN'S FIRST JOB]

Mr. President, tell me about your first job.

"Well, when I was ten, maybe eleven years old, I got a job at Jim Clinton's drugstore on the northeast corner of the square in Independence. I had to get there at six thirty in the morning and set up the place so that when Mr. Clinton came down, he would find everything in order. I'd mop the floor and dust off the bottles and wipe off the counters, and then I'd wake Jim Clinton at seven."

Did you ever have any early-morning customers?

"Oh, yes, a great many. The people who were church members, the high hats in town, the ones who were afraid to go into

13

a saloon and buy a drink, they'd come in, and I'd have to set out a bottle of whiskey, and they'd pay a dime for a drink before most people were up and around to see them. They'd put their dimes on the counter, and I'd leave all those dimes there until Mr. Clinton came in, and he'd put them in the cash register.

"All those fancy high hats, they'd say, 'Harry, give me a drink,' and I'd do it. And that's where I got my idea of what prohibitionists and high hats are. That's the reason some of them didn't like me. Because they knew I knew their background and their history.

"There were saloons all around the square, and the tough old birds who didn't give a damn about what people think, they'd go into the saloons and buy a drink when they wanted it. But as I say, the so-called *good* people, the fancy ones, they'd come in and buy a drink behind the prescription counter from a boy who didn't have any right to sell it to them.

"But that's the way I got to . . . well, feel a lack of respect for the counterfeits, and I don't care where they are. In Washington or wherever. There's a story they tell about this high hat that got to be Postmaster General of the United States. I think Mark Twain told it on him.

"He got to be Postmaster General, and he came back to his hometown to visit, and there wasn't anybody at the station to meet him but the village idiot. And the high hat wanted to know what people in the town had said when they found out he was Postmaster General.

"And the village idiot said, 'They didn't say anything. They just laughed.'

"That's what happens if you're a high hat and start taking yourself too seriously."

Do you think you ever did that, Mr. President?

"I tried not to. I did my level best not to, and if I had, the Boss and Margaret wouldn't ever have let me get away with it."

Mr. President, I understand that when you were still a boy, you got a job working as timekeeper for the Santa Fe Railroad.

14

"I worked for an old fellow named Smith. L. J. Smith his name was, and he was head of the construction company that was building the double track for the Santa Fe Railroad down here from Eaton Falls to where the Missouri Pacific comes into the Santa Fe down at Sheffield.

"I was eighteen years old, and I'd just finished high school and knew I wasn't going to get to go to West Point. So I took this job as a timekeeper. I took it to help out at home, to keep my brother, Vivian, and my sister, Mary, in school. My father was having a hard time with finances just then.

"Old man Smith had three camps, and there were about a hundred hoboes in each camp, and I got very well acquainted with them. My job was to keep tabs on them, to keep track of how much time they put in, and then I'd write out their paychecks for them. I'd usually write those checks in a saloon on the north side of the square in Independence here, a saloon called Pogunpo's or in old man Schmidt's saloon in Sheffield. I used to sit there and pay off those hoboes. And they weren't bad fellows. They'd work for two weeks. They'd get discounted if they drew their checks before that time. So they'd work two weeks, and then they'd spend all their money for whiskey in the saloon and come back to work the next Monday morning. I'd pay them off on Saturday night.

"But they weren't bad fellows. Not in any way. Most of them had backgrounds that caused them to be hoboes. Either they'd had family troubles or they'd been in jail for some damn fool thing that wasn't a penitentiary offense. But they weren't bad citizens at all. I remember one time I told the old man that ran the saloon, he was an old Dutchman and wore whiskers, I told him, I said, 'This old bastard is the blacksmith out there on the railroad, and we need him. So try to cut out on his whiskey.'

"Well, damn old Schmidt went out and told this blacksmith what I'd said, and I never got a better cussing in my life than I did for interfering with the freedom of an American citizen. And he was right. And that taught me something.

"But after that I guess the blacksmith was grateful for it because he took a file, a regular ordinary file about that long and made a butcher knife out of it and tempered it so that the edge would never come off. He made two of them for me, and I think one of them is still around the house somewhere. . . . So he didn't hold it against me that I was trying to keep him from getting drunk."

When you said camps, what were they, houses or tents?

"Tents mostly. There were tents, and I had a tricycle car on the railroad that I went up and down on. I had to make a list of the men that were working every morning at seven thirty, and then I had to go back at one thirty in the afternoon to be sure that they were still there. So when the time came for their being paid, I had the records. No one ever doubted the records I kept."

How much did those men make?

"They made eleven dollars for two weeks' work, and as I say, they'd get paid on Saturday, and by Monday morning most of them had drunk it all up. But it was one of the best experiences that I ever had because that was when I began to understand who the underdog was and what he thought about the people who were the high hats. They felt just like I did about them. They didn't have any time for them. And neither did I. I always liked the underdogs better than the high hats. I still do."

Weren't you ever uneasy? I mean, you were a reader of books and wore glasses and, as you say, you'd been called a sissy.

"No. No. I never had any trouble with those birds. They were just as nice as they could be, and when I left, the foreman down there in Sheffield said, 'Harry's all right from the navel out in every direction.' Which when you come to think of it is just about the highest compliment I ever have been paid.

"Some of those hoboes had better educations than the president of Ha-vud University, and they weren't stuck up about it either. The average of them was just as smart as the smartest people in the country, and they'd had experiences, and a lot of them told me about their experiences. I hope I profited from it, and I think I did. I had to quit at the end of the summer, but my goodness, that was a great experience for me."

I understand you learned a few cuss words that summer.

"I did. The words some of those men knew I'd never heard before, but later when I was in the Army, there was an occasion or two when those words came in handy, and I used them.

"That experience also taught me that the lower classes so called are better than the high hats and the counterfeits, and they can be trusted more, too.

"About this counterfeit business. My Grandfather Young felt the same way. We had a church in the front yard where the cemetery is now. And the Baptists and the Methodists and all of them used it. And Grandfather Young when I was six years old, he died when I was eight, he told me that whenever the customers in any of those denominations prayed too loud in the Amen corner, you'd better go home and lock your smokehouse.

"And I found that to be true. I've never cared much for the loud pray-ers or for people who do that much going on about religion."

∽ Studs Terkel ∽

(1912-   )

Studs Terkel was born in New York City, but has lived in Chicago most of his life. Work as a radio announcer led him to develop an interest in oral history. He has published three books based on his tape-recorded interviews with a wide range of Americans, most of them not prominent or professional people. The following excerpt is from his most recent book, Working (1972), and reflects Terkel's skill in getting people to speak for and about themselves.

HEATHER LAMB

[A TELEPHONE OPERATOR AND HER WORK]

For almost two years she has been working as a long distance telephone operator at Illinois Bell. A naval base is nearby. She works three nights a week, split shift, during the high-school season and a full forty hours in the summertime. She is turning eighteen.

It's a strange atmosphere. You're in a room about the size of a gymnasium, talking to people thousands of miles away. You come in contact with at least thirty-five an hour. You can't exchange any ideas with them. They don't know you, they never will. You feel like you might be missing people. You feel like they put a coin in the machine and they've got you. You're

From Studs Terkel: *Working: People Talk About What They Do All Day and How They Feel About What They Do.* Copyright © 1972, 1974 by Studs Terkel. Reprinted by permission of Pantheon Books, a Division of Random House, Inc.

there to perform your service and go. You're kind of detached. A lot of the girls are painfully shy in real life. You get some girls who are outgoing in their work, but when they have to talk to someone and look them in the face, they can't think of what to say. They feel self-conscious when they know someone can see them. At the switchboard, it's a feeling of anonymousness.

There are about seven or eight phrases that you use and that's it: "Good morning, may I help you?" "Operator, may I help you?" "Good afternoon." "Good evening." "What number did you want?" "Would you repeat that again?" "I have a collect call for you from so-and-so, will you accept the charge?" "It'll be a dollar twenty cents." That's all you can say.

A big thing is not to talk with a customer. If he's upset, you can't say more than "I'm sorry you've been having trouble." If you get caught talking with a customer, that's one mark against you. You can't help but want to talk to them if they're in trouble or if they're just feeling bad or something. For me it's a great temptation to say, "Gee, what's the matter?" You don't feel like you're really that much helping people.

Say you've got a guy on the line calling from Vietnam, his line is busy and you can't interrupt. God knows when he'll be able to get on his line again. You know he's lonesome and he wants to talk to somebody, and there you are and you can't talk to him. There's one person who feels badly and you can't do anything. When I first started, I asked the operator and she says, "No, he can always call another time."

One man said, "I'm lonesome, will you talk to me?" I said, "Gee I'm sorry, I just can't." But you *can't*. (Laughs.) I'm a communications person but I can't communicate.

I've worked here almost two years and how many girls' first names do I know? Just their last name is on their headset. You might see them every day and you won't know their names. At Ma Bell they speak of teamwork, but you don't even know the names of the people who are on your team.

It's kind of awkward if you meet someone from the company and say, "Hi there, Jones," or whatever. (Laughs.) It's very embarrassing. You sit in the cafeteria and you talk to people and you don't even know their names. (Laughs.) I've gone to a lot of people I've been talking to for a week and I've said, "Tell me your name." (Laughs.)

You have a number—mine's 407. They put your number on your tickets, so if you made a mistake they'll know who did it. You're just an instrument. You're there to dial a number. It would be just as good for them to punch out the number.

The girls sit very close. She would be not even five or six inches away from me. The big thing is elbows, especially if she's left-handed. That's why we have so many colds in the winter, you're so close. If one person has a cold, the whole office has a cold. It's very catchy.

You try to keep your fingernails short because they break. If you go to plug in, your fingernail goes. You try to wear your hair simple. It's not good to have your hair on top of your head. The women don't really come to work if they've just had their hair done. The headset flattens it.

Your arms don't really get tired, your mouth gets tired. It's strange, but you get tired of talking, 'cause you talk constantly for six hours without a break.

Half the phones have a new system where the quarter is three beeps, a dime is two beeps, and a nickel is one beep. If the guy's in a hurry and he keeps throwing in money, all the beeps get all mixed up together (laughs), and you don't know how much money is in the phone. So it's kinda hard.

When you have a call, you fill it out on this IBM card. Those go with a special machine. You use a special pencil so it'll go through this computer and pick up the numbers. It's real soft lead, it just goes all over the desk and you're all dirty by the time you get off. (Laughs.) And sometimes your back hurts if your chair isn't up at the right height and you have to bend over and write. And keeping track. You don't get just one call at a time.

There is also the clock. You've got a clock next to you that times every second. When the light goes off, you see the party has answered, you have to write down the hour, the minute, and the second. Okay, you put that in a special slot right next to the cord light. You're ready for another one. Still you've got to watch the first one. When the light goes on, they disconnect and you've got to take that card out again and time down the hour, the minute, and the second—plus keeping on taking other calls. It's hectic.

∽ Nate Shaw ∽

(1885-1975)

Nate Shaw is the pseudonym of a black man from rural Alabama who worked the land as a sharecropper and tenant farmer all his life. Shaw was active in organizing a sharecropper's union during the 1930s and was jailed for twelve years on charges related to his union activities. In 1969, Theodore Rosengarten, doing historical research on the union, interviewed Shaw and discovered a man with remarkable powers of recollection and an extraordinary narrative gift. Rosengarten taped many hours of Shaw's oral autobiography and published it as All God's Dangers *(1974).*

YOUTH

[WORKING ON THE FARM]

My daddy put me to plowin the first time at nine years old, right after my mother died. I remember the first plowin he put me to doin. She died in August and he put me to plowin in October, helpin him plow up sweet potatoes. He had two mules and he had me plowin one and him plowin the other. And the potatoes was very sorry that year—plowin em up for Mr. Shelton Clay, plowin up the white man's potatoes, hadn't been plowed up yet. And in them days the weather would be warm late on up until near Christmas. In October that year the weather was warm and the gnats was awful bad. And doggone

From Theodore Rosengarten: *All God's Dangers: The Life of Nate Shaw*. Copyright © 1974 by Theodore Rosengarten. Reprinted by permission of Alfred A. Knopf, Inc.

it, the gnats looked like they would eat me up and I was just nine years old. So I would fight the gnats and my daddy got mad with me for that and he come to me and he picked me up by the arm and he held me up and he wore out a switch nearly on me, then dropped me back down. That was the first whippin he ever give me bout plowin. I just wasn't big enough for the job, that's the truth.

And that country where we was livin was rough and rocky. And he—my poor old daddy is dead and gone but I don't tell no lies on him—he put me to plowin a regular shift at twelve, thirteen years old. And I had to plow barefooted on that rocky country; anything liable to skin up my feet. And he'd go off, take his gun every mornin and hit the woods, practically every mornin, hit the woods and the swamps, huntin. And he was a marksman if there ever has been one. He'd go off with his gun and come back just loaded with game—shootin a old double barrel muzzle-loader too. You'd pour your powder in it and put you some paper in there and pack that powder tight. And he kept little sacks full of shot in his huntin pocket. Put that powder in the gun barrel, pack it down in there, then put his shot in there, charge of shot, push it down to that powder, just tamp it in place. You couldn't pack the shot in there; you could pack the powder close as you please, but when you put the shot in, pack it light. Then he'd pull them hammers back, take out his cap box, and set a little old cap on there—that's muzzle-loader style. Then he'd shoulder that double barrel muzzle-loader up. It was a long gun, too, longer than the average breech-loader.

And so he'd hunt and some mornins he'd tell his wife, my stepmother, "Give Nate his breakfast—" and he'd get his gun and step out the door, bolt across the woods, across the swamps, and he was gone. "Give Nate his breakfast and let him get to plowin quick as he can." And he'd go off and hunt until late time of day.

White people used to say—them Clays, we lived close to the Clay family: "Hayes sure is a hard worker," and laugh about it. "Hayes is a hard worker. But he's workin to keep from work." That was funny to me too, but it was all the truth.

I've known my daddy to kill more wild turkeys, wild ducks, and catch more fish in Sitimachas Creek up between Beaufort and Pottstown—we lived on the upper end of the creek close to Apafalya and Litabixee. And my daddy would catch fish, great God almighty. Catch em in baskets, two or three baskets; sometimes he'd catch more fish than the settlement could eat. And he'd get him some steel traps and go down to the creek—trap eels. Fish, eels, wild turkeys, wild ducks, possums, coons, beavers, squirrels, all such as that. But he wouldn't shoot a rabbit if it jumped up before him; just didn't fancy rabbits out of all the beasts of the forests and fields.

Sometimes he'd come back off his hunt and come across the field—he knowed where he said for me to plow. He'd expect to find me there and he'd find me there. I'd be plowin right along and the old mule I was plowin or old horse, whatever he had, he'd begin to throw up his head, turn around and look at me and kick at the plow—I knowed I was in for a whippin then. Because it didn't suit my daddy to have his mule actin up like that and his boy can't control him, and me barefooted too, just a little old boy plowin in that rough land. I'd go on plowin and my daddy'd just stand off in a row until I plowed up pretty close to him. He'd say, "Nate."

"Yes sir?"

"What sort of plowin is this you doin here? What sort of plowin is this you doin?"

He was like to blow me down. I'd tell him, "I's doin the best I can, Papa, I's doin the best I can."

Next word, "Drop them britches. Drop them britches."

He run around then to the old horse mule and begin to untie one of the lines from the bits.

"Drop them britches."

I'd be a little slow about it. He'd get that line out loose and sling it off the handle so I'd drop the loop; run it out the traces and swing it full loose and go to doublin it—double it once or twice, enough so it wouldn't worry him to beat me with. Then he'd walk up to me and if I weren't gettin out of my britches fast enough to suit him he'd grab me and snap my little old galluses down and drop my britches, stick my head between his legs—and when he got done with me that plow line was hot.

But I had to like him, had to like him. If he thought I got a little miffed about somethin or other, any way, if he thought my mind was runnin against what he wanted to do, right there was a beatin up. O, children when I come along come along the hard way. But I say after all that: a child aint got no business buckin his parents; parents aint got no business beatin a child.

∾ Frank O'Connor ∾

(1903-1966)

Frank O'Connor was born in Cork, Ireland. O'Connor's father was a day laborer, and the family lived in poverty, sometimes made worse by the father's bouts of alcoholism. O'Connor was largely self-educated and worked at a variety of jobs until he participated in the Irish Civil War and was briefly imprisoned in 1923. While in his twenties, he began to write fiction, first in Gaelic and then in English. Although he has published verse, translations, biographies, and literary criticism, he is best known as a writer of short stories, virtually all of which have a contemporary Irish setting. The following selection is from an interview with O'Connor that originally appeared in Paris Review. *That magazine regularly features interviews in which creative writers are asked about their work and their working habits. Some of these interviews were collected in* Writers at Work *(1957), from which these excerpts were taken. The interviewer was Anthony Whittier.*

[A WRITER AT WORK]

INTERVIEWER: What determined you to become a writer?

O'CONNOR: I've never been anything else. From the time I was nine or ten, it was a toss-up whether I was goin' to be a writer or a painter, and I discovered by the time I was sixteen or seventeen that paints cost too much money, so I became a writer because you could be a writer with a pencil and a penny notebook. I did at one time get a scholarship to Paris, but I couldn't afford to take it up because of the family. That's where my life changed its course; otherwise I'd have been a painter. I have a very strongly developed imitative instinct, which I notice is shared by some of my children. I always wrote down bits of music that impressed me in staff notation, though I couldn't read staff notation—I didn't learn to read it until I was thirty-five—but this always gave me the air of being a musician. And in the same way, I painted. I remember a friend of mine who painted in water colors and he was rather shy. He was painting in the city, so he used to get up at six in the morning when there was nobody to observe him and go out and paint. And one day he was going in to work at nine o'clock and he saw a little girl sitting where he had sat, with a can of water and an old stick, pretending to paint a picture—she'd obviously been watching him from an upstairs window. That's what I mean by the imitative instinct, and I've always had that strongly developed. So I always play at knowing things until, in fact, I find I've learned them almost by accident.

INTERVIEWER: Why do you prefer the short story for your medium?

O'CONNOR: Because it's the nearest thing I know to lyric poetry—I wrote lyric poetry for a long time, then discovered that God had not intended me to be a lyric poet, and the nearest thing to that is the short story. A novel actually requires far more logic and far more knowledge of circumstances, whereas a short story can have the sort of detachment from circumstances that lyric poetry has.

. . .

INTERVIEWER: What about working habits? How do you start a story?

O'CONNOR: "Get black on white" used to be Maupassant's advice—that's what I always do. I don't give a hoot what the writing's like, I write any sort of rubbish which will cover the main outlines of the story, then I can begin to see it. When I

27

write, when I draft a story, I never think of writing nice sentences about, "It was a nice August evening when Elizabeth Jane Moriarty was coming down the road." I just write roughly what happened, and then I'm able to see what the construction looks like. It's the design of the story which to me is most important, the thing that tells you there's a bad gap in the narrative here and you really ought to fill that up in some way or another. I'm always looking at the design of a story, not the treatment. Yesterday I was finishing off a piece about my friend A. E. Coppard, the greatest of all the English storytellers, who died about a fortnight ago. I was describing the way Coppard must have written these stories, going around with a notebook, recording what the lighting looked like, what that house looked like, and all the time using metaphor to suggest it to himself, "The road looked like a mad serpent going up the hill," or something of the kind, and, "She said so-and-so, and the man in the pub said something else." After he had written them all out, he must have got the outline of his story, and he'd start working in all the details. Now, I could never do that at all. I've got to see what these people did, first of all, and *then* I start thinking of whether it was a nice August evening or a spring evening. I have to wait for the theme before I can do anything.

INTERVIEWER: Do you rewrite?

O'CONNOR: Endlessly, endlessly, endlessly. And keep on rewriting, and after it's published, and then after it's published in book form, I usually rewrite it again. I've rewritten versions of most of my early stories and one of these days, God help, I'll publish these as well.

INTERVIEWER: Do you keep notes as a source of supply for future stories?

O'CONNOR: Just notes of themes. If somebody tells me a good story, I'll write it down in my four lines; that is the secret of the theme. If you make the subject of a story twelve or fourteen lines, that's a treatment. You've already committed yourself to the sort of character, the sort of surroundings, and the moment you've committed yourself, the story is already written. It has ceased to be fluid, you can't design it any longer, you can't model it. So I always confine myself to my four lines. If it won't go into four, that means you haven't reduced it to its ultimate simplicity, reduced it to the fable.

INTERVIEWER: I have noticed in your stories a spareness of physical description of people and places. Why this apparent rejection of sense impressions?

O'CONNOR: I thoroughly agree, it's one of the things I know I do, and sometimes when I'm reading Coppard I feel that it's entirely wrong. I'd love to be able to describe people as he describes them, and landscapes as he describes them, but I begin the story in the man's head and it never gets out of the man's head. And in fact, in real life, when you meet somebody in the street you don't start recording that she had this sort of nose— at least a man doesn't. I mean, if you're the sort of person that meets a girl in the street and instantly notices the color of her eyes and of her hair and the sort of dress she's wearing, then you're not in the least like me. I just notice a feeling from people. I notice particularly the cadence of their voices, the sort of phrases they'll use, and that's what I'm all the time trying to hear in my head, how people word things—because everybody speaks an entirely different language, that's really what it amounts to. I have terribly sensitive hearing and I'm terribly aware of voices. If I remember somebody, for instance, that I was very fond of, I don't remember what he or she looked like, but I can absolutely take off the voice. I'm a good mimic; I've a bit of the actor in me, I suppose, that's really what it amounts to. I cannot pass a story as finished unless I connect it myself, unless I know how everybody in it spoke, which, as I say, can go quite well with the fact that I couldn't tell you in the least what they looked like. If I use the right phrase and the reader hears the phrase in his head, he sees the individual. It's like writing for the theater, you see. A bad playwright will "pull" an actor because he'll tell him what to do, but a really good playwright will give you a part that you can do what you like with. It's transferring to the reader the responsibility for acting those scenes. I've given him all the information I have and put it into his own life.

·   ·   ·

INTERVIEWER: Have you any particular words of encouragement for young writers?

O'CONNOR: Well, there's this: Don't take rejection slips too seriously. I don't think they ought to send them out at all. I think a very amusing anthology might be gotten up of rejection letters alone. It's largely a question of remembering, when you send something out, that So-and-so is on the other end of this one, and he has certain interests. To give an example of what I mean on this rejection business, I had a story accepted by a magazine. So I wrote it over again as I always do, and sent it back. Well, someone else got it and I got this very nice letter saying that they couldn't use it, but that they'd be very interested in seeing anything else I wrote in the future.

Possibilities for Writing

1. First join with other students in exchanging the roles of interviewer and interviewee. As an interviewer, try to find out about your subject's life, his background, interests, and ambitions. After participating in these interviews, write a list of questions that you now think it might be important for an autobiographical writer to try to answer.

2. Write a draft of an account of some early point in your life—your memories of the first grade, for example, or of some person, place, or event from an even earlier time. Then let yourself be interviewed by several members of the class and see to what extent their questions make you provide additional information or help you gain a new perspective on your subject.

3. Together with other students in the class, try to recall a recent experience that you have all shared—for example, the registration process, your first meal at the cafeteria, a school concert or dance. After each student in turn has presented his account of the experience, write a brief report explaining which student's recollection was most convincing for you.

Part Two – Diaries and Journals

Introduction: Writing for Oneself

Section two of this chapter consists of selections from diaries and journals, another grouping intended as guides for the transition to formal autobiography. With these excerpts we have moved across the line from speaking to writing, but to a type of writing that can still share some of the informality characteristic of speech. The journal writer has even greater freedom than a speaker does to decide what he will comment on, when he will suddenly shift to another subject, and how long he will continue to develop the subject before he stops entirely. While speech usually involves a participating audience, listening and responding, the writer of diaries or journals addresses either himself alone or else an imagined audience that he defines to fit his own desires. What is most important about diaries and journals is that they do encourage us to write; through them we transfer our experience to written language, a step which almost inevitably leads to greater coherence and greater detachment.

A distinction is conventionally made between a diary—a day-to-day record of the events of one's life—and a journal—a record of the intellectual or spiritual development of an individual. The two definitions do not create a hard-and-fast line; in fact, most writers of either form interweave specific memories and more general reflections. Virginia Woolf was already a professional novelist and critic when she recorded the diary entries included in this chapter, but she shows us the range of possibilities the journal can present to even the least experienced writer. In one entry she describes an eclipse of the sun, in another she records the brittle and empty chatter at a luncheon party she attended, in a third she sketches a vivid portrait of a local clergyman. Often she writes directly about herself, her private thoughts and feelings, her judgments about her own work as a writer, her opinions of friends and acquaintances.

Woolf's diary illustrates the special importance of this kind of record: its flexibility in accommodating a writer's impulses. The journal should function like an artist's sketchbook, where the artist records what strikes his eye, and he experiments, not only with a particular kind of subject, like portraiture or landscape, but also with different methods of interpreting that subject. An artist's sketchbook does not contain drawings ready to be framed and exhibited, but instead concentrates on fragments (an arm, a mouth, the petal of a flower), drawn and redrawn, that eventually may find their way into a completed work. However skillful he may be, any writer can make good use of a journal as a verbal sketchpad to test new possibilities. Preferably his journal writing should not be limited only to recording one particular situation or one particular mood. It then becomes merely a reflection of a single facet of his potential skills, lapsing into a comfortable and repetitive record of current reading, let us say, or family conversations. An inexperienced writer should make a special effort to take advantage of the freedom the journal provides to write about anything— events, ideas, feelings, passing sensations or impressions—in any conceivable way. By doing so, he can extend himself as a writer without having his desire to experiment inhibited by the need to persuade or impress an audience. The journal may ultimately become a useful source book for more ambitious writing projects, but it will already have served its major function if it helps to put a writer in touch with his own potentialities.

∽ Lorraine Hansberry ∽

(1930-1965)

Lorraine Hansberry achieved a major success with her first play, A Raisin in the Sun *(1959). Her very promising career was ended when she died of cancer at the age of 34. Her husband, Robert Nemiroff, compiled a selection of her writings,* To Be Young, Gifted and Black *(1969), in order to present a portrait of her life, her work, and her ideas. The selection here is not from a single journal, but was drawn together by Nemiroff from various journals, letters, and miscellaneous papers; the passages are unified by their common subject of Hansberry's childhood in Chicago.*

from *To Be Young, Gifted and Black*

1.

For some time now—I think since I was a child—I have been possessed of the desire to put down the stuff of my life. That is a commonplace impulse, apparently, among persons of massive self-interest; sooner or later we all do it. And, I am quite certain, there is only one internal quarrel: how much of the truth to tell? How much, how much, how much! It *is* brutal, in sober uncompromising moments, to reflect on the comedy of concern we all enact when it comes to our precious images!

Even so, when such vanity as propels the writing of such memoirs is examined, certainly one would wish at least to have some boast of social serviceability on one's side. I shall set down in these pages what shall seem to me to be the truth of my life and essences . . . which are to be found, first of all, on the Southside of Chicago, where I was born. . . .

2.

All travelers to my city should ride the elevated trains that race along the back ways of Chicago. The lives you can look into!

I think you could find the tempo of my people on their back porches. The honesty of their living is there in the shabbiness. Scrubbed porches that sag and look their danger. Dirty gray wood steps. And always a line of white and pink clothes scrubbed so well, waving in the dirty wind of the city.

My people are poor. And they are tired. And they are determined to live.

Our Southside is a place apart: each piece of our living is a protest.

3.

I was born May 19, 1930, the last of four children.

Of love and my parents there is little to be written: their relationship to their children was utilitarian. We were fed and housed and dressed and outfitted with more cash than our associates and that was all. We were also vaguely taught certain vague absolutes: that we were better than no one but infinitely superior to everyone; that we were the products of the proudest and most mistreated of the races of man; that there was nothing enormously difficult about life; that one *succeeded* as a matter of course.

Life was not a struggle—it was something that one *did*. One won an argument because, if facts gave out, one invented them—with color! The only sinful people in the world were dull people. And, above all, there were two things which were never to be betrayed: the family and the race. But of love, there was nothing ever said.

If we were sick, we were sternly, impersonally and carefully nursed and doctored back to health. Fevers, toothaches were attended to with urgency and importance; one always felt *important* in my family. Mother came with a tray to your room with the soup and Vick's salve or gave the enemas in a steaming bathroom. But we were not fondled, any of us—head held to breast, fingers about that head—until we were grown, all of us, and my father died.

At his funeral I at last, in my memory, saw my mother hold her sons that way, and for the first time in her life my sister held me in her arms I think. We were not a loving people: we were passionate in our hostilities and affinities, but the caress embarrassed us.

We have changed little. . . .

4.

Seven years separated the nearest of my brothers and sisters and myself; I wear, I am sure, the earmarks of that familial station to this day. Little has been written or thought to my knowledge about children who occupy that place: the last born separated by an uncommon length of time from the next youngest. I suspect we are probably a race apart.

The last born is an object toy which comes in years when brothers and sisters who are seven, ten, twelve years older are old enough to appreciate it rather than poke out its eyes. They do not mind diapering you the first two years, but by the time you are five you are a pest that has to be attended to in the washroom, taken to the movies and "sat with" at night. You are not a person—you are a nuisance who is not particular fun any more. Consequently, you swiftly learn to play alone. . . .

5.

My childhood Southside summers were the ordinary city kind, full of the street games which other rememberers have turned into fine ballets these days, and rhymes that anticipated what some people insist on calling modern poetry:

37

Oh, Mary Mack, Mack, Mack
With the silver buttons, buttons, buttons
All down her back, back, back.
She asked her mother, mother, mother
For fifteen cents, cents, cents
To see the elephant, elephant, elephant
Jump the fence, fence, fence.
Well, he jumped so high, high, high
'Til he touched the sky, sky, sky
And he didn't come back, back, back
'Til the Fourth of Ju—ly, ly, ly!

I remember skinny little Southside bodies by the fives and tens of us panting the delicious hours away:

"May I?"

And the voice of authority: "Yes, you may—you may take one giant step."

One drew in all one's breath and tightened one's fist and pulled the small body against the heavens, stretching, straining all the muscles in the legs to make—one giant step.

It is a long time. One forgets the reason for the game. (For children's games are always explicit in their reasons for being. To play is to win something. Or not to be "it." Or to be high pointer, or outdoer or, sometimes—just *the winner*. But after a time one forgets.)

Why was it important to take a small step, a teeny step, or the most desired of all—one GIANT step?

A giant step *to where?*

6.

Evenings were spent mainly on the back porches where screen doors slammed in the darkness with those really very special summertime sounds. And, sometimes, when Chicago nights got too steamy, the whole family got into the car and went to the park and slept out in the open on blankets. Those were, of course, the best times of all because the grownups were invariably reminded of having been children in the South and told the best stories then. And it was also cool and sweet to be on the grass and there was usually the scent of freshly cut lemons or melons in the air. Daddy would lie on his back, as fathers must, and explain about how men thought the stars above us came to be and how far away they were.

I never did learn to believe that anything could be as far away as *that*. Especially the stars. . . .

∽ John Holt ∽

(1923-)

John Holt was born in New York City and educated at Yale. He has had experience in almost every kind of academic setting, from an elementary school to a graduate program. Holt is one of the most influential American writers on educational theory and practice, and his many books draw upon his own classroom experience as a basis for his arguments. How Children Fail *(1964) began as a series of memos recording what Holt discovered while acting as an observer and a teacher in a fifth-grade class.*

from *How Children Fail*

February 27, 1958

A few days ago Nell came up to the desk, and looking at me steadily and without speaking, as usual, put on the desk her ink copy of the latest composition. Our rule is that on the ink copy there must be no more than three mistakes per page, or the page must be copied again. I checked her paper, and on the first page found five mistakes. I showed them to her, and told her, as gently as I could, that she had to copy it again, and urged her to be more careful—typical teacher's advice. She looked at me, heaved a sigh, and went back to her desk. She is left-handed, and doesn't manage a pen very well. I could see her frowning with concentration as she worked and struggled. Back she came after a while with the second copy. This time the first page had seven mistakes, and the handwriting was noticeably worse. I told her to copy it again. Another bigger sigh, and she went back to her desk. In time the third copy arrived, looking much worse than the second, and with even more mistakes.

At that point Bill Hull asked me a question, one I should have asked myself, one we ought all to keep asking ourselves: "Where are you trying to get, and are you getting there?"

The question sticks like a burr. In schools—but where isn't it so?—we so easily fall into the same trap: the means to an end becomes an end in itself. I had on my hands this three-mistake rule meant to serve the ends of careful work and neat compositions. By applying it rigidly was I getting more careful work and neater compositions? No; I was getting a child who was so worried about having to recopy her paper that she could not concentrate on doing it, and hence did it worse and worse, and would probably do the next papers badly as well.

We need to ask more often of everything we do in school, "Where are we trying to get, and is this thing we are doing helping us to get there?" Do we do something because we want to help the children and can see that what we are doing is helping them? Or do we do it because it is inexpensive or convenient for school, teachers, administrators? Or because everyone else does it? We must beware of making a virtue of necessity, and cooking up high-sounding educational reasons for doing what is done really for reasons of administrative economy or convenience. The still greater danger is that, having started to do something for good enough reasons, we may go on doing it stubbornly and blindly, as I did that day, unable or unwilling to see that we are doing more harm than good.

October 30, 1958
Everyone around here talks as if, except for a few hopeless characters, these children know most of the math they are supposed to know. It just isn't so. Out of the twenty kids in the class, there are at least six who don't even know simple "addition facts," and many more who, whether they know the facts or not, habitually add by counting on their fingers, usually keeping them well out of sight. There are still more who don't

understand and can't do multiplication and division. I hate to think what we will find about their understanding of place value.

It would be easy to make up an arithmetic test that without being too long, or unfairly tricky, or covering anything but what these kids are supposed to know, would stump all but a few of the children in fifth grade. Or any grade. The ninth graders I taught came to me with respectable school records in arithmetic, yet they knew little about division, less about fractions, and next to nothing about decimals.

It begins to look as if the test-examination-marks business is a gigantic racket, the purpose of which is to enable students, teachers, and schools to take part in a joint pretense that the students know everything they are supposed to know, when in fact they know only a small part of it—if any at all. Why do we always announce exams in advance, if not to give students a chance to cram for them? Why do teachers, even in graduate schools, always say quite specifically what the exam will be about, even telling the type of questions that will be given? Because otherwise too many students would flunk. What would happen at Harvard or Yale if a prof gave a surprise test in March on work covered in October? Everyone knows what would happen; that's why they don't do it.

March 20, 1959
Today Jane did one of those things that, for all her rebellious and annoying behavior in class, make her one of the best and most appealing people, young or old, that I have ever known. I was at the board, trying to explain to her a point on long division, when she said, in self-defense, "But Miss W. (her fourth-grade teacher) told us that we should take the first number . . ." Here she saw the smallest shadow of doubt on my face. She knew instantly that I did not approve of this rule, and without so much as a pause she continued, ". . . it wasn't Miss W., it was someone else . . ." and then went on talking about long division.

I was touched and very moved. How many adults would have seen what she saw, that what she was saying about Miss W.'s teaching was, in some slight degree, lowering my estimate of Miss W.? Even more to the point, how many adults, given this opportunity to shift the blame for their difficulties onto the absent Miss W., would instead have instantly changed their story to protect her from blame? For all our yammering about loyalty, not one adult in a thousand would have shown the loyalty that this little girl gave to her friend and former teacher. And she scarcely had to think to do it; for her, to defend one's friends from harm, blame, or even criticism was an instinct as natural as breathing.

Teachers and schools tend to mistake good behavior for good character. What they prize above all else is docility, suggestibility; the child who will do what he is told; or even better, the child who will do what is wanted without even having to be told. They value most in children what children least value in themselves. Small wonder that their effort to build character is such a failure; they don't know it when they see it. Jane is a good example. She has been a trial to everyone who has taught her. Even this fairly lenient school finds her barely tolerable; most schools long since would have kicked her out in disgrace. Of the many adults who have known her, probably very few have recognized her extraordinary qualities or appreciated their worth. Asked for an estimate of her character, most of them would probably say that it was bad. Yet, troublesome as she is, I wish that there were more children like her.

April 11, 1959
The things children talk about in class, when they are allowed to talk at all, are seldom close to their hearts. Only once in a great while do I feel, at the end of a class discussion, that I have come close to the real life of these children. One such discussion was about hiding places; another, just a few days ago, was about names.

This latter came up in Roman history. The time arrived in

Rome when the mob gained political power, so that the ability to arouse and inflame the mob was a sure key to high office. The kids wanted to know how this was done. I said it was done mostly with names. The way to arouse a mob against your political opponent was to call him names, the kind of names the mob hates most, or can be talked into hating. The mob spirit is weaker in these children than it will be in a few years, and they were skeptical; they wanted to know what kind of names would arouse a mob.

For answer, I asked them, "Well, what kind of names do you hate to be called?" We were off. Before the end of the period the board was covered with names. About half were what I expected, the usual ten-year-old insults—idiot, stupid, nuthead, fat slob, chicken, dope, scaredy-cat, etc. The rest surprised me. They were all terms of endearment.

It was quite a scene. There were all these bright-faced, lively children, eyes dancing with excitement and enthusiasm, seeing who could most strongly express their collective contempt and disgust for all the names that adults might suppose they like most. Someone would say, "Dearie—ug-g-g-g-gh!" Chorus of agreement. Someone else would say, "Honey—ic-c-c-c-ch!" More agreement. Every imaginable term of affection and endearment came in for its share. Not one was legitimate, not one was accepted. Nobody said of any term, "Well, that's not too bad." To some extent the children may have been carried away by the excitement of the game, but from the way they looked and sounded I felt sure, and do now, that they really meant what they were saying, that their dislike of these terms of endearment was genuine and deeply felt.

Why should this be? Of course, ten is a heroic age for most kids. They remind me in many ways of the Homeric Greeks. They are quarrelsome and combative; they have a strong and touchy sense of honor; they believe that every affront must be repaid, and with interest; they are fiercely loyal to their friends, even though they may change friends often; they have little sense of fair play, and greatly admire cunning and trickery; they are both highly possessive and very generous—no smallest trifle may be taken from them, but they are likely to give anything away, if they feel so disposed. Most of the time, they don't feel like little children, and they don't like being talked to as if they were little children.

But there is more to it than this. They suspect and resent these terms of endearment because they have too often heard them used by people who did not mean them. Everyone who deals with children these days has heard the dictum that children need to be loved, must be loved. But even to those who like them most, children are not always a joy and delight to be with. Often they are much like older people, and often they are exasperating and irritating. It is not surprising that there are many adults who do not like children much, if at all. But they feel that they ought to like them, have a duty to like them, and they try to discharge this duty by acting, particularly by talking, as if they liked them. Hence the continual and meaningless use of words like *honey*, *dearie*, etc. Hence, the dreadful, syrupy voice that so many adults use when they speak to children. By the time they are ten, children are fed up with this fake affection, and ready to believe that, most of the time, adults believe and mean very little of what they say.

∾ Henry Thoreau ∾

(1817-1862)

Henry Thoreau was born in Concord and educated at Harvard. He became interested in Transcendentalism, in part through his association with a Concord neighbor, Ralph Waldo Emerson. Thoreau was deeply appreciative of nature, and in his life and writings he combined the careful observation of a trained surveyor and botanist with the idealism of his Transcendentalist belief in the natural world as a manifestation of spiritual realities. Thoreau began keeping a journal in 1837, shortly after graduating from college, and maintained it until November, 1861, six months before his death. He frequently incorporated materials from his journals in his published writings, as can be seen by comparing some of the passages here (October, 1852) with the selection from Walden *included in Chapter Four.*

from *The Journals*

Oct. 10. Burdock, *Ranunculus acris*, rough hawkweed. A drizzling rain to-day. The air is full of falling leaves. The streets are strewn with elm leaves. The trees begin to look thin. The butternut is perhaps the first on the street to lose its leaves. Rain, more than wind, makes the leaves fall. Glow-worms in the evening.

Oct. 11. Monday. Most leaves are already somewhat faded and withered. Their tints are not so bright. The chestnut leaves already rustle with a great noise as you walk through the

From Henry Thoreau: *The Journals,* eds. Bradford Torrey and Francis Allen. Reprinted by permission of Houghton Mifflin Company.

woods, as they lie light, firm, and crisp. Now the chestnuts are rattling out. The burs are gaping and showing the plump nuts. They fill the ruts in the road, and are abundant amid the fallen leaves in the midst of the wood. The jays scream, and the red squirrels scold, while you are clubbing and shaking the trees. Now it is true autumn; all things are crisp and ripe.

I observed the other day (October 8) that those insects whose ripple I could see from the Peak were water-bugs. I could detect the progress of a water-bug over the smooth surface in almost any part of the pond, for they furrow the water slightly, making a conspicuous ripple bounded by two diverging lines, but the skaters slide over it without producing a perceptible ripple. In this clear air and with this glassy surface the motion of every water-bug, ceaselessly progressing over the pond, was perceptible. Here and there amid the skaters.

Oct. 12. I am struck by the superfluity of light in the atmosphere in the autumn, as if the earth absorbed none, and out of this profusion of dazzling light came the autumnal tints. Can it be because there is less vapor? The delicacy of the stratification in the white sand by the railroad, where they have been getting out sand for the brick-yards, the delicate stratification of this great globe like the leaves of the choicest volume just shut on a lady's table. The piled-up history! I am struck by the slow and delicate process by which the globe was formed.

Paddled on Walden. A rippled surface. Scared up ducks. Saw them first far over the surface, just risen,—two smaller, white-bellied, one larger, black. They circled round as usual, and the first went off, but the black one went round and round and over the pond five or six times at a considerable height and distance, when I thought several times he had gone to the river, and at length settled down by a slanting flight of a quarter of a mile into a distant part of the pond which I had left free; but what beside safety these ducks get by sailing in the middle of Walden I don't know. That black rolling-pin with wings, circling round you half a mile off for a quarter of an hour, at that height, from which he sees the river and Fair Haven all the while, from which he sees so many things, while I see almost him alone. Their wings set so far back. They are not handsome, but wild.

What an ample share of the light of heaven each pond and lake on the surface of the globe enjoys! No woods are so dark and deep but it is light above the pond. Its window or skylight is as broad as its surface. It lies out patent to the sky. From the mountain-top you may not be able to see out because of the woods, but on the lake you are bathed in light.

I can discern no skaters nor water-bugs on the surface of the pond, which is now rippled. Do they, then, glide forth to the middle in calm days only, by short impulses, till they have completely covered it?

A new carpet of pine leaves is forming in the woods. The forest is laying down her carpet for the winter. The elms in the village, losing their leaves, reveal the birds' nests.

I dug some ground-nuts in the railroad bank with my hands this afternoon, the vine being now dead. They were nearly as large as hen's eggs, six inches or a foot beneath the surface, on the end of a root or strung along on it. I had them roasted and boiled at supper time. The skin came readily off like a potato. Roasted, they have an agreeable taste very much like a potato, though somewhat fibrous in texture. With my eyes shut, I should not know but I was eating a rather soggy potato. Boiled, they were unexpectedly quite dry, and though in this instance a little strong, had a more nutty flavor. With a little salt, a hungry man would make a very palatable meal on them. It would not be easy to find them, especially now that the vines are dead, unless you knew beforehand where they grew.

· · ·

Oct. 16. Saturday. The sidewalks are covered with the impressions of leaves which fell yesterday and were pressed into the soil by the feet of the passers, leaving a myriad dark spots—like bird-tracks or hieroglyphics to a casual observer.

What are the sparrow-like birds with striped breasts and two

triangular chestnut-colored spots on the breasts which I have
seen some time, picking the seeds of the weeds in the garden?

. . .

Oct. 20. Canada snapdragon, tansy, white goldenrod, blue-
stemmed ditto. *Aster undulatus*, autumnal dandelion, tall but-
tercup, yarrow, mayweed. Picking chestnuts on Pine Hill. A
rather cold and windy, somewhat wintry afternoon, the heavens overcast. The clouds have lifted in the northwest, and I see
the mountains in sunshine, all the more attractive from the
cold I feel here, with a tinge of purple on them, a cold but
memorable and glorious outline. This is an advantage of
mountains in the horizon: they show you fair weather from
the midst of foul. The small red Solomon's-seal berries spot the
ground here and there amid the dry leaves. The witch-hazel is
bare of all but flowers.

Many a man, when I tell him that I have been on to a mountain, asks if I took a glass with me. No doubt, I could have seen
further with a glass, and particular objects more distinctly,—
could have counted more meeting-houses; but this has nothing
to do with the peculiar beauty and grandeur of the view which
an elevated position affords. It was not to see a few particular
objects, as if they were near at hand, as I had been accustomed
to see them, that I ascended the mountain, but to see an infinite
variety far and near in their relation to each other, thus reduced to a single picture. The facts of science, in comparison
with poetry, are wont to be as vulgar as looking from the
mountain with a telescope. It is a counting of meeting-houses.
At the public house, the mountain-house, they keep a glass to
let, and think the journey to the mountain-top is lost, that you
have got but half the view, if you have not taken a glass with
you.

. . .

Oct. 23. P. M.—To Conantum.
This may be called an Indian-summer day. It is quite hazy
withal, and the mountains invisible. I see a horehound turned

49

lake or steel-claret color. The yellow lily pads in Hubbard's ditch are fresh, as if recently expanded. There are some white lily pads in river still, but very few indeed of the yellow lily. A pasture thistle on Conantum just budded, but flat with the ground. The fields generally wear a russet hue. A striped snake out. The milkweed (*Syriaca*) now rapidly discounting. The lanceolate pods having opened, the seeds spring out on the least jar, or when dried by the sun, and form a little fluctuating white silky mass or tuft, each held by the extremities of the fine threads, until a stronger puff of wind sets them free. It is a pleasant sight to see it dispersing its seeds. The bass has lost its leaves. I see where boys have gathered the mockernut, though it has not fallen out of its shells. The red squirrel chirrups in the walnut grove. The chickadees flit along, following me inquisitively a few rods with lisping, tinkling note,—flit within a few feet of me from curiosity, head downward on the pines. The white pines have shed their leaves, making a yellow carpet on the grass, but the pitch pines are yet parti-colored. Is it the procumbent speedwell (*Veronica agrestis*) still in flower on Lee's Cliff? But its leaves are neither heart-ovate nor shorter than the peduncles. The sprays of the witch-hazel are sprinkled on the air, and recurved. The pennyroyal stands brown and sere, though fragrant still, on the shelves of the Cliff. The elms in the street have nearly lost their leaves.

October has been the month of autumnal tints. The first of the month the tints began to be more general, at which time the frosts began, though there were scattered bright tints long before; but not till then did the forest begin to be painted. By the end of the month the leaves will either have fallen or be sered and turned brown by the frosts for the most part. Also the month of barberries and chestnuts.

My friend is one whom I meet, who takes me for what I am. A stranger takes me for something else than I am. We do not speak, we cannot communicate, till we find that we are recognized. The stranger supposes in our stead a third person whom we do not know, and we leave him to converse with that one. It is suicide for us to become abetters in misapprehending ourselves. Suspicion creates the stranger and substitutes him for the friend. I cannot abet any man in misapprehending myself.

What men call social virtues, good fellowship, is commonly but the virtue of pigs in a litter, which lie close together to keep each other warm. It brings men together in crowds and mobs in barrooms and elsewhere, but it does not deserve the name of virtue.

∾ Virginia Woolf ∾

(1882-1941)

Born into a family of literary distinction, Virginia Stephen Woolf became an important novelist and critic in her own right and a central figure in the London intellectual circle known as the Bloomsbury Group. As a novelist, she is distinguished by her penetrating understanding of the inner lives of her characters, by her subtle depiction of relations between the sexes, and by her experimentation with symbolism and stream of consciousness technique. At the time these entries were made in her diary (1927), she had already published more than a half-dozen works of fiction and had achieved considerable public recognition. Woolf suffered from periods of acute anxiety and depression; the recurrence of her illness led to her suicide in 1941. She had written in her diary regularly from 1915 until the time of her death.

from *A Writer's Diary*

Thursday, June 30

All the fields were aburn with June grasses and red tasselled plants none coloured as yet, all pale. Pale and grey too were the little uncompromising Yorkshire farms. As we passed one, the farmer and his wife and sister came out, all tightly and tidily dressed in black, as if they were going to church. At another ugly square farm, two women were looking out of the upper windows. These had white blinds drawn down half across them. We were a train of 3 vast cars, one stopping to let the others go on; all very low and powerful; taking immensely steep hills. The driver once got out and put a small stone behind our wheel—inadequate. An accident would have been natural; there were also many motor cars. These suddenly increased as we crept up to the top of Bardon Fell. Here were people camping beside their cars. We got out and found ourselves very high, on a moor, boggy, heathery, with butts for grouse shooting. There were grass tracks here and there and people had already taken up positions. So we joined them, walking out to what seemed the highest point looking over Richmond. One light burned down there. Vales and moors stretched, slope after slope, round us. It was like the Haworth country. But over Richmond, where the sun was rising, was a soft grey cloud. We could see by a gold spot where the sun was. But it was early yet. We had to wait, stamping to keep warm. Ray had wrapped herself in the blue striped blanket off a double bed. She looked incredibly vast and bedroomish. Saxon looked very old. Leonard kept looking at his watch. Four great red setters came leaping over the moor. There were sheep feeding behind us. Vita had tried to buy a guinea pig—Quentin advised a savage—so she observed the animals from time to time. There were thin places in the clouds and some complete holes. The question was whether the sun would show through a cloud or through one of these hollow places when the time came. We began to get anxious. We saw rays coming through the bottom of the clouds. Then, for a moment, we saw the sun, sweeping— it seemed to be sailing at a great pace and clear in a gap; we had out our smoked glasses; we saw it crescent, burning red; next moment it had sailed fast into the cloud again; only the red streamers came from it; then only a golden haze, such as one has often seen. The moments were passing. We thought we were cheated; we looked at the sheep; they showed no fear; the setters were racing round; everyone was standing in long lines, rather dignified, looking out. I thought how we were like very old people, in the birth of the world—druids on Stonehenge;

(this idea came more vividly in the first pale light though). At the back of us were great blue spaces in the cloud. These were still blue. But now the colour was going out. The clouds were turning pale; a reddish black colour. Down in the valley it was an extraordinary scrumble of red and black; there was the one light burning; all was cloud down there, and very beautiful, so delicately tinted. Nothing could be seen through the cloud. The 24 seconds were passing. Then one looked back again at the blue; and rapidly, very very quickly, all the colours faded; it became darker and darker as at the beginning of a violent storm; the light sank and sank; we kept saying this is the shadow; and we thought now it is over—this is the shadow; when suddenly the light went out. We had fallen. It was extinct. There was no colour. The earth was dead. That was the astonishing moment; and the next when as if a ball had rebounded the cloud took colour on itself again, only a sparky ethereal colour and so the light came back. I had very strongly the feeling as the light went out of some vast obeisance; something kneeling down and suddenly raised up when the colours came. They came back astonishingly lightly and quickly and beautifully in the valley and over the hills—at first with a miraculous glittering and ethereality, later normally almost, but with a great sense of relief. It was like recovery. We had been much worse than we had expected. We had seen the world dead. This was within the power of nature. Our greatness had been apparent too. Now we became Ray in a blanket, Saxon in a cap etc. We were bitterly cold. I should say that the cold had increased as the light went down. One felt very livid. Then—it was over till 1999. What remained was the sense of the comfort which we get used to, of plenty of light, and colour. This for some time seemed a definitely welcome thing. Yet when it became established all over the country, one rather missed the sense of its being a relief and a respite, which one had had when it came back after the darkness. How can I express the darkness? It was a sudden plunge, when one did not expect it; being at the mercy of the sky; our own nobility; the druids;

Stonehenge; and the racing red dogs; all that was in one's mind. Also, to be picked out of one's London drawing room and set down on the wildest moors in England, was impressive. For the rest, I remember trying to keep awake in the gardens at York while Eddy talked and falling asleep. Asleep again in the train. It was hot and we were messy. The carriage was full of things. Harold was very kind and attentive. Eddy was peevish. Roast beef and pineapple chunks, he said. We got home at 8:30 perhaps.

. . .

Tuesday, September 25th
On the opposite page I wrote notes for Shelley, I think, by mistake for my writing book.

Now let me become the annalist of Rodmell.

Thirty-five years ago, there were 160 families living here where there are now no more than 80. It is a decaying village, which loses its boys to the towns. Not a boy of them, said the Rev. Mr. Hawkesford, is being taught to plough. Rich people wanting weekend cottages buy up the old peasants' houses for fabulous sums. Monks House was offered to Mr. H. for £400; we gave £700. He refused it, saying he didn't wish to own country cottages. Now Mr. Allison will pay £1,200 for a couple and we he said might get £2,000 for this. He (Hawkesford) is an old decaying man, run to seed. His cynicism and the pleasant turn it gives his simple worn out sayings amuses me. He is sinking into old age, very shabby, loose limbed, wearing black woollen mittens. His life is receding like a tide, slowly; or one figures him as a dying candle, whose wick will soon sink into the warm grease and be extinct. To look at, he is like some aged bird; a little, small featured face, with heavily lidded smoky bright eyes; his complexion is still ruddy; but his beard is like an unweeded garden. Little hairs grow weakly all over his cheeks and two strands are drawn, like pencil marks, across his bald head. He tumbles into an armchair and tells over his stock of old village stories which always have this slightly mocking flavour as though, completely unambitious and by no means successful himself, he recouped himself by laughing slyly at the humours of the more energetic. The outlay these flashy newcomers make on their field and farms makes him sardonic. But he won't raise a finger either way; likes his cup of Indian tea, which he prefers to China, and doesn't much mind what anybody thinks. He smokes endless cigarettes and his fingers are not very clean. Talking of his well, he said, "It would be a different thing if one wanted baths"—which for some 70 years, presumably, he has done without. Then he likes a little practical talk about Aladdin lamps, for instance, and how the Rector at Iford has a device by which he makes the globe of the Veritas lamp, which is cheaper, serve. It appears that the Aladdin costs 10d. and 2/-. But it blackens suddenly and is useless. Leaning over stiles, it is of lamp mantles that the two rectors talk. Or he will advise about making a garage; how Percy should cut a trench and then old Fears should line the walls with cement. That is what he advises; and I fancy many many hours of his life have passed hobnobbing with Percies and Fears about cement and trenches. Of his clerical character there is little visible. He would not buy Bowen a riding school he said; her sister did that. He didn't believe in it. She has a school at Rottingdean, keeps 12 horses, employs grooms and has to be at it all day, Sundays included. But having expressed his opinion in the family conclave he would leave it at that. Mrs. H. would back Bowen. She would get her way. The Rector would slouch off to his study, where he does heaven knows what. I asked him if he had work to do: a question which amused him a little. Not work, he said; but a young woman to see. And then he settled into the armchair again and so sat out a visit of over an hour and a half.

Wednesday, October 5th
I wrote in the sordid doss house atmosphere of approaching departure. Pinker is asleep in one chair; Leonard is signing cheques at the little deal table under the glare of the lamp.

The fire is covered with ashes, since we have been burning it all day and Mrs. B. never cleans. Envelopes lie in the grate. I am writing with a pen which is feeble and wispy; and it is a sharp fine evening with a sunset, I daresay.

We went to Amberley yesterday and think of buying a house there. For it is an astonishing forgotten lovely place, between water meadows and downs. So impulsive we both are, in spite of our years.

But we are not as old as Mrs. Gray, who came to thank us for our apples. She won't send to buy, as it looks like begging, since we never take money. Her face is cut into by wrinkles; they make weals across her. She is 86 and can never remember such a summer. In her youth it was so hot in April often that they couldn't bear a sheet on them. Her youth must have been almost the same time as my father's. She is 9 years younger, I make out; born in 1841. And what did she see of Victorian England I wonder.

I can make up situations, but I cannot make up plots. That is: if I pass a lame girl I can, without knowing I do it, instantly make up a scene: (now I can't think of one). This is the germ of such fictitious gift as I have. And by the way I get letter after letter about my books and they scarcely please me.

If my pen allowed, I should now try to make out a work table, having done my last article for the *Tribune*, and now being free again. And instantly the usual exciting devices enter my mind: a biography beginning in the year 1500 and continuing to the present day, called *Orlando:* Vita; only with a change about from one sex to another. I think, for a treat, I shall let myself dash this in for a week, while . . .

. . .

Wednesday, November 30th
A hurried note about the lunch party, L. dining at the Cranium. An art of light talk; about people. Bogey Harris; Maurice Baring. B. H. "knows" everyone: that is no one. Freddy

57

Fossle? Oh yes I know him; knows Lady so-and-so. Knows everyone: can't admit to not knowing. A polished, burnished diner out—Roman Catholic. In the middle M. Baring says: "But Lady B. died this morning." Sibyl says: "Say that again." "But R. M. was lunching with her yesterday," says Bogey. "Well it's in the papers she's dead," says M. B. Sibyl says: "But she was quite young. Lord Ivor asked me to meet the young man his daughter's to marry." "I know Lord Ivor," says, or would say, Bogey. "Well it's odd," says Sibyl, giving up the attempt to wrestle with the death of the young at a lunch party. So on to wigs: "Lady Charlie used to have hers curled by a sailor on deck before she got up," says Bogey. "Oh, I've known her all my life. Went yachting with them. Lady . . . eyebrows fell into the soup. Sir John Cook was so fat they had to hike him up. Once he got out of bed in the middle of the night and fell on the floor, where he lay 5 hours—couldn't move. B. M. sent me a pear by the waiter with a long letter." Talk of houses and periods. All very smooth and surface talk; depends on knowing people; not on saying anything interesting. Bogey's cheeks are polished daily.

Tuesday, December 20th

This is almost the shortest day and perhaps the coldest night of the year. We are in the black heart of a terrific frost. I notice that look of black atoms in a clear air, which for some reason I can never describe to my liking. The pavement was white with great powdery flakes the other night, walking back with Roger and Helen; this was from Nessa's last Sunday—last, I fear, for many a month. But I have as usual "no time": let me count the things I should be doing this deep winter's night with Leonard at his last lecture and Pinker asleep in her chair. I should be reading Bagenal's story; Julian's play; Lord Chesterfield's letters; and writing to Hubert (about a cheque from the *Nation*). There is an irrational scale of values in my mind which puts these duties higher than mere scribbling.

This flashed to my mind at Nessa's children's party last night. The little creatures acting moved my infinitely sentimental throat. Angelica so mature and composed; all grey and silver; such an epitome of all womanliness; and such an unopened bud of sense and sensibility; wearing a grey wig and a sea coloured dress. And yet oddly enough I scarcely want children of my own now. This insatiable desire to write something before I die, this ravaging sense of the shortness and feverishness of life, make me cling, like a man on a rock, to my one anchor. I don't like the physicalness of having children of one's own. This occurred to me at Rodmell; but I never wrote it down. I can dramatise myself a parent, it is true. And perhaps I have killed the feeling instinctively; or perhaps nature does.

I am still writing the third chapter of *Orlando*. I have had of course to give up the fancy of finishing by February and printing this spring. It is drawing out longer than I meant. I have just been thinking over the scene when O. meets a girl (Nell) in the Park and goes with her to a neat room in Gerrard Street. There she will disclose herself. They will talk. This will lead to a diversion or two about women's love. This will bring in O.'s night life; and her clients (that's the word). Then she will see Dr. Johnson and perhaps write (I want somehow to quote it) To all you Ladies. So I shall get some effect of years passing; and then there will be a description of the lights of the eighteenth century burning; and the clouds of the nineteenth century rising. Then on to the nineteenth. But I have not considered this. I want to write it all over hastily and so keep unity of tone, which in this book is very important. It has to be half laughing, half serious; with great splashes of exaggeration. Perhaps I shall pluck up courage to ask *The Times* for a rise. But could I write for my Annual I would never write for another paper. How extraordinarily unwilled by me but potent in its own right, by the way, *Orlando* was! as if it shoved everything aside to come into existence. Yet I see looking back just now to March that it is almost exactly in spirit, though not in actual facts, the book I planned then as an escapade; the spirit to be satiric, the structure wild. Precisely.

Yes, I repeat, a very happy, a singularly happy autumn.

Thursday, December 22nd

I just open this for a moment, being dull of the head, to enter a severe reprimand of myself to myself. The value of society is that it snubs one. I am meretricious, mediocre, a humbug; am getting into the habit of flashy talk. Tinsel it seemed last night at the Keynes. I was out of humour and so could see the transparency of my own sayings. Dadie said a true thing too; when V. lets her style get on top of her, one thinks only of that; when she uses clichés, one thinks what she means. But, he says, I have no logical power and live and write in an opium dream. And the dream is too often about myself.

Now with middle age drawing on and age ahead it is important to be severe on such faults. So easily might I become a harebrained egotistic woman, exacting compliments, arrogant, narrow, withered. Nessa's children (I always measure myself against her and find her much the largest, most humane of the two of us), think of her now with an admiration that has no envy in it; with some trace of the old childish feeling that we were in league together against the world; and how proud I am of her triumphant winning of all our battles; as she takes her way so nonchalantly, modestly, almost anonymously, past the goal, with her children round her; and only a little added tenderness (a moving thing in her) which shows me that she too feels wonder, surprise, at having passed so many terrors and sorrows safe. . . .

The dream is too often about myself. To correct this; and to forget one's own sharp absurd little personality, reputation and the rest of it, one should read; see outsiders; think more; write more logically; above all be full of work; and practise anonymity. Silence in company; or the quietest statement, not the showiest; is also "medicated" as the doctors say. It was an empty party, rather, last night. Very nice here, though.

❧ George Orwell ❧

(1903-1950)

*George Orwell was born in India, educated as a scholarship
student at a private school in England, and completed his academic training at Eton in 1921. He then returned to the East
as a member of the Indian Imperial Police and served in
Burma until 1927. Disgusted with colonialism, he returned to
England and tried to begin a career as a writer. His life during
those impoverished years became the subject of his first book,*
Down and Out in Paris and London *(1933). All of these form-
ative experiences gave Orwell a strong sympathy with the oppressed classes, a sympathy reflected in his later writings as a
political journalist. He published a number of works of fiction
and nonfiction, of which the best known are* Homage to Cata-
lonia *(1938), an account of his participation in the Spanish
Civil War,* Animal Farm *(1945), an allegorical satire on the
social and political aftermath of the Russian Revolution, and*
Nineteen Eighty-Four *(1949), a novel envisioning a totali-
tarian society of the future. Orwell's political conscience, the
honesty and accuracy of his observation, and the clarity of his
style characterize all his work, including his autobiographical
writings. The selections that follow are from a diary that Orwell began after the outbreak of the Second World War and
continued until November, 1942.*

from "A War-time Diary"

7 September

Air-raid alarms now frequent enough, and lasting long enough,
for people habitually to forget whether the alarm is on at the

From *The Collected Essays, Journalism and Letters of George Orwell*, vol. II,
eds. Sonia Orwell and Ian Angus. © 1968 by Sonia Brownell Orwell. Reprinted
by permission of Harcourt Brace Jovanovich, Inc.

moment, or whether the All Clear has sounded. Noise of bombs and gunfire, except when very close (which probably means within two miles) now accepted as a normal background to sleep or conversation. I have still not heard a bomb go off with the sort of bang that makes you feel you are personally involved.

In Churchill's speech, number killed in air raids during August given as 1075. Even if truthful, probably a large understatement as it includes only civilian casualties. . . . The secretiveness officially practised about raids is extraordinary. Today's papers report that a bomb fell in a square "in central London". Impossible to find out which square it was, though thousands of people must know.

10 September

Can't write much of the insanities of the last few days. It is not so much that the bombing is worrying in itself as that the disorganisation of traffic, frequent difficulty of telephoning, shutting of shops whenever there is a raid on etc etc, combined with the necessity of getting on with one's ordinary work, wear one out and turn life into a constant scramble to catch up lost time. . . .

The delayed-action bombs are a great nuisance, but they appear to be successful in locating most of them and getting all the neighbouring people out until the bomb shall have exploded. All over South London, little groups of disconsolate-looking people wandering about with suitcases and bundles, either people who have been rendered homeless or, in more cases, who have been turned out by the authorities because of an unexploded bomb. . . .

Most of last night in the public shelter, having been driven there by recurrent whistle and crash of bombs not very far away at intervals of about a quarter of an hour. Frightful discomfort owing to overcrowding, though the place was well-appointed, with electric light and fans. People, mostly elderly working class, grousing bitterly about the hardness of the seats and the longness of the night, but no defeatist talk. . . .

People are now to be seen every night about dusk queuing up at the doors of the Shelters with their bedding. Those who come in first grab places on the floor and probably pass a reasonably good night. Day raids apart, the raiding hours are pretty regularly 8 pm to 4.30 am i.e. dusk to just before dawn.

I should think 3 months of continuous raids at the same intensity as the last 4 nights would break down everyone's morale. But it is doubtful whether anyone could keep up the attack on such a scale for 3 months, especially when he is suffering much the same himself.

12 September

As soon as the air raids began seriously, it was noticeable that people were much readier than before to talk to strangers in the street. . . . This morning met a youth of about 20, in dirty overalls, perhaps a garage hand. Very embittered and defeatist about the war, and horrified by the destruction he had seen in South London. He said that Churchill had visited the bombed area near the Elephant and at a spot where 20 out of 22 houses had been destroyed, remarked that it was "not so bad." The youth: "I'd have wrung his bloody neck if he'd said it to me." He was pessimistic about the war, considered Hitler was sure to win and would reduce London to much the same state as Warsaw. He spoke bitterly about the people rendered homeless in South London and eagerly took up my point when I said the empty houses in the West End should be requisitioned for them. He considered that all wars were fought for the profit of the rich, but agreed with me that this one would probably end in revolution. With all this, he was not unpatriotic. Part of his grouch was that he had tried to join the Air Force 4 times in the last 6 months, and always been put off.

Tonight and last night they have been trying the new device of keeping up a continuous AA barage, apparently firing blind or merely by sound, though I suppose there is some kind of sound-detector which estimates the height at which they must make the shells burst. . . . The noise is tremendous and almost continuous, but I don't mind it, feeling it to be on my side. Spent last night at Stephen Spender's place with a battery firing in the square at short intervals throughout the night. Slept through it easily enough, no bombs being audible in that place.

The havoc in the East End and South London is terrible, by all accounts. . . . Churchill's speech last night referred very seriously to danger of imminent invasion. If invasion is actually attempted and this is not a feint, the idea is presumably either to knock out our air bases along the South Coast, after which the ground defences can be well bombed, at the same time causing all possible confusion in London and its southward communications, *or* to draw as much as possible of our defensive forces south before delivering the attack on Scotland or possibly Ireland.

Meanwhile our platoon of Home Guards, after 3½ months, have about 1 rifle for 6 men, no other weapons except incendiary bombs, and perhaps 1 uniform for 4 men. After all, they have stood out against letting the rifles be taken home by individual men. They are all parked in one place, where a bomb may destroy the whole lot of them any night.

14 September
On the first night of the barrage, which was the heaviest, they are said to have fired 500,000 shells, i.e. at an average cost of £5 per shell, £2½ millions worth. But well worth it, for the effect on morale.

15 September
This morning, for the first time, saw an aeroplane shot down. It fell slowly out of the clouds, nose foremost, just like a snipe that has been shot high overhead. Terrific jubilation among the people watching, punctuated every now and then by the question, "Are you sure it's a German?" So puzzling are the directions given, and so many the types of aeroplane, that no one even knows which are German planes and which are our

own. My only test is that if a bomber is seen over London it must be a German, whereas a fighter is likelier to be ours.

17 September
Heavy bombing in this area last night till about 11 pm. . . . I was talking in the hallway of this house to two young men and a girl who was with them. Psychological attitude of all 3 was interesting. They were quite openly and unashamedly frightened, talking about how their knees were knocking together, etc and yet at the same time excited and interested, dodging out of doors between bombs to see what was happening and pick up shrapnel splinters. Afterwards in Mrs C's little reinforced room downstairs, with Mrs C and her daughter, the maid, and three young girls who are also lodgers here. All the women, except the maid, screaming in unison, clasping each other and hiding their faces, every time a bomb went past, but between-whiles quite happy and normal, with animated conversation proceeding. The dog subdued and obviously frightened, knowing something to be wrong. Marx is also like this during raids, i.e. subdued and uneasy. Some dogs, however, go wild and savage during a raid and have had to be shot. They allege here, and E says the same thing about Greenwich, that all the dogs in the park now bolt for home when they hear the siren.

Yesterday, when having my hair cut in the City, asked the barber if he carried on during raids. He said he did. And even if he was shaving someone? I said. Oh, yes, he carried on just the same. And one day a bomb will drop near enough to make him jump, and he will slice half somebody's face off.

Later, accosted by a man, I should think some kind of commercial traveller, with a bad type of face, while I was waiting for a bus. He began a rambling talk about how he was getting himself and his wife out of London, how his nerves were giving way and he suffered from stomach trouble, etc etc. I don't know how much of this kind of thing there is. . . . There has of course been a big exodus from the East End, and every night what amount to mass migrations to places where there is sufficient shelter accommodation. The practice of taking a 2d ticket and spending the night in one of the deep Tube stations, e.g. Piccadilly, is growing. . . . Everyone I have talked to agrees that the empty furnished houses in the West End should be used for the homeless; but I suppose the rich swine still have enough pull to prevent this from happening. The other day 50 people from the East End, headed by some of the Borough Councillors, marched into the Savoy and demanded to use the air-raid shelter. The management didn't succeed in ejecting them till the raid was over, when they went voluntarily. When you see how the wealthy are *still* behaving, in what is manifestly developing into a revolutionary war, you think of St Petersburg in 1916.

(Evening). Almost impossible to write in this infernal racket. (Electric lights have just gone off. Luckily I have some candles.) So many streets in (lights on again) the quarter roped off because of unexploded bombs, that to get home from Baker Street, say 300 yards, is like trying to find your way to the heart of a maze.

21 September

Have been unable for some days to buy another volume to continue this diary because, of the three or four stationers' shops in the immediate neighbourhood, all but one are cordoned off because of unexploded bombs.

Regular features of the time: neatly swept-up piles of glass, litter of stone and splinters of flint, smell of escaping gas, knots of sightseers waiting at the cordons.

Yesterday, at the entry to a street near here, a little crowd waiting with an ARP man in a black tin hat among them. A devastating roar, with a huge cloud of dust, etc. The man with the black hat comes running towards the ARP headquarters, where another with a white hat is emerging munching at a mouthful of bread and butter.

The man with the black hat: "Dorset Square, sir."

The man with the white hat: "OK." (Makes a tick in his notebook.)

Nondescript people wandering about, having been evacuated from their houses because of delayed-action bombs. Yesterday two girls stopping me in the street, very elegant in appearance except that their faces were filthily dirty: "Please, sir, can you tell us where we are?"

Withal, huge areas of London almost normal, and everyone quite happy in the daytime, never seeming to think about the coming night, like animals which are unable to foresee the future so long as they have a bit of food and a place in the sun.

24 September

Oxford Street yesterday, from Oxford Circus up to the Marble Arch, completely empty of traffic, and only a few pedestrians, with the late afternoon sun shining straight down the empty roadway and glittering on innumerable fragments of broken glass. Outside John Lewis's, a pile of plaster dress models, very pink and realistic, looking so like a pile of corpses that one could have mistaken them for that at a little distance. Just the same sight in Barcelona, only there it was plaster saints from desecrated churches.

Much discussion as to whether you would hear a bomb (i.e. its whistle) which was coming straight at you. All turns upon whether the bomb travels faster than sound. . . . One thing I have worked out, I think satisfactorily, is that the further away from you a bomb falls, the longer the whistle you will hear. The short whizz is therefore the sound that should make you dive for cover. I think this is really the principle one goes on in dodging a shell, but there one seems to know by a kind of instinct.

Possibilities for Writing

1. Try different kinds of relatively uncontrolled writing: free writing in which you keep going without any interruptions for a specific period of time; a more controlled version in which you occasionally pause briefly to see what new thought you might follow, but where you never take any lengthy break; a final version in which you concentrate on some particular memory of your past and try to write down everything you associate with that past experience, writing without regard to structure or complete statements, but keeping your attention on a single topic. Each of these exercises should be tried several times in different circumstances and should continue for ten to thirty minutes. Then compare how comfortable and productive each of these starting methods was for you and continue using the method of your choice regularly during the semester.

2. Try for a period of a week or two to maintain two journals. One would be a journal of experience, emphasizing your thoughts, feelings, fantasies, and those experiences which gave you a sense of the uniqueness of your own life. The other would be a journal of observation, in which you would record what you perceived in your environment, trying to capture through precise detail anything in the world that struck you as interesting and distinctive. Then compare the two journals to see what strengths as a writer you have revealed in each.

3. Keep a writer's diary of the course. Such a diary could be a

record of how you felt about your own writing, what subjects you chose to write about and why, what decisions you made as you were in the process of writing, and what surprised or interested or excited you when you were reviewing your own writing.

CHAPTER TWO

BEGINNINGS

Introduction: Engaging the Reader

This chapter turns us from the kinds of informal self-expression represented in Chapter One to the more formal task of putting oneself into words for an unknown audience whom we can reach only through the medium of our writing. Each selection has been limited to the first few paragraphs of a published autobiography, to show how each writer chooses to introduce himself to his readers. The variety among the selections demonstrates that there is no set way to manage this introduction. An inexperienced writer might suppose that a proper autobiography begins at the beginning, with some necessary facts about date and place of birth, parents' names and ages, and so forth. If he has such expectations, he is probably remembering situations in which he has been autobiographical while filling out forms, not really telling someone about himself but merely classifying himself in convenient categories: male, single, employed. In social situations, however, where we are really introducing ourselves to someone else—someone we would like to know and to be known by—we avoid engulfing the other person with all sorts of quantifiable data about ourselves. Instead we try to present ourselves as interesting and worth knowing. We offer some interesting anecdote, make some humorous remarks or some comments on whatever may be going on around us, hoping that we will awaken some lively response in the stranger. Our primary intention is not to furnish specific information; in fact, it is usually much later, when two people are better acquainted, that they begin to take an interest in factual details about each other's lives. Instead, an introductory social meeting is a time for presenting some facet of ourselves that is particularly engaging or impressive.

The same condition holds true with written autobiography, with one important difference. Writing is a monologue rather than a dialogue, at least to the extent that no actual person is present before the writer moment by moment, to cue him or urge him on by facial expression or verbal response. Because of this difference, some attributes of the talker are lost to the writer. For example, one way to make people we meet like us is to be sympathetic, interested in their experiences and judgments, and thus to impress them by the warmth and the intelligent attention we bestow on them. But the autobiographical writer has to, in effect, keep talking, compelling his audience's attention exclusively through what he says. To do this he must imagine an audience and respond to its questions and needs, so that ultimately his writing is not really a monologue but a special kind of dialogue with the other party located in the writer's own head. This other party must be intrigued by what the writer has to say; his anticipated questions have to be dealt with, and his intelligence and goodwill must be assumed and never imposed on.

One final connection should be made between meeting someone interesting in actual life and writing or reading interesting autobiographies. The word "interesting" is exasperatingly imprecise, but at least we know that saying "I met someone interesting today" is different from saying "I met someone important today." We should keep this distinction in mind when writing autobiography; it is not necessary to start off by recounting some grand and exceptional accomplishment or to worry if nothing in our lives strikes us as being very exceptional. Important people, after all, are often called self-important, meaning that they are so absorbed in their own accomplishments that they forget their responsibilities to their audience—including, if they are writers, that imaginary audience mentioned earlier. In writing autobiography we have to be interesting rather than important, for interest is clearly something created by the writer's attitude toward himself, his subject, and his audience. It may help clarify the point to review some of the beginnings reprinted here. Both George Kennan and Margaret Bourke-White were distinguished public figures, one a notable American diplomat, the other a famous photographer, yet both ignore their public careers as they begin their autobiographies. Instead, Bourke-White recalls her parents and the humorous circumstances of her birth, while Kennan involves the reader in the general problem of how one remembers the past.

What is interesting in writing, then, is whatever is capable of engaging the reader's attention. The selections here are assembled to prove that broad and liberating definition. By their variety they should encourage us to try things out ourselves. As we read we can see how Claude Brown chooses to thrust the reader suddenly into the midst of a highly dramatic moment, full of violence and danger, while Dylan Thomas provides a catalogue of the people and objects and events that struck a small boy as magical and wonderful. Each has found his own appropriate way to catch our ear and our eye. Thus Brown begins with abrupt dialogue and action because it evokes the sudden violence that he feels has been so much a part of his ghetto existence as a young black in Harlem. Thomas wants to suggest how the exotic and the ordinary tend to intermingle for a young child, and how, for such a child, life seems an endless series of marvelous moments. The last selection, by Raymond Mungo, is an appropriate conclusion, for Mungo dramatizes himself as a dropout from conventional society by making fun of many of the ways conventional autobiographies might begin, turning all of our usual expectations into jokes.

∽ Claude Brown ∽

(1937-   )

Claude Brown was born and raised in Harlem where he lived the violent life of an adolescent gang member in the ghetto. He spent time in the Wiltwyck School for disturbed boys and in reform school. He left Harlem for Greenwich Village, completed high school, and graduated from Howard University in 1965. Manchild in the Promised Land *(1965) is his account of his early life and his self-rehabilitation.*

from Manchild in the Promised Land

"Run!"

Where?

Oh, hell! Let's get out of here!

"Turk! Turk! I'm shot!"

I could hear Turk's voice calling from a far distance, telling me not to go into the fish-and-chips joint. I heard, but I didn't understand. The only thing I knew was that I was going to die.

I ran. There was a bullet in me trying to take my life, all thirteen years of it.

I climbed up on the bar yelling, "Walsh, I'm shot. I'm shot." I could feel the blood running down my leg. Walsh, the fellow who operated the fish-and-chips joint, pushed me off the bar and onto the floor. I couldn't move now, but I was still completely conscious.

Walsh was saying, "Git outta here, kid. I ain't got no time to play."

A woman was screaming, mumbling something about the Lord, and saying, "Somebody done shot that poor child."

Mama ran in. She jumped up and down, screaming like a crazy woman. I began to think about dying. The worst part of dying was thinking about the things and the people that I'd never see again. As I lay there trying to imagine what being dead was like, the policeman who had been trying to control Mama gave up and bent over me. He asked who had shot me. Before I could answer, he was asking me if I could hear him. I told him that I didn't know who had shot me and would he please tell Mama to stop jumping up and down. Every time Mama came down on that shabby floor, the bullet lodged in my stomach felt like a hot poker.

Another policeman had come in and was struggling to keep the crowd outside. I could see Turk in the front of the crowd. Before the cops came, he asked me if I was going to tell them that he was with me. I never answered. I looked at him and wondered if he saw who shot me. Then his question began to ring in my head: "Sonny, you gonna tell 'em I was with you?" I was bleeding on a dirty floor in a fish-and-chips joint, and Turk was standing there in the doorway hoping that I would die before I could tell the cops that he was with me. Not once did Turk ask me how I felt.

Hell, yeah, I thought, I'm gonna tell 'em.

It seemed like hours had passed before the ambulance finally arrived. Mama wanted to go to the hospital with me, but the ambulance attendant said she was too excited. On the way to Harlem Hospital, the cop who was riding with us asked Dad what he had to say. His answer was typical: "I told him about hanging out with those bad-ass boys." The cop was a little surprised. This must be a rookie, I thought.

The next day, Mama was at my bedside telling me that she had prayed and the Lord had told her that I was going to live. Mama said that many of my friends wanted to donate some blood for me, but the hospital would not accept it from narcotics users.

This was one of the worst situations I had ever been in. There was a tube in my nose that went all the way to the pit of my stomach. I was being fed intravenously, and there was a drain in my side. Everybody came to visit me, mainly out of curiosity. The girls were all anxious to know where I had gotten shot. They had heard all kinds of tales about where the bullet struck. The bolder ones wouldn't even bother to ask: they just snatched the cover off me and looked for themselves. In a few days, the word got around that I was in one piece.

~ George Kennan ~

(1904-   )

George Kennan was born in Wisconsin and educated at Prince-
ton. He has had a distinguished career as a diplomat, serving
primarily in Germany, Russia, and Eastern Europe. Since the
early 1950s, he has pursued scholarly interests as a historian
associated with the Institute for Advanced Studies at Princeton
and has published a series of studies of Soviet-American rela-
tions in the twentieth century. The opening pages of his Memoirs: 1925–1950 *are reprinted below.*

A PERSONAL NOTE

There are, of course, great variations in people's capacity to remember consciously their early youth. My own, I fear, falls at
the weaker end of the spectrum. Beyond this, I wonder
whether, in this rapidly moving age, every older man does not
stand at a greater distance from his own childhood and adolescence than was the case when the pace of change was less
precipitate—whether the immediacy of remembered experience is not impaired by the ruthless destruction of setting
which the explosions of population and technological change
have so often worked. I, in any case, see only dimly and uncertainly—too uncertainly to permit of confident judgments—the
thin, tense, introverted Princeton student whose physical
frame and reflexes I know myself to have inherited. More
dimly do I perceive, behind him, the grubby military school

cadet. Wholly untrustworthy and inadequate are the glimpses of the grade school boy, clad in the knickerbockers of the period, traveling back and forth between school and home on the new "pay-as-you-enter" streetcars of the Milwaukee street railways system (which thrilled him inordinately), retiring into sullen rages and sit-down strikes when required to attend Bournique's dancing school on Saturday afternoons, dreaming daydreams so intense and satisfying that hours could pass in oblivion of immediate surroundings. And when one moves still further into the past and arrives at the small child, the resources of memory fail altogether. I have found myself tempted to relate that this child was deeply affected, and in a certain sense scarred for life, by the loss of his mother shortly after his birth. This is, perhaps, a rational deduction, supported by a certain amount of circumstantial evidence from later years. But it is not really anything drawn from memory.

The fact is that one moves through life like someone moving with a lantern in a dark woods. A bit of the path ahead is illuminated, and a bit of the path behind. But the darkness follows hard on one's footsteps, and envelopes our trail as one proceeds. Were one to be able, as one never is, to retrace the steps by daylight, one would find that the terrain traversed bears, in reality, little relationship to what imagination and memory had pictured. We are, toward the end of our lives, such different people, so far removed from the childhood figures with whom our identity links us, that the bond to those figures, like that of nations to their obscure prehistoric origins, is almost irrelevant.

There is another difficulty that confronts me when I try to describe the early self. In my own youthful consciousness, more, perhaps, than in the case of many others, the borderline between external and internal reality was unfirm. I lived, particularly in childhood but with lessening intensity right on to middle age, in a world that was peculiarly and intimately my own, scarcely to be shared with others or even made plausible to them. I habitually read special meanings into things, scenes,

and places—qualities of wonder, beauty, promise, or horror—
for which there was no external evidence visible, or plausible, to
others. My world was peopled with mysteries, seductive hints,
vague menaces, "intimations of immortality." For example, at
the foot of the street we lived on in Milwaukee there was a particular entryway in a particular brick building—a dark, cav-
ernous aperture, lurking behind a heavy romanesque archway
of grimy brick, flush with the street—that held for me a sinis-
ter significance all its own. Behind it, I never doubted, lay a
house of horror—horror unnamed, unmentionable, not to be
imagined. It was plain, on the other hand, that the trunks of
the trees in Juneau Park were populated by fairies. My cousin
Catherine had told my older sister Frances that this was the
case, and long, respectful contemplation of the park on my
part convinced me that the hypothesis was probably correct.

How, then, if I am to consider my youth today in terms that
could have meaning to other people, am I to weave my way effectively between what others could accept as reality and what
they could not? How do I know what was real and what was
not? To the extent that memory can carry me back at all into
those dim recesses, it can do no more than to confront me with
these uncertainties. Perhaps the house at the end of our street
had indeed been the scene of some horrible unmentionable
tragedy; perhaps it was affected by this, as houses sometimes
are; and perhaps the fine antennae of the child picked up something of the ensuing desolation. Can I even be sure, for that
matter, that there were not really fairies in Juneau Park?
Things scarcely less strange have been known to happen. That
it would be difficult to find the fairies there today I have no
doubt. The automobiles have probably done them in, as they
have done in so many other things in that now blighted region
of central Milwaukee. But who can be sure what was there in
1910? Things are as we see them. It took two of us—the park
and myself—to make possible a given view, a given apprehension, if you will, of the place. Fairies were a part of this view.
To what extent they had their existence in the park and to what

extent in me we shall never know. Perhaps a long and intensive self-analysis, along Freudian lines, would clarify such things. Were I a great artist, a great criminal, the subject of some highly complex and unusual experience, or one of exceptional personal failings and virtues, there might be reason for it. I am none of these things.

～ Margaret Bourke-White ～

(1906-1971)

Margaret Bourke-White was an exceptional photographer and journalist. She created award-winning photographic essays for many national magazines during a professional career of more than thirty years. Her autobiography, Portrait of Myself *(1963), recalls many of her assignments as a photographic correspondent, as well as her struggle against the effects of Parkinson's disease later in her life.*

MY INVITATION INTO THE WORLD

"Margaret, you can always be proud that you were invited into the world," my mother told me.

I don't know where she got this fine philosophy that children should come because they were wanted and should not be the result of accidents. She came from a poor family with a multitude of children, and she had little chance to get an education, although she made up for this after marriage by going to college at intervals until she was over sixty. When each of her own three children was on the way, Mother would say to those closest to her, "I don't know whether this will be a boy or girl and I don't care. But this child was invited into the world and *it* will be a wonderful child."

She was explicit about the invitation and believed the child should be the welcomed result of a known and definite act of love between man and wife (which Mahatma Gandhi believed—I was to learn much later—although Mother never would have gone along with the Mahatma on his ideas of celibacy between invitations. Mother believed in warmth and ardor between married partners).

Mother's plan of voluntary parenthood was so outstandingly successful in my case that not only did I come along as requested, but I arrived on the specific date that had been decided upon.

This fine flourish to my orderly entry into upper Manhattan was as much the doctor's doing as my mother's. In the early evening of June 13 my arrival was imminent, and the doctor had directed my mother to walk the floor to ease and speed the process. He noticed that my father was placing some packages wrapped as gifts on the dining room table, and inquired about it.

"Tomorrow is our wedding anniversary," said my father.

"Put that woman to bed," ordered the doctor, and devoting himself to postponing my arrival, he held me off till two o'clock the next morning.

This was a good birthday in any case for a little American girl, as on June 14 the whole nation hangs out the Stars and Stripes to commemorate the day when Betsy Ross hung the first American flag. But my friends who know my bad habits, and hear the story of my delayed arrival, are apt to complain that I have never been on time for an appointment since.

∽ Dylan Thomas ∽

(1914-1953)

Welshman Dylan Thomas published his first volume of poetry by the time he was twenty. During a relatively short lifetime, he established a reputation as a major British poet and attracted additional public attention through his flamboyant and somewhat disreputable life style. The passage that follows begins his essay "Reminiscences of Childhood" (1943), a lyrical evocation of his boyhood in Wales.

REMINISCENCES OF CHILDHOOD

I like very much people telling me about their childhood, but they'll have to be quick or else I'll be telling them about mine.

I was born in a large Welsh town at the beginning of the Great War—an ugly, lovely town (or so it was and is to me), crawling, sprawling by a long and splendid curving shore where truant boys and sandfield boys and old men from nowhere, beachcombed, idled and paddled, watched the dockbound ships or the ships steaming away into wonder and India, magic and China, countries bright with oranges and loud with lions; threw stones into the sea for the barking outcast dogs; made castles and forts and harbours and race tracks in the sand; and on Saturday summer afternoons listened to the brass band, watched the Punch and Judy, or hung about on the fringes of the crowd to hear the fierce religious speakers who shouted at the sea, as though it were wicked and wrong to roll in and out like that, white-horsed and full of fishes.

One man, I remember, used to take off his hat and set fire to his hair every now and then, but I do not remember what it proved, if it proved anything at all, except that he was a very interesting man.

This sea-town was my world; outside a strange Wales, coal-pitted, mountained, river-run, full, so far as I knew, of choirs and football teams and sheep and storybook tall hats and red flannel petticoats, moved about its business which was none of mine.

∾ Isadora Duncan ∾

(1878-1927)

Isadora Duncan was born in San Francisco, but her great fame as an interpretive dancer was achieved on the European continent. She combined her dance theories of natural movement with an outspoken advocacy of greater personal freedom for women and of democratic political principles. Her autobiography, My Life *(1927), a candid account of her unconventional private and public behavior, was written the same year that she was killed in a freak accident.*

INTRODUCTORY

I confess that when it was first proposed to me I had a terror of writing this book. Not that my life has not been more interesting than any novel and more adventurous than any cinema and, if really well written, would not be an epoch-making recital, but there's the rub—the writing of it!

It has taken me years of struggle, hard work and research to learn to make one simple gesture, and I know enough about the Art of writing to realise that it would take me again just so many years of concentrated effort to write one simple, beautiful sentence. How often have I contended that although one man might toil to the Equator and have tremendous exploits with lions and tigers, and try to write about it, yet fail, whereas another, who never left his verandah, might write of the killing of tigers in their jungles in a way to make his readers feel that he was actually there, until they can suffer his agony and apprehension, smell lions and hear the fearful approach of the rattle-snake. Nothing seems to exist save in the imagination, and all the marvellous things that have happened to me may lose their savour because I do not possess the pen of a Cervantes or even of a Casanova.

Then another thing. How can we write the truth about ourselves? Do we even know it? There is the vision our friends have of us; the vision we have of ourselves, and the vision our lover has of us. Also the vision our enemies have of us—and all these visions are different. I have good reason to know this, because I have had served to me with my morning coffee newspaper criticisms that declared I was beautiful as a goddess, and that I was a genius, and hardly had I finished smiling contentedly over this, than I picked up the next paper and read that I was without any talent, badly shaped and a perfect harpy.

I soon gave up reading criticisms of my work. I could not stipulate that I should only be given the good ones, and the bad were too depressing and provocatively homicidal. There was a critic in Berlin who pursued me with insults. Among other things he said that I was profoundly unmusical. One day I wrote imploring him to come and see me and I would convince him of his errors. He came and as he sat there, across the tea-table, I harangued him for an hour and a half about my theories of visional movement created from music. I noticed that he seemed most prosaic and stolid, but what was my uproarious dismay when he produced from his pocket a deafaphone and informed me he was quite deaf and even with his instrument could hardly hear the orchestra; although he sat in the first row of the stalls! This was the man whose views on myself had kept me awake at night!

So, if at each point of view others see in us a different person how are we to find in ourselves yet another personality of whom to write in this book? Is it to be the Chaste Madonna, or the Messalina, or the Magdalen, or the Blue Stocking? Where can I find the woman of all these adventures? It seems to me there was not one, but hundreds—and my soul soaring aloft, not really affected by any of them.

It has been well said that the first essential in writing about anything is that the writer should have no experience of the matter. To write of what one has actually experienced in words, is to find that they become most evasive. Memories are less tangible than dreams. Indeed, many dreams I have had seem more vivid than my actual memories. Life is a dream, and it is well that it is so, or who could survive some of its experiences? Such, for instance, as the sinking of the *Lusitania*. An experience like that should leave forever an expression of horror upon the faces of the men and women who went through it, whereas we meet them everywhere smiling and happy. It is only in romances that people undergo a sudden metamorphosis. In real life, even after the most terrible experiences, the main character remains exactly the same. Witness the number of Russian princes who, after losing everything they possessed, can be seen any evening at Montmartre supping as gaily as ever with chorus girls, just as they did before the war.

Any woman or man who would write the truth of their lives would write a great work. But no one has dared to write the truth of their lives. Jean-Jacques Rousseau made this supreme sacrifice for Humanity—to unveil the truth of his soul, his most intimate actions and thoughts. The result is a great book. Walt Whitman gave his truth to America. At one time his book was forbidden to the mails as an "immoral book." This term seems absurd to us now. No woman has ever told the whole truth of her life. The autobiographies of most famous women are a series of accounts of the outward existence, of petty details and anecdotes which give no realisation of their real life. For the great moments of joy or agony they remain strangely silent.

∽ Norman Podhoretz ∽

(1930-   )

*Norman Podhoretz was born in Brooklyn of Jewish immigrant
parents and was educated at Columbia University and Cambridge University. He supported himself as a freelance writer
on literary and cultural subjects and in 1960 became editor of*
Commentary Magazine. *His autobiography,* Making It *(1967),
describes his ambitious effort to establish himself as an intellectual celebrity in New York.*

THE BRUTAL BARGAIN

One of the longest journeys in the world is the journey from
Brooklyn to Manhattan—or at least from certain neighbor-
hoods in Brooklyn to certain parts of Manhattan. I have made
that journey, but it is not from the experience of having made
it that I know how very great the distance is, for I started on
the road many years before I realized what I was doing, and
by the time I did realize it I was for all practical purposes already there. At so imperceptible a pace did I travel, and with
so little awareness, that I never felt footsore or out of breath or
weary at the thought of how far I still had to go. Yet whenever
anyone who has remained back there where I started—remained not physically but socially and culturally, for the
neighborhood is now a Negro ghetto and the Jews who have
"remained" in it mostly reside in the less affluent areas of
Long Island—whenever anyone like that happens into the
world in which I now live with such perfect ease, I can see that
in his eyes I have become a fully acculturated citizen of a coun-

try as foreign to him as China and infinitely more frightening.

That country is sometimes called the upper middle class; and indeed I am a member of that class, less by virtue of my income than by virtue of the way my speech is accented, the way I dress, the way I furnish my home, the way I entertain and am entertained, the way I educate my children—the way, quite simply, I look and I live. It appalls me to think what an immense transformation I had to work on myself in order to become what I have become: if I had known what I was doing I would surely not have been able to do it, I would surely not have wanted to. No wonder the choice had to be blind; there was a kind of treason in it: treason toward my family, treason toward my friends. In choosing the road I chose, I was pronouncing a judgment upon them, and the fact that they themselves concurred in the judgment makes the whole thing sadder but no less cruel.

When I say that the choice was blind, I mean that I was never aware—obviously not as a small child, certainly not as an adolescent, and not even as a young man already writing for publication and working on the staff of an important intellectual magazine in New York—how inextricably my "noblest" ambitions were tied to the vulgar desire to rise above the class into which I was born; nor did I understand to what an astonishing extent these ambitions were shaped and defined by the standards and values and tastes of the class into which I did not know I wanted to move. It is not that I was or am a social climber as that term is commonly used. High society interests me, if at all, only as a curiosity; I do not wish to be a member of it; and in any case, it is not, as I have learned from a small experience of contact with the very rich and fashionable, my "scene." Yet precisely because social climbing is not one of my vices (unless what might be called celebrity climbing, which very definitely *is* one of my vices, can be considered the contemporary variant of social climbing), I think there may be more than a merely personal significance in the fact that class has played so large a part both in my life and in my career.

∽ Raymond Mungo ∽

(1946-   )

Raymond Mungo attended Boston University and edited the school newspaper there. He was involved in revolutionary politics during the late 1960s and helped to found the Liberation News Service, an underground press syndicate. His autobiography, Famous Long Ago *(1970), tells of his political activities and of the changes in his outlook that prompted him to take up life on a communal farm in Vermont.*

MY LIFE AND HARD TIMES

I was born in a howling blizzard in February, 1946, in one of those awful mill towns in eastern Massachusetts, and lived to tell about it. My parents were and are hard-working, ordinary people lacking the "benefits" of higher education and the overwhelming *angst* and cynicism which come with it. I was thus not raised in what most of you would call a middle-class environment, lucky for me. Were I true to my roots I'd now be a laborer in a paper or textile mill, married and the father of two children, a veteran of action in Vietnam, and a reasonably brainwashed communicant in a Roman Catholic, predominantly Irish parish. Instead, I am a lazy good-for-nothing dropout, probably a Communist dupe, and live on a communal farm way, way into the backwoods of Vermont. What went wrong?

At the age of one, I can clearly recall, I was rocked on my mother's lap in the middle of some dark New England winter night, the light from our kitchen lamp shone on the ceiling, and the rocking motion gave it a moving, undulating shape which formed beautiful patterns in my infant mind—obviously the forerunner of the psychedelic experience for me.

At the age of four, I read books—Dick and Jane readers, Bobbsey Twins, Tom Swift, and my parents' encyclopedia of human anatomy, which featured dirty pictures.

At four and one half years, I went to kindergarten, but the girl who sat next to me (her name was Patty) had clammy wet hands and since I was always made to hold her hand during ring-around-the-rosy, I dropped out.

At five and one half, I entered Sister Joseph Anthony's first grade classroom and, being physically puny, elected to become the smartest kid in school to compensate. And did.

In the second grade, I was primed for my First Holy Communion. My parents had spent money we couldn't afford on a beautiful white suit in which I was to receive Jesus for the first time. The night before this holy event, I could not sleep, and rose from my bed—over which the picture of Jesus was broadly smiling upon me—to investigate the pantry. There, I ate a whole box of peanuts reserved for First Holy Communion festivities the next day; then noticed that it was 3:30 A.M., and realized I had *broken the fast*. (In those days, Catholics were required to fast from midnight on the day they received Communion. To receive the host without having fasted was a mortal sin; that means you go to hell if you suddenly die under the wheels of a runaway car, a tableau which had often been presented to me in Sisters' school.) My alternatives were to refuse Holy Communion, thus obeying the sacred law of Rome and disappointing my parents and all my relatives, or else to receive Holy Communion, thus insulting Jesus and Mary but pleasing the family. The picture of Jesus was now crying over my bed. Next morning, I said nothing of the peanuts, just took the First Holy Communion, and nobody was the wiser. Except me, I had nightmares of runaway cars and eternal damnation for a year, until I got up the courage to confess the mortal sin to Father Gallivan.

In the eighth grade, puberty came between me and the

93

Church, and I went through a harrowing Stephen Dedalus thing for about three years; you know all about stuff like that so I won't bore you with the details.

For four years, I hitchhiked thirty miles twice a day to attend an R.C. prep school where everybody except me was rich and my tuition was paid by a full scholarship, for I was seen as a promising lad and a likely candidate for the priesthood. I knew the only way out of the mills was through college, so I kept my Stephen Dedalus secrets from everybody until I was safely out of that school with a bundle of college scholarships.

Life began at seventeen. I left home, which was a good and simply virtuous place, and my parents, with whom I have never had a really bad scene, and moved to Boston to get hip about the big big world out there. During my freshman year, I was a violent Marxist, friend of the working class and all that, and relished my background among the oppressed. I was also the victim of a burning need for and involvement with the theatre, having graduated from all the usual precocious-adolescent trips with Romantic poets, Italian composers, Surrealist painters, and dirty novelists. I wrote plays for Theater of the Absurd, which was a big thing back in 1963.

During my sophomore year at college, somebody (God bless him) turned me on to dope. I grew very fond of it, all kinds of it. Dope didn't really become an all-American college preoccupation until 1966 or 1967, so I was a few years ahead in that department. I was then a pacifist and in the process of getting educated about the war in Vietnam, which in 1964 most of my classmates didn't even know was going on. From Vietnam I learned to despise my countrymen, my government, and the entire English-speaking world, with its history of genocide and international conquest. I was a normal kid.

By my junior year, I had lost my virginity and that changed everything. I was living in a wretched Boston slum and working my way through school. I traveled around the country participating in demonstrations against the war in Vietnam, and lived from day to day, smoked a lot of dope and fornicated every night. It was glorious.

In my senior year, I edited the college newspaper and put a lot of stuff about draft resistance, the war, abortions, dope, black people, and academic revolutions in it. Which, even though it was 1966, people seemed to think was pretty far-out stuff indeed. I walked with Mr. LSD and met God, who taught me to flow with it and always seek to be kind. "I am striving to understand."

Toward the very end of my college daze, I had a fat fellowship to Harvard University for graduate school and for lack of anything more exciting to do, intended to use it. But a madman named Marshall Bloom flew into Boston from London one cold April day and put the question to me, did I want to join him in overthrowing the state down in Washington, D.C.? Overthrowing the state seemed to me an excellent idea, it desperately needed to get done, and since if you want something done right you must do it yourself, I said OK why not? Fare thee well simple hometown and good parents, good riddance Catholicism, so long Boston it was nice while it lasted, goodbye school and teachers and warm fat books, I'm off to make my fortune in Washington, D.C., the nation's capital. I'm out to show the emperor without his clothes and tear down the walls of the rotten imperial city and have fun doing it. Fair New England, we'll meet again in the New Age and not before.

That's me on the Merritt Parkway, hauling my cat, her kittens, my friend Steve who turned me on, and all my worldly belongings. There's me on the New Jersey Turnpike puffing on a lighthearted cigarette and leaving behind my debts, hangups, and unborn child. On to Washington to fulfill my years of dreaming of Revolution in my time! Got my manuscripts, my one oil painting, two or three dollars in change, a few records, and my friend. This is the way a young man starts his career.

Now, dear friend, you know as much about me as you need to know. What follows is a story, by no means complete, of what happened to me during the few years after I started. Please don't try to learn anything from it, for there is no message. Try to enjoy it, as I have (at least much of the time) enjoyed putting it down for you. Take it slow, don't try to read it in one sitting, by all means get distracted from time to time. Read it stoned, read it straight, give up and never finish it, it's all the same between friends. Take care of your health and get plenty of rest.

Possibilities for Writing

1. Write a beginning for your own autobiography, then make an exchange with someone else in the class and write a brief response to his beginning. In your response, comment on what you found interesting and suggest possible directions in which the autobiography could continue.

2. Experiment by writing two or three different beginnings for your own autobiography, perhaps starting one with your earliest memories, one with a formal sketch of your family background, and one with a vivid account of an important moment in your life. The selections reprinted in this section might give you some other ideas about ways of beginning your own story.

3. Choose three of the autobiographical beginnings in this section and write at least a one-page continuation for each, maintaining the style and attitude that you feel the author has tried to establish.

CHAPTER THREE

~~~~~~

EVENTS

Introduction: Narration and Point of View

When we say that autobiography is the writer's own story, we are reminding ourselves not only that autobiography is a form of personal expression, but also that it is a story, an account of what happened to the writer. What happened can mean what he did or felt or thought, for the events of his story can just as easily emphasize the inner, private life or the outer, public one. But wherever and however the writer chooses to begin, he is sure to find himself caught up in the creative process of telling a story.

It is important to remember that creative storytelling begins when we first choose an event in our lives as an autobiographical subject. When writing about a memorable day we would not simply follow the clock ("At 7:30 I got up; at 7:45 I had breakfast") any more than we would answer a friend's casual "What've you been doing?" by taking out our appointment calendar. These examples sound absurd because such lists of what happened by clock or calendar are highly impersonal—like records of police calls and fire alarms. No individual really experiences life as an unvarying succession of equally important moments and so naturally no one remembers the past in that way either. Any writer's explanation of what happened is from the beginning a creative shaping of past experience based on what his own memory establishes as vivid and meaningful. Once the writer recognizes that memory is the storehouse of the memorable, he can call upon his memory as a creative resource.

The memory of a day on a college campus would certainly take different forms for a freshman student, a visitor from a foreign country, and a city building inspector because the things each found worth remembering would vary so widely. But even if we chose two freshmen who were close friends and compared their memories of a single hour in the same class, we could still expect to find significant differences in the kinds of selection and emphasis that govern what they remember. Obviously their accounts would overlap, but they would never be identical; we all see the world with different eyes and from the vantage point of different lives. The uniqueness of our individual perspective is something we rarely celebrate or even think about, since it is universal and inescapable, but because of it, when we begin to remember an autobiographical event, we are already regarding that event in a distinctive way.

Although our memory does a good deal of shaping and selecting, giving our experience an initial form, something more is necessary to realize that form effectively in our writing. First, and perhaps most important, we need to exploit our greatest resource, memory, to the fullest, coaxing and prodding it to yield to us more and more of the usable past. Sometimes, of course, memories can overwhelm us with extraordinary power, evoking a past whose vividness virtually displaces the present moment, and our writing seems to share this rush of energy, proceeding fluently, almost without a pause, to say everything we wish to say. But we are much more likely to remember only the outline of an event, our general feelings, and a few stray details. The writer who settles for such fragments has impoverished himself unnecessarily by not making a greater effort to have more of his past accessible for his purposes. There are many ways to make such an exploratory effort. A writer can become his own interviewer, following the methods illustrated in the first chapter, pursuing himself like a trained journalist; he can follow a process of association, linking images and ideas in ways that may eventually reveal a pattern or form; he can concentrate on producing a mental

picture of the event, painstakingly visualizing detail after detail. He may simply drift in reverie, giving in to memory
rather than trying to control it. Whatever method or combination of methods a writer uses in order to produce a more intense or a more expansive sense of some event in his past life,
his immediate goal is to activate clusters of recollection, not
necessarily connected with one another or coherently assembled, but piled high like backstage scenery. The value of
such clusters is that they give the writer confidence to proceed,
and they give him options about how to proceed. The more
material he has at hand and the more fertile he comes to believe his own inventive powers are, the more confidently he will
approach any later tasks of reorganizing his material. If he is
pinched or strained for things to say, he will resist revising or
cutting anything he already has on paper because he cannot
be sure he will be able to produce anything in its place. Possibly the most valuable kind of confidence for a writer is his
feeling that his subject (whether autobiographical or not) is
richly and variously his, so that he could write about it in
many different ways.

After exploring his memory and keeping as many notes and
jottings as possible about what he remembers, the writer may
feel that what he sees in front of him is not a record of an autobiographical event, but merely a crazy jumble of disorganized
data. All writing of any imaginative power, however, exists as
jumble at some stage, either at an early phase of mental groping, at a later point with successive reroutings of our trains of
thought, or at a still later point when the process of translation
into words written on a page begins. While most writers experience all of these stages in varying intensity, they are of
course particularly aware of the last stage because the jumble
is written out before their eyes. We may feel vaguely embarrassed and inferior when we see our own jumble on the page,
but that is because we are so accustomed to reading written
language in its published form, clear, controlled, and convincing. We assume that the sprawl and mess is leading us away

from effective writing rather than toward it, but this is not the case. Instead, we need to see jumble differently, as a necessary precondition to most good writing, for jumble is part of the process by which creativity discovers itself.

At this point, the writer is ready to test out possibilities in a written draft. Creating the first draft leads him from the first crucial stage of the writing process to the second. On the one hand, the first draft should try to sustain the kind of imaginative freedom and flexibility that the process of exploration encouraged in the prewriting stage. On the other hand, the first draft also introduces in a very broad way elements of conscious choice, for the writer has to decide which memories he will use and emphasize and how he will connect one memory with another. Conscious choice, already important as the first draft gets underway, becomes crucial when the draft is completed. As he looks over his first draft, the writer must decide whether he is satisfied with what he has accomplished and whether he now approves the preliminary choices he has already made. It is possible that the first draft may also be the last draft, if he finds that his intuitions and his preliminary choices have resulted in a satisfying narrative. More often, however, as the writer reviews where he chose to begin and end, what kinds of consistency he has established within his story, and what sort of order he has used to present events, he finds something, major or minor, that he wishes to alter. When he decides to do so, he enters fully into what can be called the editing process, the conscious search for the style and the structure most appropriate to a particular subject. It is the editing process that this text will discuss, here and in subsequent chapters, by suggesting what some of a writer's most frequent decisions are likely to be and by providing some examples of the choices made by other writers in similar situations.

The episode for Maya Angelou's autobiography shows how one published writer shapes a subject already mentioned in the discussion of the exploratory stage in writing—the experience of a school graduation. It is important to remember that

Angelou must have gone through the exploratory stage and the editing stage herself, but that what we see and can discuss is the result of that process, with no indication of how short or how long, how simple or how complex the process proved to be for her. What we can be sure of is her persistent and intense exploration of memory, for her account is vividly detailed and convincing. What seems to have struck Angelou as one important part of her experience is the gap between the kind of expectations she had for her graduation and the actual feelings that came over her during the ceremony. In order to make her readers feel this contrast, she has to give prominence to those memories that have some bearing on this special subject. She takes particular care to describe at length the preparations for the great event, the days and weeks of anticipation, the pleasure and pride she felt in her own success. In the same way she dramatizes in detail how the ceremony illustrates the painful injustices of a segregated society and turns her sense of triumph into humiliation. Finally she shows how the singing of James Weldon Johnson's anthem by the graduating class alters her feelings once more, giving her a new sense of pride in the courage and determination of black people. This pattern of changing feelings is created by Angelou as she makes three choices in the editorial process: what to include or exclude, where to begin and end, and whether to emphasize something or treat it casually. None of these choices are simple either/or decisions, but they are basic choices that give to day-to-day experience the meaningful shape and proportion of narrative.

To say that selection and emphasis always play a part in good writing does not mean that all good writing narrows down to a single focus of interest. The Angelou selection includes many details that have no direct bearing on the graduation but that help to evoke the conditions of life in a small Arkansas town and to characterize her relations with members of her family—to give us, in short, the sense of the texture of her life, regardless of any particular dramatic event. Nevertheless, another writer might want to go much further than Angelou in creating the impression that he is telling us everything about his life by including far more random detail, justifying the more chaotic organization by pointing to the way he came closer to capturing the immediacy and variety of experience. Similarly, another writer might not stay within the time scheme of a single sequence of events, as Angelou does. Instead, he might want his writing to reflect a freer range of recollection, linking one event to another by a loose association of thought and feeling. In such cases, the writer is not abandoning the editing process, but is using it to stretch out the narrative sequence and to bring out complexities in the story he is telling.

A writer may also simply move out of the narrative sequence altogether, in order to explain or argue, interpret or justify, for the purpose of giving his readers an explicit commentary on the importance and meaning of the narrative. Angelou's final paragraph

> If we were a people much given to revealing secrets, we might raise monuments and sacrifice to the memories of our poets, but slavery cured us of that weakness. It may be enough, however, to have it said that we survive in exact relationship to the dedication of our poets (include preachers, musicians and blues singers).

is an example of how she can detach herself from the graduation event to give us her views on one aspect of its meaning. The selection by George Orwell, for example, makes us even more aware of a narrator for whom events are memories from a different kind of world. Orwell exemplifies the most flexible approach to autobiographical narrative, just as Piri Thomas shows how effective straightforward narrative with no shifts or deviations can be. The other selections in this chapter can be compared with both Orwell and Thomas, since they occupy different places on a spectrum bounded by narratives that comment extensively on experience and narratives that present experience directly.

The passage from Maya Angelou quoted above also suggests one final issue connected with autobiographical narrative—the question of point of view. Any writer of autobiography is telling us about himself as he was at some time in the past, but he is also writing about that past from the perspective of the present, with whatever advantages hindsight provides. The comment by Angelou about black poets and the survival of a black heritage illustrates this perspective, for it is not a comment that the ten-year-old Angelou would have been capable of making at the time of her graduation. Obviously, no writer is going to erase entirely the passage of time and re-create exactly the thoughts and feelings of the younger person he once was, but the writer must decide to what extent he wants to create some form of dramatic illusion and to reproduce the point of view of a much younger self. The writer who persistently reflects and interprets, like Orwell, is keeping the reader constantly aware of his mature self; the writer who dramatizes, like Thomas, projects the reader more forcefully into the time and conditions of his earlier life. Angelou expresses a more customary balance between thoughts and attitudes of the present interwoven with the continuing drama of past experience. These various arrangements simply show that some relationship between a past and a present self must be in any writer's mind as he attempts to recover the past and interpret it.

The awareness of how one views one's own past is part of the general issue of how the writer sees what he writes about—the issue of point of view. Progression and dramatic momentum in autobiography are created by the writer's selection of events and the emphasis he gives them, but the way that a narrative holds together depends on the writer's ability to create a point of view toward the events. Temporal sequence (how events are related to one another in time) is central to our understanding of narrative; point of view (the vantage point from which these events are seen and presented) is central to our understanding of the narrator.

We can best appreciate how point of view influences autobiographical narrative by comparing the selections by George Plimpton and Jerry Kramer, each of which describes how the writer participated in several crucial plays in a football game. There are some obvious distinctions between the two situations, the most important being that one game is a preseason scrimmage, while the other is a championship playoff. The most important contrast, however, involves the difference in points of view. George Plimpton describes the situation as a writer and magazine editor who has never before played tackle football, let alone worked with a professional team; Jerry Kramer reports the feelings and reactions of a seasoned professional player caught up in a game where money and prestige ride on every play. Plimpton sees things from the point of view of the anxious outsider. He stresses his own uncertainty and sense of imminent disaster, and he describes what happens in the language of someone whose frame of reference is quite different from that of the football player. When Plimpton tells of a player lifting his head in the offensive huddle and looking across at the defense, "the egg-smooth surface of the helmet, its cage pointed at me, adding to the sense of that impersonal scrutiny, like a robot monster's," he clearly records the impressions of someone who sees the conventional uniforms of players as strange and inhuman. The reference to "robot monster" is a good example of how Plimpton's language establishes his viewpoint as that of an outsider. Kramer, on the other hand, pays no attention to how players looked, since the conditions of the game are so familiar to him. Instead he concentrates on the tactics and strategies of the game, on the ebb and flow of his team's success. He depends much more on the technical language of football ("halfback-option," "out of the pocket") and even on the special shorthand used in the huddle ("give-65") in order to convey an insider's view of what happened on the field during a championship game. We trust his account because certain elements in it—the familiarity with special terminology, the attention to tactics and execution—create a point of view which gives authority and consistency to his narration.

The distinctions made between Plimpton's and Kramer's accounts say nothing about the relative quality of the selections;

they simply mark how the language of each piece establishes the writer's way of seeing and interpreting events. Moreover, point of view, like selection and emphasis, is an aspect of the writer's craft that can begin to emerge without conscious effort, as soon as the writer puts some·words on a page. The basic contours of Plimpton's and Kramer's points of view depend on the images and language that come most readily to their minds, not on some highly deliberate procedure of creation. But the great majority of writers benefit by knowing something about how and why they shape a narrative to give their story its interest and intensity. Those elements of the writer's craft that have been discussed in this introduction are not the sources of autobiography, but they are the necessary means of turning an autobiographical awareness into communicable forms of expression.

∽ Frank Conroy ∽

(1936-)

Frank Conroy was born in New York and educated at Haverford College. He is now a writer and an occasional piano player in New York jazz clubs. Stop-Time (1965), his first book, is an account of his boyhood in Florida and New York.

THE COLDNESS OF PUBLIC PLACES

[IN TROUBLE AT SCHOOL]

Three boys were on the bench. I sat down with them and watched the floor for a moment, not, as a naïve observer might have thought, to dramatize penitence, but simply to maintain my privacy in an important moment. Drawn close by their delinquency, the other boys whispered and passed notes, holding off fear with artificial camaraderie. I kept quiet, acclimating slowly to the electric air, knowing that where there was danger there might also be salvation.

I never rehearsed a defense. I must have thought the Dean preferred a boy who walked in and took his medicine to one who groveled, however cleverly. And of course when the moment of recognition came, when the barriers fell and we stood revealed, I didn't want to be in the midst of an elaborate lie. To hasten the emergence of love I could only be completely honest. Lies might make it difficult for him to reach me, and vice-versa.

I wanted to be won over by him, but not cheaply. If he won

me cheaply he might betray me. The sense in which I knew this is hard to explain. It wasn't a principle I'd deduced from experience, it was knowledge without thought. Had someone asked me at the time what it meant to be betrayed by another person I couldn't have answered. Without being able to conceive betrayal I none the less protected myself against it, unconsciously, in my expectation of a commitment from the other person equal to my own. A perfectly valid stance between individuals but a tragic absurdity between a child and authority.

A side door I'd never noticed before opened and a student came out smiling. I caught a glimpse of a man at a desk, and for no reason at all I became convinced he was a policeman.

"Fischberg," the Dean's secretary called without looking up. The boy next to me left the bench and went through the side door. I heard the man inside tell him to close it.

The smiling student picked up a pass from the secretary and started out. As he passed I touched his arm. "Who's that in there?"

"I don't know. Some jerk asking if I had a happy home life."

"No talking there!"

A soft buzz sounded on the secretary's intercom. "Next," she said.

There was a momentary paralysis on the bench.

"Well, what are you waiting for?" She shuffled some papers on her desk. "Conroy? Is one of you Conroy?"

I walked to the Dean's door and went in.

"All right Conroy; step over here."

I crossed the carpet and stood in front of his desk. He took off his glasses, rubbed the bridge of his nose, and put them on again. After a moment he pushed against the edge of the desk and swiveled away to face the wall, leaning back with a sigh and then letting his chin come down slowly like a man dozing off.

"Why were you late?" he asked the wall.

"There was no reason, I guess."

"No reason?"

"I mean I don't have an excuse."

"You didn't miss your bus? You didn't forget your transit pass? The subways didn't break down?"

"No sir."

"I suppose not, since you've been late three times this week. You can't possibly have an excuse so you don't give one. Isn't that right?" He stared at the wall.

I didn't answer.

"Isn't that right?" he asked again in exactly the same flat tone.

"If you say so, sir."

He turned his head to look at me for a moment, his face expressionless, and then went back to watching the wall. "I don't have time for trouble-makers, Conroy. I get rid of them."

"I don't know why I'm late so often. I try to get here on time but somehow it just happens."

"Don't make a mystery out of it, Conroy. You're late because you're lazy and inattentive."

I could feel myself beginning to close down inside, as if my soul were one of those elaborate suitcases street peddlers use to display their wares, the kind that fold up from all directions at the approach of the law.

He lifted some papers from his desk. "You're nothing but trouble. Constantly late if you get here at all, inattentive in class, disrespectful to your teachers, twice reprimanded for gambling . . ."

"It was just pitching pennies, sir."

"I know what it was. Don't interrupt."

"Yes sir."

"At this moment you are failing three subjects."

"We haven't had any tests yet. I'm sure I'll pass the tests."

He looked up, his eyes narrowing in irritation. "You're failing three subjects. That leaves the decision up to me. You stay here or you get transferred to another school. You're in that category now."

I turned away, instinctively hiding the fear that might be on my face. Getting kicked out of Stuyvesant would be a catastrophe surpassing anything in my experience, perhaps because it seemed to eliminate the possibility of turning over a new leaf. I disbelieved in self-betterment. By turning a new leaf I meant no more than avoiding the more obvious forms of trouble.

Secretly, I did hope that things would get better. That I didn't know *how* they'd get better was balanced by my inability to understand why they were bad in the first place. It was a delicate world in which one had to move carefully, dealing with elements one understood vaguely if at all, knowing only that some elements seemed to sustain life and some to threaten it. Getting thrown out of school would disrupt things profoundly. I would no longer be able to experiment with those balanced elements, probing them gingerly here and there, adding some, taking away some, trying, in the least dangerous way, to find out what they were. In a trade school, my bridges burned behind me, I imagined myself in total isolation and darkness, unable to reorganize, unable to make the slightest adjustments in the course of my life, finally and irrevocably in the hands of a disinterested fate.

"What do you think I should do?" he asked.

"I want to stay. I can make it."

"What the hell is the matter with you, Conroy?"

I looked down at the edge of the desk. Something strange was happening. I seemed to be at two removes from reality, crouching behind my own body like a man manipulating a puppet through a curtain. "I don't know." My arms were reaching in through my back to make me talk. "That's the truth."

"If you don't," he said slowly, "you had better find out."

I climbed back into myself and nodded.

He opened the drawer of his desk and took out a small notebook. "Early report for two weeks. Get here fifteen minutes before the first bell and sign in with the hall monitor." He uncapped his pen and made a notation. "Leave plenty of time. Miss once and you're out. Understand?"

"Yes sir."

"That's all." He didn't look up.

I had my hand on the doorknob when he spoke again. "And see the man in the other room before you go back to class."

The bench had refilled and the boys turned as if to read their fates in my expression. I walked past and went up to the secretary. "He says I should see the man in there."

"Go on in, then. There's nobody with him."

I tapped the door lightly and entered.

"Come in. Sit down." He was standing over a desk. "You are . . . ah . . . ." He looked down at his papers.

"Conroy."

"Oh yes, Conroy." He smiled nervously, poking one of the papers across the surface of the desk with his fingers. Hunched over, he coughed into his fist as he quickly read it. "Well now, Frank," he began. (It was a slight shock to be so addressed. My official name was Conroy, and neither teachers nor students called me anything else.) "I want to ask you some questions. Understand that I have nothing to do with the school or the Dean. I'm here simply as an observer, and to help if I can. You can answer freely without fear of . . ." he hesitated, searching for the right word.

"Repercussions?"

"Yes. That's right." He sat down. "Now let's see. You're fourteen years old. Any brothers or sisters?"

"An older sister," I said. "And oh yes, the baby. Jessica. She's only a few months old."

"I see. She would be your half-sister, I imagine, since I see here your father passed away some time ago."

"Yes." I began to pick at some lint on my trousers, feeling slightly uncomfortable.

"Do you get along with them all right?"

"What do you mean?" I understood him, but the question irritated me.

"Well, there are always little fights now and then. We all lose our tempers occasionally, I wondered if outside of that you got along with them all right."

"Of course I do."

"Okay." He paused, watching me indirectly. There was no more lint to pick from my leg so I began to brush out the cuff with a finger. "Do you have a job in the morning?"

"Yes. I work in a library."

"How do you like that?"

"It's okay."

"What do you do when you get home from school at night? Do you have any hobbies? Stamp collecting, that sort of thing?"

"No hobbies."

"Well, how do you pass the time?"

"I read a lot. Sometimes I play the piano."

"What kind of books?"

I hesitated, not sure how to answer. "All kinds, I guess."

"I suppose you don't like school very much."

"I don't think about it very much."

The bell rang, all over the building, and was followed instantly by the sound of thousands of students moving through the halls. I listened abstractedly, luxuriating in the knowledge that for the moment I'd escaped the routine. How can I explain the special pleasure of listening to the machine operating all around me while I myself was removed from it? I'd cut class and climb the stairs past the top floor to the deserted landing above. I'd sit with my back against the door to the roof listening to the bells, to the boys shouting on the stairs below, and to the long silences after the halls had emptied. The mood was quietly Olympian.

I hadn't realized how much the Dean had shaken me up, but now, as the bell I didn't have to answer rang again, I felt a tremor of release play over my body. Muscles everywhere began to relax and I threw back my head in an enormous involuntary yawn.

"What does your stepfather do for a living, Frank?"

115

Instantly I was alert. I knew the man was harmless, but my deepest rule, a rule so deep I maintained it without the slightest conscious effort, was never to reveal anything important about life at home. "He's a cab driver," I said slowly.

"Does your mother work too?"

I stared at the floor. "Sometimes." It occurred to me that my initial relief at getting away from the Dean might have made me careless with the man I now faced. He obviously had some image of me in his mind, some psychological cliché, and by answering carelessly I might unknowingly have supported it. I moved to the edge of my chair and sat up straight.

"Is there trouble at home?" he asked quietly.

My face flushed. A stupid question. An insulting question, as if I were a case to be dealt with by the book, as if he suspected some hidden deprivation or abnormality. "No, of course not. Nothing like that." I knew what he had in his mind. He held images of drunken fathers who beat their kids, slut mothers who roamed the house in old nightgowns, and long, screaming fights with crockery flying through the air. We weren't like that. I knew we were much better than that. I stood up. "Is that all?"

He fiddled with his papers for a moment, looking off into space. "Yes, I guess so," he said reluctantly. "If and when I come back to Stuyvesant I'd like to talk to you again."

I hiked my books high under my arm and went out the door. Standing motionless in the small room, I looked at the secretary and the four boys on the bench. The bell rang.

---

1. *What initial sense of Conroy do you get from the first three paragraphs of the selection? What kind of expectations does he have before he goes in to see the Dean? Do those expectations seem to you realistic? What do they suggest about Conroy's character?*

2. *Conroy uses a great deal of dialogue in presenting this scene. What are the most significant features of the conversations he presents? What relation do they have to Conroy's expectations while waiting in the outer office?*

3. Do you see the Dean and the second interviewer as quite different or quite similar figures? What details in the way they are described or in their conversation seem to you most important in conveying their characters? Do you think Conroy's decision to tell us very little about the second interviewer adds to the effectiveness of the scene?

4. Conroy's own role here is generally passive—he answers a few questions, nothing more. How does he still keep himself at the center of the scene? What sense of Conroy's own character emerges during the scene?

5. Do you expect some kind of vivid climax as you are reading this selection? What does happen at the end? Is it an effective ending? What sense of schools and of the problems of students does Conroy's narrative create?

∽ James Herndon ∽

(1926-   )

James Herndon was a teacher in an inner-city junior high school in Los Angeles when he wrote The Way It Spozed To Be *(1965). In the book he tells of his situation as a white teacher in a school where the students were virtually all black, and of his struggle to educate himself as well as his students. This selection presents a brief (and unusual) moment of violence in the classroom and its resolution. In a later book,* How To Survive in Your Native Land *(1971), Herndon describes his experiences teaching in a suburban middle-class junior high school.*

MAURICE

[A NEW STUDENT COMES TO CLASS]

I determined to pass out English books and spellers to 9D, to make everything official, and get down to work. The main work, I'd decided, was going to be composition, freely done and at length. With a lot of written material on hand, theirs—in which, having written it themselves, they were bound to be interested—we could later get down to making some corrections, show up some common faults, use the books to find practical standards for usage and punctuation. The spellers I'd use for regularity; they weren't much good, being just lists of words and a number of rather silly things to do with those words, but I thought we'd do them anyway, half the period twice a week perhaps. They were simple enough and it would be a kind of breather for everybody.

9D, however, having received the free gift, wasn't about to let go of it as easy as that. It's true they scrambled around for the books and spellers, but they quickly withdrew into a more dignified aloofness as soon as it became clear there were enough to go around, which was only when every single person had one of each. Cosmetics came out, kids got up and began searching for new places to sit, a boy took out a transistor radio, the C's withdrew to the back table. I passed out paper; I began to talk about what we were going to do. Cosmetics and conversation continued—not loudly or aggressively, but just as if I weren't addressing them. I began to insist on everyone's attention. Perhaps ten kids had their backs to me by now. I called kids by name, requiring their attention. They began to resent it. Finally a voice said, Teacher, why don't you let us alone?

That stopped it. Ooooooh? they all went. The speaker was Verna, a tall, lanky girl, brown, lithe and strong-looking, plain-faced, kinky-haired, without makeup. She was making a stand. The tone of the class implied apprehension and excitement: I was now going to throw Verna out. Actually I didn't give a damn. Verna and I had everyone's attention; the others had momentarily lost. Verna had to say something, if only to get the last word before being thrown out. I expected an outburst, but instead she said, You should have made us get to work yesterday. All the other teachers made us get to work. If you want us to do work, why didn't you make us yesterday?

She stopped talking and immediately turned around, her back toward me. The class rallied to her support by taking up their conversations where they had left off. Now I was losing. I got ready to start insisting again, wondering what I was going to say if and when they started listening.

Then the door swung open, and a kid walked in, came over and handed me a slip and found a seat near the back of the room. The class turned around and conversed in a different key. The subject was the newcomer, Maurice, particularly the fact that he had just gotten out of Juvenile Hall in time to make the second day of school. Teacher, Maurice just back from Juvi! shouted out somebody, so I didn't have any trouble finding out. Maurice himself was subdued and quiet, having been warned, I suppose, to be nice or find himself right back in Juvi. But I was winning again; they were so curious about what I was going to say to Maurice about Juvi that they had to recognize me, just to make sure I knew about it. I passed a book and a speller down the row to Maurice. You supposed to report to the parole officer about Maurice, teacher! How he do, if he do his work! Do he get in trouble or fighting! . . . I began to get advice from all sides.

Well, now, I said, actually this is not a class about Juvi, but about English. Whooo-eee! That broke them up. But when they stopped laughing they were attentive enough. I began to talk about how English meant using the language however they wanted; I was well into my speech about figuring out together what was relatively interesting to do and then figuring out how to do it—which was, naturally, crap since I already had the business of composition in mind and how we were going to go about it—and they were just beginning to get bored (they knew it was crap too), seeing as how I wasn't going to either lecture Maurice about Crime Not Paying or say anything humorous again, when *bang!* Maurice and another boy, locked in each other's arms, fell over their desks and across the desks of the next row and lay there stretched out, struggling. Books, papers and kids scattered. Hell!

Whoooo-eee! I got over there. Silence. Let go! Both of you! I shouted, but nothing happened. Maurice was on top, the other kid across a desk, and as I got there Maurice loosed an arm and belted the other kid in the face. Cut it out! I grabbed Maurice. He didn't come. The kid on the bottom let go, but Maurice didn't. I tugged him rather gently. He belted the kid again. I got mad, grabed Maurice under the arms and heaved as hard as I could. Maurice flew backward over the row of desks and landed with a crash on the next row. He landed plenty hard; I imagine it hurt, and also he must have thought it was all up with him, back to Juvi. He was frantic and mad. He jumped up and started for me. I stood there; he stopped and stood there. He glared. Everybody was scared. No one in the class looked forward, suddenly, to what was going to happen, which was that Maurice was going to come for me and hit me or I him; the end would be the speedy return of Maurice to Juvenile Hall, beaten up by me previously or not. It was inevitable.

We stood there quite a few seconds and then I nodded, turned and walked swiftly back to my desk and sat down. I hoped I was implying a mutual ceasefire among equals. When I turned around toward the class, Maurice had likewise retreated and was sitting at his desk. We carefully didn't look right at each other, but still in the same general direction, so as not to be accused of avoiding anything either. Maurice had seen the issue—I'd say we saw it exactly alike. We both had something at stake, and he cooperated perfectly. It was like a play, or an improvisation which came off just right. We were winning.

The class was dumbfounded. They waited, disappointed but certainly somewhat relieved. Students at GW courted disaster; that doesn't mean they liked it. They didn't believe the action was over. They knew better. So they were all attention when I got ready to say something—considering the last thing I'd said about Juvi, they had high hopes. Instead I said, All right, I guess we can start classwork. The first English assignment is to write a story about what just happened. You can begin writing now, finish it tonight, and have it ready for tomorrow's class.

Whatever they'd expected, that wasn't it. It suddenly seemed like a lousy idea to me, and I decided to admit it and do something else, but before I could Verna said Shhh! loudly and turned around in her seat so her back was to me. The class woke up at that signal and began to yell demands and questions at me. All of a sudden they were just like 7H.

What to write! How we spozed to write without no paper!

That ain't no schoolwork, teacher! You can't make us write about that! I ain't got no pencil! You trying to get us into trouble! No pen! No paper! What to write! What to do!

Panic. Instead of the moral lecture they expected to enjoy from an indignant teacher, here I was making them supply the lecture themselves. Everything was going wrong. Quiet! I yelled a few times. That was more like it, and everyone subsided. Thirty-year-old May raised her hand placidly. I called on her gratefully, but she said, Teacher, why don't we do our spellers? I got furious at once. Spellers? I was proposing to write seriously about this exciting event and she wanted instead to put a silly list of words in alphabetical order or backward according to last letter, or whatever it was for Unit 1 in the goddam speller! You teaching this class or am I? I snapped at her. Whoooo-eee! He sure cut down old May! By now I was determined on the assignment again.

What's the problem? I asked the class. Things happened in here today. All I'm asking you to do is to write about it. Why don't you get started?

What to write? everyone started asking again. Quiet! I shouted at once. A series of sarcastic questions tempted me. You were here, weren't you? Right? You have eyes? Right? You all have ears? OK. Now think about what happened in this same room, describe it, tell it to yourself, remember it, and then write it down. Never mind the spelling for now, never mind ink, just write it down however you can. That's all!

Shhh—loudly again. This time not from Verna, but from Leon LaTore in the back. No one ever said *shit* at GW, only *shhh!* or, to express extreme disgust, *sheee!* Shhh! said Leon LaTore, nobody going to write that. He was addressing the class, not me. He just want to pin it on somebody. He want to find out about it. He want to pull you in on it!

Twenty-five protestations of innocence and as many accusations and counter-accusations followed that. Finally people's mamas began to be mentioned, and I had to yell Quiet! again. Well, what if I do want to know? I yelled. Do you know? Some-

thing started it, didn't it? Here's Maurice pounding on somebody, on Fletcher there, all of a sudden. Do you think he
wanted to? So who did start it, then?

Accusations, etc. Leon LaTore grinned in the back. Finally
Verna jumped up and yelled, Hush up, you-all! Sit down,
big-leg! came an unidentified voice. Forget you! said Verna
coldly, and everybody hushed. You don't have to get all shook
up, said Verna. She was talking to me. Everybody know who
start it. Robert he took hold of Maurice's notebook while Maurice writing on them cards you give him for the books, and slip
it over onto Fletcher's desk, and Maurice look up and find it
gone and then he see it on Fletcher's desk and grab it, but
Fletcher don't know it Maurice's because he didn't see that.
Robert put it there so he grab it back and there they go.

No one denied it. Robert was out of his seat and backed up
in the corner of the room like John Dillinger facing the FBI.
He looked like an authentic fourteen-year-old, small, stocky,
black. Sit down, Robert, I said. Oooooh? went the class softly.
Shhh! said Leon LaTore. Verna wasn't convinced. Ain't you
sendin' Robert to the office, teacher? she said flatly.

I was tired of the whole thing. Property. Your mama. It
seemed likely that at the moment Robert was slipping Maurice's notebook over, every other kid in the class was grabbing,
poking, pushing or pulling at some piece of someone else's
stuff. I told them so. Robert waited warily in the corner. Sit
down, Robert, I said again. I looked at the clock; there were
only about five minutes left. OK, I said, now go on and write
the assignment, now we all know all about it.

Actually no one wrote the assignment; no one, that is, except for Maurice, who perhaps figured he'd better. No one remembered it the next day; all denied any knowledge of its
being assigned. I read Maurice's "Composition," as it was entitled: A boy took another boy('s) (notebook) in the class and
so the boy jump(ed) him to beat (him) the teacher broke it up.
But the teacher didn't send the boys to the office.

(Corrections mine.)

1. What sense of Herndon as a teacher do you get from reading this account? Usually a teacher is thought of as someone on the other side of the desk from students. Does Herndon try to emphasize that distance or diminish it? How do you know? How would you describe his attitudes toward students and toward the work they are doing in his class?

2. If Herndon's methods as a teacher strike you as unconventional, how do you think he tries to justify them or make his readers understand them? In what ways could the class hour be described as "educational"?

3. How is Maurice characterized? How does Herndon present his account of the incident with Maurice? What does he seem most concerned about? What do you think Herndon means when he writes "We were winning"?

4. Take one or two of the longer paragraphs from the story and try to figure out which language is that of the students and which is that of Herndon then and Herndon now. Are these different languages clearly marked off or not? Do you think they make the selection more effective or not?

∽ Maya Angelou ∽

(1929-   )

Maya Angelou grew up living with her maternal grandmother in Stamps, Arkansas, and her childhood experiences form the basis of her autobiography, I Know Why the Caged Bird Sings *(1969). As an adult she has been a dancer, a nightclub singer, and an actress. Her involvement as a black woman with social issues led to her work for the Southern Christian Leadership Conference in the early 1960s. Her books include a volume of poetry,* Give Me a Cool Drink of Water 'fore I Die *(1970) and, more recently, a second volume of autobiography,* Gather Together in My Name *(1974).*

[GRADUATION DAY]

The weeks until graduation were filled with heady activities. A group of small children were to be presented in a play about buttercups and daisies and bunny rabbits. They could be heard throughout the building practicing their hops and their little songs that sounded like silver bells. The older girls (nongraduates, of course) were assigned the task of making refreshments for the night's festivities. A tangy scent of ginger, cinnamon, nutmeg and chocolate wafted around the home economics building as the budding cooks made samples for themselves and their teachers.

In every corner of the workshop, axes and saws split fresh timber as the woodshop boys made sets and stage scenery. Only the graduates were left out of the general bustle. We were free to sit in the library at the back of the building or look in quite detachedly, naturally, on the measures being taken for our event.

Even the minister preached on graduation the Sunday before. His subject was, "Let your light so shine that men will see your good works and praise your Father, Who is in Heaven." Although the sermon was purported to be addressed to us, he used the occasion to speak to backsliders, gamblers and general ne'er-do-wells. But since he had called our names at the beginning of the service we were mollified.

Among Negroes the tradition was to give presents to children going only from one grade to another. How much more important this was when the person was graduating at the top of the class. Uncle Willie and Momma had sent away for a Mickey Mouse watch like Bailey's. Louise gave me four embroidered handkerchiefs. (I gave her three crocheted doilies.) Mrs. Sneed, the minister's wife, made me an underskirt to wear for graduation, and nearly every customer gave me a nickel or maybe even a dime with the instruction "Keep on moving to higher ground," or some such encouragement.

Amazingly the great day finally dawned and I was out of bed before I knew it. I threw open the back door to see it more clearly, but Momma said, "Sister, come away from that door and put your robe on."

I hoped the memory of that morning would never leave me. Sunlight was itself still young, and the day had none of the insistence maturity would bring it in a few hours. In my robe and barefoot in the backyard, under cover of going to see about my new beans, I gave myself up to the gentle warmth and thanked God that no matter what evil I had done in my life He had allowed me to live to see this day. Somewhere in my fatalism I had expected to die, accidentally, and never have the chance to walk up the stairs in the auditorium and gracefully receive my hard-earned diploma. Out of God's merciful bosom I had won reprieve.

Bailey came out in his robe and gave me a box wrapped in Christmas paper. He said he had saved his money for months to pay for it. It felt like a box of chocolates, but I knew Bailey wouldn't save money to buy candy when we had all we could want under our noses.

He was as proud of the gift as I. It was a soft-leatherbound copy of a collection of poems by Edgar Allan Poe, or, as Bailey and I called him, "Eap." I turned to "Annabel Lee" and we walked up and down the garden rows, the cool dirt between our toes, reciting the beautifully sad lines.

Momma made a Sunday breakfast although it was only Friday. After we finished the blessing, I opened my eyes to find the watch on my plate. It was a dream of a day. Everything went smoothly and to my credit. I didn't have to be reminded or scolded for anything. Near evening I was too jittery to attend to chores, so Bailey volunteered to do all before his bath.

Days before, we had made a sign for the Store, and as we turned out the lights Momma hung the cardboard over the doorknob. It read clearly: CLOSED. GRADUATION.

My dress fitted perfectly and everyone said that I looked like a sunbeam in it. On the hill, going toward the school, Bailey walked behind with Uncle Willie, who muttered, "Go on, Ju." He wanted him to walk ahead with us because it embarrassed him to have to walk so slowly. Bailey said he'd let the ladies walk together, and the men would bring up the rear. We all laughed, nicely.

Little children dashed by out of the dark like fireflies. Their crepe-paper dresses and butterfly wings were not made for running and we heard more than one rip, dryly, and the regretful "uh uh" that followed.

The school blazed without gaiety. The windows seemed cold and unfriendly from the lower hill. A sense of ill-fated timing crept over me, and if Momma hadn't reached for my hand I would have drifted back to Bailey and Uncle Willie, and possibly beyond. She made a few slow jokes about my feet getting cold, and tugged me along to the now-strange building.

Around the front steps, assurance came back. There were my fellow "greats," the graduating class. Hair brushed back, legs oiled, new dresses and pressed pleats, fresh pocket handkerchiefs and little handbags, all homesewn. Oh, we were up to snuff, all right. I joined my comrades and didn't even see my family go in to find seats in the crowded auditorium.

The school band struck up a march and all classes filed in as had been rehearsed. We stood in front of our seats, as assigned, and on a signal from the choir director, we sat. No sooner had this been accomplished than the band started to play the national anthem. We rose again and sang the song, after which we recited the pledge of allegiance. We remained standing for a brief minute before the choir director and the principal signaled to us, rather desperately I thought, to take our seats. The command was so unusual that our carefully rehearsed and smooth-running machine was thrown off. For a full minute we fumbled for our chairs and bumped into each other awkwardly. Habits change or solidify under pressure, so in our states of nervous tension we had been ready to follow our usual assembly pattern: the American national anthem, then the pledge of allegiance, then the song every Black person I knew called the Negro National Anthem. All done in the same key, with the same passion and most often standing on the same foot.

Finding my seat at last, I was overcome with a presentiment of worse things to come. Something unrehearsed, unplanned, was going to happen, and we were going to be made to look bad. I distinctly remember being explicit in the choice of pronoun. It was "we," the graduating class, the unit, that concerned me then.

The principal welcomed "parents and friends" and asked the Baptist minister to lead us in prayer. His invocation was brief and punchy, and for a second I thought we were getting back on the high road to right action. When the principal came back to the dais, however, his voice had changed. Sounds always affected me profoundly and the principal's voice was one of my favorites. During assembly it melted and lowed weakly into the audience. It had not been in my plan to listen to him, but my curiosity was piqued and I straightened up to give him my attention.

He was talking about Booker T. Washington, our "late great leader," who said we can be as close as the fingers on the hand, etc. . . . Then he said a few vague things about friendship and the friendship of kindly people to those less fortunate than themselves. With that his voice nearly faded, thin, away. Like a river diminishing to a stream and then to a trickle. But he cleared his throat and said, "Our speaker tonight, who is also our friend, came from Texarkana to deliver the commencement address, but due to the irregularity of the train schedule, he's going to, as they say, 'speak and run.' " He said that we understood and wanted the man to know that we were most grateful for the time he was able to give us and then something about how we were willing always to adjust to another's program, and without more ado—"I give you Mr. Edward Donleavy."

Not one but two white men came through the door offstage. The shorter one walked to the speaker's platform, and the tall one moved over to the center seat and sat down. But that was our principal's seat, and already occupied. The dislodged gentleman bounced around for a long breath or two before the Baptist minister gave him his chair, then with more dignity than the situation deserved, the minister walked off the stage.

Donleavy looked at the audience once (on reflection, I'm sure that he wanted only to reassure himself that we were really there), adjusted his glasses and began to read from a sheaf of papers.

He was glad "to be here and to see the work going on just as it was in the other schools."

At the first "Amen" from the audience I willed the offender to immediate death by choking on the word. But Amens and Yes, sir's began to fall around the room like rain through a ragged umbrella.

He told us of the wonderful changes we children in Stamps had in store. The Central School (naturally, the white school was Central) had already been granted improvements that would be in use in the fall. A well-known artist was coming from Little Rock to teach art to them. They were going to have the newest microscopes and chemistry equipment for their laboratory. Mr. Donleavy didn't leave us long in the dark over who made these improvements available to Central High. Nor were we to be ignored in the general betterment scheme he had in mind.

He said that he had pointed out to people at a very high level that one of the first-line football tacklers at Arkansas Agricultural and Mechanical College had graduated from good old Lafayette County Training School. Here fewer Amen's were heard. Those few that did break through lay dully in the air with the heaviness of habit.

He went on to praise us. He went on to say how he had bragged that "one of the best basketball players at Fisk sank his first ball right here at Lafayette County Training School."

The white kids were going to have a chance to become Galileos and Madame Curies and Edisons and Gauguins, and our boys (the girls weren't even in on it) would try to be Jesse Owenses and Joe Louises.

Owens and the Brown Bomber were great heroes in our world, but what school official in the white-goddom of Little Rock had the right to decide that those two men must be our only heroes? Who decided that for Henry Reed to become a scientist he had to work like George Washington Carver, as a bootblack, to buy a lousy microscope? Bailey was obviously always going to be too small to be an athlete, so which concrete angel glued to what country seat had decided that if my brother wanted to become a lawyer he had to first pay penance for his skin by picking cotton and hoeing corn and studying correspondence books at night for twenty years?

The man's dead words fell like bricks around the auditorium and too many settled in my belly. Constrained by hard-learned manners I couldn't look behind me, but to my left and right the proud graduating class of 1940 had dropped their heads. Every girl in my row had found something new to do with her handkerchief. Some folded the tiny squares into love knots, some into triangles, but most were wadding them, then pressing them flat on their yellow laps.

On the dais, the ancient tragedy was being replayed. Professor Parsons sat, a sculptor's reject, rigid. His large, heavy body seemed devoid of will or willingness, and his eyes said he was no longer with us. The other teachers examined the flag (which was draped stage right) or their notes, or the windows which opened on our now-famous playing diamond.

Graduation, the hush-hush magic time of frills and gifts and congratulations and diplomas, was finished for me before my name was called. The accomplishment was nothing. The meticulous maps, drawn in three colors of ink, learning and spelling decasyllabic words, memorizing the whole of *The Rape of Lucrece*—it was for nothing. Donleavy had exposed us.

We were maids and farmers, handymen and washerwomen, and anything higher that we aspired to was farcical and presumptuous.

Then I wished that Gabriel Prosser and Nat Turner had killed all whitefolks in their beds and that Abraham Lincoln had been assassinated before the signing of the Emancipation Proclamation, and that Harriet Tubman had been killed by that blow on her head and Christopher Columbus had drowned in the *Santa María*.

It was awful to be Negro and have no control over my life. It was brutal to be young and already trained to sit quietly and listen to charges brought against my color with no chance of defense. We should all be dead. I thought I should like to see us all dead, one on top of the other. A pyramid of flesh with the whitefolks on the bottom, as the broad base, then the Indians with their silly tomahawks and teepees and wigwams and treaties, the Negroes with their mops and recipes and cotton sacks and spirituals sticking out of their mouths. The

Dutch children should all stumble in their wooden shoes and break their necks. The French should choke to death on the Louisiana Purchase (1803) while silkworms ate all the Chinese with their stupid pigtails. As a species, we were an abomination. All of us.

Donleavy was running for election, and assured our parents that if he won we could count on having the only colored paved playing field in that part of Arkansas. Also—he never looked up to acknowledge the grunts of acceptance—also, we were bound to get some new equipment for the home economics building and the workshop.

He finished, and since there was no need to give any more than the most perfunctory thank-you's, he nodded to the men on the stage, and the tall white man who was never introduced joined him at the door. They left with the attitude that now they were off to something really important. (The graduation ceremonies at Lafayette County Training School had been a mere preliminary.)

The ugliness they left was palpable. An uninvited guest who wouldn't leave. The choir was summoned and sang a modern arrangement of "Onward, Christian Soldiers," with new words pertaining to graduates seeking their place in the world. But it didn't work. Elouise, the daughter of the Baptist minister, recited "Invictus," and I could have cried at the impertinence of "I am the master of my fate, I am the captain of my soul."

My name had lost its ring of familiarity and I had to be nudged to go and receive my diploma. All my preparations had fled. I neither marched up to the stage like a conquering Amazon, nor did I look in the audience for Bailey's nod of approval. Marguerite Johnson, I heard the name again, my honors were read, there were noises in the audience of appreciation, and I took my place on the stage as rehearsed.

I thought about colors I hated: ecru, puce, lavender, beige and black.

There was shuffling and rustling around me, then Henry Reed was giving his valedictory address, "To Be or Not to Be."

Hadn't he heard the whitefolks? We couldn't *be*, so the question was a waste of time. Henry's voice came out clear and strong. I feared to look at him. Hadn't he got the message? There was no "nobler in the mind" for Negroes because the world didn't think we had minds, and they let us know it. "Outrageous fortune"? Now, that was a joke. When the ceremony was over I had to tell Henry Reed some things. That is, if I still cared. Not "rub," Henry, "erase." "Ah, there's the erase." Us.

Henry had been a good student in elocution. His voice rose on tides of promise and fell on waves of warnings. The English teacher had helped him to create a sermon winging through Hamlet's soliloquy. To be a man, a doer, a builder, a leader, or to be a tool, an unfunny joke, a crusher of funky toadstools. I marveled that Henry could go through with the speech as if we had a choice.

I had been listening and silently rebutting each sentence with my eyes closed; then there was a hush, which in an audience warns that something unplanned is happening. I looked up and saw Henry Reed, the conservative, the proper, the A student, turn his back to the audience and turn to us (the proud graduating class of 1940) and sing, nearly speaking,

> "Lift ev'ry voice and sing
> Till earth and heaven ring
> Ring with the harmonies of Liberty . . ."

It was the poem written by James Weldon Johnson. It was the music composed by J. Rosamond Johnson. It was the Negro national anthem. Out of habit we were singing it.

Our mothers and fathers stood in the dark hall and joined the hymn of encouragement. A kindergarten teacher led the small children onto the stage and the buttercups and daisies and bunny rabbits marked time and tried to follow:

> "Stony the road we trod
> Bitter the chastening rod

Felt in the days when hope, unborn, had died.
Yet with a steady beat
Have not our weary feet
Come to the place for which our fathers sighed?"

Every child I knew had learned that song with his ABC's
and along with "Jesus Loves Me This I Know." But I personally had never heard it before. Never heard the words, despite
the thousands of times I had sung them. Never thought they
had anything to do with me.

On the other hand, the words of Patrick Henry had made
such an impression on me that I had been able to stretch myself tall and trembling and say, "I know not what course others
may take, but as for me, give me liberty or give me death."

And now I heard, really for the first time:

"We have come over a way that with tears
has been watered,
We have come, treading our path through
the blood of the slaughtered."

While echoes of the song shivered in the air, Henry Reed
bowed his head, said "Thank you," and returned to his place
in the line. The tears that slipped down many faces were not
wiped away in shame.

We were on top again. As always, again. We survived. The
depths had been icy and dark, but now a bright sun spoke to
our souls. I was no longer simply a member of the proud graduating class of 1940; I was a proud member of the wonderful,
beautiful Negro race.

Oh, Black known and unknown poets, how often have your
auctioned pains sustained us? Who will compute the lonely
nights made less lonely by your songs, or the empty pots made
less tragic by your tales?

If we were a people much given to revealing secrets, we
might raise monuments and sacrifice to the memories of our

poets, but slavery cured us of that weakness. It may be enough, however, to have it said that we survive in exact relationship to the dedication of our poets (include preachers, musicians and blues singers).

1. *How would you describe the mood Angelou creates when she writes about the morning of graduation day? What details help to establish that mood?*

2. *How do her feelings change as the day progresses? What causes the change in her feelings? How are her feelings related to her situation as a black student in a segregated school?*

3. *What perspective on the relations between black people and white people do you think Angelou is trying to give the reader? Does she dramatize these relations through one major incident or through many minor details?*

4. *To what extent does Angelou narrate the story of the graduation as she would have experienced it as a child? To what extent does she make you aware of herself as a mature woman seeing her past through more experienced eyes?*

5. *Do you think the end of the episode (the singing of the Negro national anthem) is an effective one? Does it change your sense of the situation and of the mood of the students? How would you explain what Angelou is doing in the last three paragraphs, since she no longer seems to be referring directly or exclusively to her graduation from grade school?*

∽ George Plimpton ∽

(1927-   )

George Plimpton is a member of a wealthy New York family and was educated at Exeter and Harvard. He became a founder and the editor-in-chief of the literary magazine The Paris Review *in 1953, and combined his editorial work with writing and teaching during the 1950s. Since that time, he has written several books based on his experiences as an eager but not very talented amateur athlete trying to play competitively in professional sports.* Paper Lion *(1964) is an account of Plimpton's participation in the 1963 preseason training camp of the Detroit Lions, a professional football team. Plimpton endured all the hardships of an ordinary rookie trying out for the team, and the selection printed here reports his brief appearance in a practice scrimmage.*

[GETTING A CHANCE TO PLAY]

In the defensive huddle they did not seem surprised when I trotted in and joined them. A few helmets turned. Past the helmet bars the eyes looked tired, staring from faces slick with sweat. We leaned toward Schmidt. "The coverage is red, George," he said to me. "That means you stick with the flanker—one on one, you just stay with him. I'll have your ass if you don't."

The huddle broke and I trotted back to the cornerman position. I looked over at Night Train, close by, fifteen yards or so away, standing on the sidelines. He offered up an encouraging smile, a shine of teeth in his dark face.

"It's red," I hissed at him.

"Stick with the flanker," he called back, cupping his hands to his mouth. "Scramble back when he come, and don' give up."

A knot of spectators had collected around him, looking out. All of them, in Bermuda shorts, seemed to have soft-drink bottles in their hands. I avoided their stares. I felt the heat build up inside my helmet. I jogged in place, working the stiffness out, and watched the offensive huddle break finally with a crack of hands in unison and move up to their positions. Jake Greer was the flanker and he came loping out along the line of scrimmage, split ten yards or so from his nearest lineman. I moved along opposite, watching him.

Plum began to call the signals. At the hike of the ball, Greer started toward me with his high, bouncy steps, slow at first, like the slow-motion advance of a klipspringer, coming head on. Then his speed picked up.

"Fetch him!" I heard Night Train yell. "Scrabble aroun'!"

I began to back-pedal, trying to keep my eye on Greer's belt buckle. He sailed up to me, and then cut to my left for the sidelines, with a little grunt, and I could hear the *shu-shu* of his football trousers as he went by, and the creak of his shoulder pads. I was leaning left to the outside when he cut, just chancing he would move for the sidelines on a down-and-out pattern, and when I reached after him I was not too far behind. He pulled up after two or three strides, and I almost cracked into him. The play was over—a pass to the other side had been knocked down by a lineman rearing up. Greer started trotting back to his huddle. I doubted he noticed that I was opposing him at cornerback. I had not seen the pass thrown—the action there as distant as if it had taken place on another practice field. I had no sense of identification with the play. Greer and I had been alone in my zone. My confrontation with him could have been an inadvertent bumbling into the track of a high hurdler out practicing in the evening.

Night Train came hurrying up to his précis. The whole action hadn't taken more than four or five seconds. I was left with a sense of anticlimax.

"I didn't feel part of that play," I said.

"Not too much to quibble," he said. "You scare the man so much they throw to the other side." He grinned. "Now," he said, "you mus' keep the angle so you see the quarterback. Look," he said. He showed me how I should have controlled Greer, a fast crablike scuttle that allowed him to keep facing downfield to watch the play, both the flanker and the quarterback in his field of vision.

I began to see what he meant by the angle of the receiver.

"Get on up there," he said. The defensive huddle was forming. I trotted up in time to hear Joe Schmidt call out a red coverage—man-to-man again.

Back in my position, Night Train called to me from the sidelines: "Jawge, this time, recall to shout out there . . . talk it up."

The spectators, their soft-drink bottles poised, leaned in behind Train, listening.

It was awkward, their being there, but I called to Train nonetheless: "What . . . what sort of thing do I say?"

"Dis*close* what your man doing," he called out. "If they float your zone with people, disclose that. Disclose the defense what is goin' on."

The offense was alternating flankers, so Terry Barr appeared opposite me on the next play. Staring downfield, being sure not to give away a move by a flick of the eyes, he stood upright, with hands on hips, his right leg slightly bent to push off. At the hike signal, he was immediately in high gear, quite unlike Greer's klipspringer bounce; with his sprinter's run, his head steady as he came, he was nearly up to me before I had a chance to plan what to do. "Barr! Barr! Barr!" I called out as he came—an identification being all I could think of to divulge. Having to announce his maneuvers nearly rooted me to the ground. It was difficult to react physically and keep up a shouted commentary at the same time, particularly as I was unsure of the appropriate vocabulary. So Barr went by me very fast, straight downfield, as I stood announcing his name, calling those loonlike wails, "Barr! Barr! Barr!" before I turned and lit out after him, with one arm outstretched in the classic pose of hopeless pursuit.

Once again, the play itself was to be to the opposite sideline, but as Barr came by on his way back he looked at me, perhaps puzzled to have heard the demonic repetition of his name, and he said, "Well, now, look who's here."

"For God's sake, keep it to yourself," I said, breathing hard from the run.

I could see him grinning behind the cage of his helmet, before he turned and began trotting back to his team. Train was at my elbow as I stared after him.

"I think he's got something to disclose," I said. "Things may get a little warmer."

"It's possible. Interception time," Train said hopefully. "You got to scatter them feet around some, and *move*. Yo' look a little stiff las' time."

As I walked in toward Schmidt I watched the offense's huddle form, keeping a nervous eye out for helmets turned in my direction. Most were turned toward Scooter McLean, just on the periphery of the huddle, still criticizing the last play; Aldo Forte was with him, talking to his offensive linemen. A play would run, and the coaches talk about it for five minutes, the players shifting their weight from foot to foot, getting their assignments straight.

Finally, the coaches backed away. "O.K., the last play of the day," George Wilson called out. Schmidt had given the same coverage, and I was back at my position. I saw the helmets duck down in the huddle, then one of them, Plum's, I supposed, rise and face in my direction, just briefly, the egg-smooth surface of the helmet, its cage pointed at me, adding to the sense of that impersonal scrutiny, like a robot monster's, and I thought, "I'm for it. Barr's told Plum."

"Train, I'm a goner," I called out.

"Get yo' angle right," Night Train replied through cupped hands. He offered a last odd flurry of instructions: "Scrabble 'roun'! Don' regard the jukin'! Recovah! Disclose! In*form!*"

The huddle broke. The flanker coming out opposite me was Barr again—being rewarded, the thought crossed my mind, for suggesting that there was a flaw, a serious one, in the defense. His face was no longer expressionless. I suspected a big grin behind the helmet bar.

The strength was lined up to his side. Bent over his center, Plum began the signals, his the only helmet turning as he surveyed the defense in that cataleptic instant, around him the whole frieze of his teammates' helmets motionless, and then he unleashed them as the ball slapped back into his palm, yielding them to the quick imperative of action.

Since in the two preceding plays the concentration of the play had been elsewhere, I had felt alone with the flanker. Now, the whole heave of the play was toward me, flooding the zone not only with confused motion but noise—the quick stomp of feet, the creak of football gear, the strained grunts of effort, the faint *ah-ah-ah*, of piston-stroke regularity, and the stiff calls of instruction, like exhalations. "Inside, inside! Take him inside!" Someone shouted, tearing by me, his cleats thumping in the grass. A call—a parrot squawk—may have erupted from me. My feet splayed in hopeless confusion as Barr came directly toward me, feinting in one direction, and then stopping suddenly, drawing me toward him for the possibility of a buttonhook pass, and as I leaned almost off balance toward him, he turned and came on again, downfield, moving past me at high speed, leaving me poised on one leg, reaching for him, trying to grab at him despite the illegality, anything to keep him from getting by. But he was gone, and by the time I had turned to set out after him, he had ten yards on me, drawing away fast with his sprinter's run, his legs pinwheeling, the row of cleats flicking up a faint wake of dust behind.

"Ball! Ball! Ball!" I could hear Night Train yelling.

I looked up as I ran, and straight above, against the sky, I could see the football heading downfield, as high as a punt it seemed—the bomb!—and I put up a hand instinctively though the ball must have been twenty feet over my head. It was astonishingly distinct—I suppose because my eyes were concentrated on it with such longing—the white laces turning, a faint wobble to its nose, even the literature on it discernable, the trade name "Duke" turning, DUKE, DUKE, DUKE. It sailed downfield, then seemed to drift down, and there was Barr running under it, barely having to reach up for it as he collected it to him. He kept on sprinting with the football, across the goal line, never looking back, finally slowing to a trot as he headed for the gym.

1. However much you know about football, choose at least two passages where you feel Plimpton gives you a sense of the game you were never conscious of before. Then examine the passages in order to decide what aspects of the game Plimpton has emphasized and how as a writer he has made them vivid and interesting to you.
2. Plimpton obviously needs to characterize himself as someone who is an amateur, not a true insider in the world of professional football. Choose at least two passages where you feel that the football world is being described by someone who comes from another background and explain how this different perspective changes the way in which football is seen.
3. Contrast the way Plimpton writes about a seasoned professional, Night Train Lane, and the way he writes about himself. What differences do you find in the portraits?
4. How does Plimpton manage to keep you interested in the episode? Do you find that he creates some suspense? If so, how?
5. Who do you think Plimpton has in mind as an audience when he writes: dedicated football fans or people who know very little about football? Or do you think he is appealing to both in different ways? Explain your choice.

∽ Jerry Kramer ∽

(1936-   )

Jerry Kramer played football at the University of Idaho and went on to become a professional star. He played offensive guard for the Green Bay Packers in the National Football League from 1958 to 1968 and was selected as an all-pro player in five of those years. The Packers won the league championship several times during Kramer's career, and this selection from his account of the 1967 season, Instant Replay *(1968), describes the last half of what was probably his team's most difficult championship victory.*

WAR'S END

[WINNING A CHAMPIONSHIP]

We just couldn't get unwound in the third quarter. I still felt I had Jethro under control, but he caught Bart two more times, not back deep, but out of the pocket, after Bart had had enough time to throw if he could have found anyone open. The ends were having trouble cutting. On the first play of the last quarter, they used the halfback-option—an old favorite play of ours—and Dan Reeves passed 50 yards for a touchdown. We were losing, 17-14, and the wind was whipping us, too.

Five minutes later, my roommate was wide with an attempted field goal, and when the ball sailed by to the left I had a little sinking feeling, a little fear that the clock might run out on us. I thought maybe the time had come for us to lose. Dallas controlled the ball for about ten plays, staying on the ground as much as they could, eating up the clock, and all the time my frustration built up, my eagerness to get back on the field, to have another chance to score.

With five minutes to go, we got the ball on our own 32-yard line, and, right away, Bart threw a little pass out to Anderson and Andy picked up five, six yards. The linebackers were laying back; they were having trouble with their footing, trouble cutting. Chuck Mercein ran for the first down, and then Bart hit Dowler for another first down, and we were inside Dallas territory. I began to feel we were going to make it, we were going to go for a touchdown. At the worst, I figured we'd go down swinging.

On first down, Willie Townes got through and caught Andy for a big loss, and we had second and about twenty. But Bart capitalized on the Dallas linebackers' difficulties getting traction. Twice, with the ends still having problems with their footing, he threw safety-valve passes to Anderson and twice Andy went for about ten yards, and we had a first down on the Dallas 30, and I could feel the excitement building in the huddle. But we had only a minute and a half to play. Bart passed out to Mercein on the left and Chuck carried the ball down to the Dallas eleven. I walked back to the huddle, wondering what Bart was going to call, and he called a give-65, and I thought, "What a perfect call. We haven't used it all day. What a smart call."

It's a potentially dangerous play, a give-65. We block as though we're going through the "five" hole, outside me. Gilly pulls and comes over my way, and everything depends on the tackle in front of him, Bob Lilly, taking the fake and moving to his left. The play can't work against a slow, dumb tackle; it can only work against a quick, intelligent tackle like Lilly. We figured Lilly would key on Gilly and follow his move, but we didn't know for sure. Everybody blocks my way on this play, Anderson coming for the hole as though he's carrying the ball, and nobody blocks the actual target area, Lilly's area. If Lilly doesn't take the fake, if he ignores Gilly pulling, he kills the actual ballcarrier, Mercein.

But Lilly followed Gillingham, and the hole opened up, and Chuck drove down to the 3-yard line. With less than a minute to play, Anderson plunged for a first down on the one, and, with only two time-outs left, we huddled quickly. "Run over there," Gilly said, in the huddle. "Run that 55-special. They can't stop that."

Bart called the 55, and I thought to myself, "Well, this is it, toad. They're putting it directly on your back, yours and Forrest's." I didn't make a very good block, and the five hole didn't open up, and Andy got stopped at the line of scrimmage. We called a time-out with twenty seconds to play. Then Bart called the same play again, and this time Andy slipped coming toward the hole—I don't know whether he could have gotten through—and slid to about the one-foot line, and we called time out with sixteen seconds to play, our last time-out, and everybody in the place was screaming.

We could have gone for the field goal right then, for a tie, hoping that we'd win in overtime. We decided to go for the victory. In the huddle, Bart said, "Thirty-one wedge and I'll carry the ball." He was going to try a quarterback sneak. He wasn't going to take a chance on a handoff, or on anybody slipping. He was going to go for the hole just inside me, just off my left shoulder. Kenny Bowman, who had finally worked his way back to the lineup, and I were supposed to move big Jethro out of the way. It might be the last play of the game, our last chance.

The ground was giving me trouble, the footing was bad down near the goal line, but I dug my cleats in, got a firm hold with my right foot, and we got down in position, and Bart called the "hut" signal. Jethro was on my inside shoulder, my left shoulder. I came off the ball as fast as I ever have in my life. I came off the ball as fast as anyone could. In fact, I wouldn't swear that I didn't beat the center's snap by a fraction of a second. I wouldn't swear that I wasn't actually offside on the play.

I slammed into Jethro hard. All he had time to do was raise his left arm. He didn't even get it up all the way and I charged into him. His body was a little high, the way we'd noticed in the movies, and, with Bowman's help, I moved him outside. Willie Townes, next to Jethro, was down low, very low. He was supposed to come in low and close to the middle. He was low, but he didn't close. He might have filled the hole, but he didn't, and Bart churned into the opening and stretched and fell and landed over the goal line. It was the most beautiful sight in the world, seeing Bart lying next to me and seeing the referee in front of me, his arms over his head, signaling the touchdown. There were thirteen seconds to play.

The fans poured on the field, engulfing us, engulfing the Cowboys, pummeling all of us. Chuck Howley, the Dallas linebacker, got knocked down three or four times accidentally, and he was furious. I had to fight my way through the crowd to the sidelines; Bart came off the field looking like he was crying, and he probably was. The Cowboys still had time to get off two plays, two incomplete passes, and the game was over. I tried to get to the dressing room quickly, but I got caught around the 30-yard line, trapped in a mass of people beating me on the back, grabbing at my chin strap, grabbing at my gloves, trying to get anything for a souvenir. I had a sudden moment of panic, wondering whether I was ever going to get out of that mess alive.

Finally I reached the dressing room and I was immediately aware that the whole place was wired for sound. Cameramen and cameras were all around, and Coach Lombardi cussed the cameramen and ordered them, flatly, to get the hell out. When we were alone, just the team and the coaches, Vince told us how proud he was of us. "I can't talk anymore," he said. "I can't say anymore." He held the tears back and we all kneeled and said the Lord's Prayer, and then we exploded, with shouts of joy and excitement, the marks of battle, the cuts, the bruises, and the blood, all forgotten.

1. Kramer tells us about a game situation from the point of view of an experienced player. How does this account differ from Plimpton's, whose point of view is that of an amateur?

2. Does Kramer's story of the game make you feel that you are being taken inside the subject by an expert? What kind of interest does Kramer's narrative generate in a reader? How would this account differ, for example, from that of a sports announcer broadcasting the game?

3. What use does Kramer make of the complicated language of football tactics and strategy? Does he use more or less of this language than Plimpton does? Does he use such language in a different way?

4. How does Kramer characterize himself? What is his attitude to his own profession? Do you think he is proud of what he does and, if so, why?

∽ Piri Thomas ∽

(1928-   )

Piri Thomas was born in Spanish Harlem. Growing up in a world of gangs, drugs, and petty crime, he became an addict while in his teens, was convicted of attempted armed robbery in 1950, and served six years of a fifteen-year sentence. Thomas has since worked for and organized drug rehabilitation programs in New York and Puerto Rico and has begun a career as a writer. Down These Mean Streets *(1967), from which this selection is taken, was his first book. This incident begins with an account of Thomas's difficulties, as a Puerto Rican schoolboy, when his family moves into a predominantly Italian block in one of the poorer sections of New York City.*

ALIEN TURF

[SURVIVING IN THE NEIGHBORHOOD]

I got through the days trying to play it cool and walk on by Rocky and his boys like they weren't there. One day I passed them and nothing was said. I started to let out my breath. I felt great; I hadn't been seen. Then someone yelled in a high, girlish voice, "Yoo-hoo . . . Hey, *paisan* . . . we see yoo . . ." And right behind that voice came a can of evaporated milk—whoosh, clatter. I walked cool for ten steps then started running like mad.

This crap kept up for a month. They tried to shake me up. Every time they threw something at me, it was just to see me jump. I decided that the next fucking time they threw something at me I was gonna play bad-o and not run. That next time came about a week later. Momma sent me off the stoop to the Italian market on 115th Street and First Avenue, deep in Italian country. Man, that was stompin' territory. But I went, walking in the style which I had copped from the colored cats I had seen, a swinging and stepping down hard at every step. Those cats were so down and cool that just walking made a way-out sound.

Ten minutes later I was on my way back with Momma's stuff. I got to the corner of First Avenue and 114th Street and crushed myself right into Rocky and his fellas.

"Well-l, fellas," Rocky said. "Lookee who's here."

I didn't like the sounds coming out of Rocky's fat mouth. And I didn't like the sameness of the shitty grins spreading all over the boys' faces. But I thought, *No more! No more! I ain't gonna run no more.* Even so, I looked around, like for some kind of Jesus miracle to happen. I was always looking for miracles to happen.

"Say, *paisan*," one guy said, "you even buying from us *paisans*, eh? Man, you must wantta be Italian."

Before I could bite that dopey tongue of mine, I said, "I wouldn't be a guinea on a motherfucking bet."

"Wha-at?" said Rocky, really surprised. I didn't blame him; I was surprised myself. His finger began digging a hole in his ear, like he hadn't heard me right. "Wha-at? Say that again?"

I could feel a thin hot wetness cutting itself down my leg. I had been so ashamed of being so damned scared that I had peed on myself. And then I wasn't scared any more; I felt a fuck-it-all attitude. I looked real bad at Rocky and said, "Ya heard me. I wouldn't be a guinea on a bet."

"Ya little sonavabitch, we'll kick the shit outta ya," said one guy, Tony, who had made a habit of asking me if I had any sen-your-ritas for sisters.

"Kick the shit outta me yourself if you got any heart, you motherfuckin' fucker," I screamed at him. I felt kind of happy, the kind of feeling that you get only when you got heart.

148

Big-mouth Tony just swung out, and I swung back and heard all of Momma's stuff plopping all over the street. My fist hit Tony smack dead in the mouth. He was so mad he threw a fist at me from about three feet away. I faked and jabbed and did fancy dance steps. Big-mouth put a stop to all that with a punch in my mouth. I heard the home cheers of "Yea, yea, bust that spic wide open!" Then I bloodied Tony's nose. He blinked and sniffed without putting his hands to his nose, and I remembered Poppa telling me, "Son, if you're ever fighting somebody an' you punch him in the nose, and he just blinks an' sniffs without holding his nose, you can do one of two things: fight like hell or run like hell—'cause that cat's a fighter."

Big-mouth came at me and we grabbed each other and pushed and pulled and shoved. *Poppa*, I thought, *I ain't gonna cop out. I'm a fighter, too.* I pulled away from Tony and blew my fist into his belly. He puffed and butted my nose with his head. I sniffed back. *Poppa, I didn't put my hands to my nose.* I hit Tony again in that same weak spot. He bent over in the middle and went down to his knees.

Big-mouth got up as fast as he could, and I was thinking how much heart he had. But I ran toward him like my life depended on it; I wanted to cool him. Too late, I saw his hand grab a fistful of ground asphalt which had been piled nearby to fix a pothole in the street. I tried to duck; I should have closed my eyes instead. The shitty-gritty stuff hit my face, and I felt the scrappy pain make itself a part of my eyes. I screamed and grabbed for two eyes with one hand, while the other I beat some kind of helpless tune on air that just couldn't be hurt. I heard Rocky's voice shouting, "Ya scum bag, ya didn't have to fight the spic dirty; you could've fucked him up fair and square!" I couldn't see. I heard a fist hit a face, then Big-mouth's voice: "Whatta ya hittin' me for?" and then Rocky's voice: *"Putana!* I ought ta knock all your fuckin' teeth out."

I felt hands grabbing at me between my screams. I punched out. *I'm gonna get killed*, I thought. Then I heard many voices:

"Hold it, kid." "We ain't gonna hurt ya." "Je-*sus*, don't rub your eyes." "Ooooohhhh, shit, his eyes is fulla that shit."

You're fuckin' right, I thought, *and it hurts like* coño.

I heard a woman's voice now: "Take him to a hospital." And an old man asked: "How did it happen?"

"Momma, Momma," I cried.

"Comon, kid," Rocky said, taking my hand. "Lemme take ya home." I fought for the right to rub my eyes. "Grab his other hand, Vincent," Rocky said. I tried to rub my eyes with my eyelids. I could feel hurt tears cutting down my cheeks. "Come on, kid, we ain't gonna hurt ya," Rocky tried to assure me. "Swear to our mudders. We just wanna take ya home."

I made myself believe him, and trying not to make pain noises, I let myself be led home. I wondered if I was gonna be blind like Mr. Silva, who went around from door to door sell-ing dish towels and brooms, his son leading him around.

"You okay, kid?" Rocky asked.

"Yeah," what was left of me said.

"A-huh," mumbled Big-mouth.

"He got much heart for a nigger," somebody else said.

A *spic*, I thought.

"For anybody," Rocky said. "Here we are, kid," he added. "Watch your step."

I was like carried up the steps. "What's your apartment number?" Rocky asked.

"One-B—inna back—ground floor," I said, and I was led there. Somebody knocked on Momma's door. Then I heard running feet and Rocky's voice yelling back, "Don't rat, huh, kid?" And I was alone.

I heard the door open and Momma say, "*Bueno*, Piri, come in." I didn't move. I couldn't. There was a long pause; I could hear Momma's fright. "My God," she said finally. "What's happened?" Then she took a closer look. "Ai-eeee," she screamed. "*Dios mío!*"

"I was playing with some kids, Momma," I said, "an' I got some dirt in my eyes." I tried to make my voice come out with-out the pain, like a man.

"*Dios eterno*—your eyes!"

"What's the matter? What's the matter?" Poppa called from the bedroom.

"*Está ciego!*" Momma screamed. "He is blind!"

I heard Poppa knocking things over as he came running. Sis began to cry. Blind, hurting tears were jumping out of my eyes. "Whattya mean, he's blind?" Poppa said as he stormed into the kitchen. "What happened?" Poppa's voice was both scared and mad.

"Playing, Poppa."

"Whatta ya mean, 'playing'?" Poppa's English sounded different when he got warm.

"Just playing, Poppa."

"Playing? Playing got all that dirt in your eyes? I bet my ass. Them damn Ee-ta-liano kids ganged up on you again." Poppa squeezed my head between the fingers of one hand. "That settles it—we're moving outta this damn section, outta this damn block, outta this damn shit."

Shit, I thought, *Poppa's sure cursin' up a storm*. I could hear him slapping the side of his leg, like he always did when he got real mad.

"Son," he said, "you're gonna point them out to me."

"Point who out, Poppa? I was playin' an'—"

"Stop talkin' to him and take him to the hospital!" Momma screamed.

"*Pobrecito*, poor Piri," cooed my little sister.

"You sure, son?" Poppa asked. "You was only playing?"

"Shit, Poppa, I said I was."

Smack—Poppa was so scared and mad, he let it out in a slap to the side of my face.

"*Bestia!* Ani-*mul!*" Momma cried. "He's blind, and you hit him!"

"I'm sorry, son, I'm sorry," Poppa said in a voice like almost-crying. I heard him running back into the bedroom, yelling, "Where's my pants?"

Momma grabbed away fingers that were trying to wipe away the hurt in my eyes. "*Caramba*, no rub, no rub," she said, kissing me. She told Sis to get a rag and wet it with cold water.

Poppa came running back into the kitchen. "Let's go, son, let's go. Jesus! I didn't mean to smack ya, I really didn't," he said, his big hand rubbing and grabbing my hair gently.

"Here's the rag, Momma," said Sis.

"What's that for?" asked Poppa.

"To put on his eyes," Momma said.

I heard the smack of a wet rag, *blapt*, against the kitchen wall. "We can't put nothing on his eyes. It might make them worse. Come on, son," Poppa said nervously, lifting me up in his big arms. I felt like a little baby, like I didn't hurt so bad. I wanted to stay there, but I said, "Let me down, Poppa, I ain't no kid."

"Shut up," Poppa said softly. "I know you ain't, but it's faster this way."

"Which hospeetal are you taking him to?" Momma asked.

"Nearest one," Poppa answered as we went out the door. He carried me through the hall and out into the street, where the bright sunlight made a red hurting color through the crap in my eyes. I heard voices on the stoop and on the sidewalk: "Is that the boy?"

"A-huh. He's probably blinded."

"We'll get a cab, son," Poppa said. His voice loved me. I heard Rocky yelling from across the street, "We're pulling for ya, kid. Remember what we . . ." The rest was lost to Poppa's long legs running down to the corner of Third Avenue. He hailed a taxi and we zoomed off toward Harlem Hospital. I felt the cab make all kinds of sudden stops and turns.

"How do you feel, *hijo?*" Poppa asked.

"It burns like hell."

"You'll be okay," he said, and as an afterthought added, "Don't curse, son."

I heard cars honking and the Third Avenue el roaring above us. I knew we were in Puerto Rican turf, 'cause I could hear our language.

"Son."

"Yeah, Poppa."

"Don't rub your eyes, fer Christ sake." He held my skinny wrists in his one hand, and everything got quiet between us.

The cab got to Harlem Hospital. I heard change being handled and the door opening and Poppa thanking the cabbie for getting here fast. "Hope the kid'll be okay," the driver said.

I will be, I thought. *I ain't gonna be like Mr. Silva.*

Poppa took me in his arms again and started running. "Where's emergency, mister?" he asked someone.

"To your left and straight away," said a voice.

"Thanks a lot," Poppa said, and we were running again. "Emergency?" Poppa said when we stopped.

"Yes, sir," said a girl's voice. "What's the matter?"

"My boy's got his eyes full of ground-up tar an'—"

"What's the matter?" said a man's voice.

"Youngster with ground tar in his eyes, doctor."

"We'll take him, mister. You just put him down here and go with the nurse. She'll take down the information. Uh, you the father?"

"That's right, doctor."

"Okay, just put him down here."

"Poppa, don't leave me," I cried.

"Sh, son, I ain't leaving you. I'm just going to fill out some papers, an' I'll be right back."

I nodded my head up and down and was wheeled away. When the rolling stretcher stopped, somebody stuck a needle in me and I got sleepy and started thinking about Rocky and his boys, and Poppa's slap, and how great Poppa was, and how my eyes didn't hurt no more . . .

I woke up in a room blind with darkness. The only lights were the ones inside my head. I put my fingers to my eyes and felt bandages. "Let them be, sonny," said a woman's voice.

I wanted to ask the voice if they had taken my eyes out, but I didn't. I was afraid the voice would say yes.

"Let them be, sonny," the nurse said, pulling my hand away

from the bandages. "You're all right. The doctor put the bandages on to keep the light out. They'll be off real soon. Don't you
worry none, sonny."

I wished she would stop calling me sonny. "Where's Poppa?"
I asked cool-like.

"He's outside, sonny. Would you like me to send him in?"

I nodded, "Yeah." I heard walking-away shoes, a door opening, a whisper, and shoes walking back toward me. "How do
you feel, *hijo?*" Poppa asked.

"It hurts like shit, Poppa."

"It's just for awhile, son, and then off come the bandages.
Everything's gonna be all right."

I thought, *Poppa didn't tell me to stop cursing.*

"And son, I thought I told you to stop cursing," he added.

I smiled. Poppa hadn't forgotten. Suddenly I realized that
all I had on was a hospital gown. "Poppa, where's my clothes?"
I asked.

"I got them. I'm taking them home an'—"

"Whatta ya mean, Poppa?" I said, like scared. "You ain't
leavin' me here? I'll be damned if I stay." I was already sitting
up and feeling my way outta bed. Poppa grabbed me and
pushed me back. His voice wasn't mad or scared any more. It
was happy and soft, like Momma's.

"Hey," he said, "get your ass back in bed or they'll have to
put a bandage there too."

"Poppa," I pleaded. "I don't care, wallop me as much as you
want, just take me home."

"Hey, I thought you said you wasn't no kid. Hell, you ain't
scared of being alone?"

Inside my head there was a running of *Yeah, yeah, yeah,*
but I answered, "Naw, Poppa, it's just that Momma's gonna
worry and she'll get sick an' everything, and—"

"Won't work, son," Poppa broke in with a laugh.

I kept quiet.

"It's only for a couple days. We'll come and see you an'
everybody'll bring you things."

I got interested but played it smooth. "What kinda things, Poppa?"

Poppa shrugged his shoulders and spread his big arms apart and answered me like he was surprised that I should ask. "Uh . . . fruits and . . . candy and ice cream. And Momma will probably bring you chicken soup."

I shook my head sadly. "Poppa, you know I don't like chicken soup."

"So we won't bring chicken soup. We'll bring what you like. Goddammit, whatta ya like?"

"I'd like the first things you talked about, Poppa," I said softly. "But instead of soup I'd like"—I held my breath back, then shot it out—"some roller skates!"

Poppa let out a whistle. Roller skates were about $1.50, and that was rice and beans for more than a few days. Then he said, "All right, son, soon as you get home, you got 'em."

But he had agreed too quickly. I shook my head from side to side. Shit, I was gonna push all the way for the roller skates. It wasn't every day you'd get hurt bad enough to ask for something so little like a pair of roller skates. I wanted them right away.

"Fer Christ sakes," Poppa protested, "you can't use 'em in here. Why, some kid will probably steal 'em on you." But Poppa's voice died out slowly in a "you win" tone as I just kept shaking my head from side to side. "Bring 'em tomorrow," he finally mumbled, "but that's it."

"Thanks, Poppa."

"Don't ask for no more."

My eyes were starting to hurt like mad again. The fun was starting to go outta the game between Poppa and me. I made a face.

"Does it hurt, son?"

"Naw, Poppa. I can take it." I thought how I was like a cat in a movie about Indians, taking it like a champ, tied to a stake and getting like burned toast.

Poppa sounded relieved. "Yeah, it's only at first it hurts."

His hand touched my foot. "Well, I'll be going now . . ." Poppa rubbed my foot gently and then slapped me the same gentle way on the side of my leg. "Be good, son," he said and walked away. I heard the door open and the nurse telling him about how they were gonna move me to the ward 'cause I was out of danger. "Son," Poppa called back, "you're *un hombre*."

I felt proud as hell.

"Poppa."

"Yeah, son?"

"You won't forget to bring the roller skates, huh?"

Poppa laughed. "Yeah, son."

I heard the door close.

1. Thomas uses a great deal of dialogue in presenting this event. What do you think a writer gains when he depends primarily on dialogue? What elements of this story are most memorable?

2. The two most important characters in the scene are Thomas and his father: show how Thomas is able to convey the strength of their relationship without ever stating how important his father is to him.

3. Thomas is portraying life in the "mean streets" of a ghetto in New York City. What conditions of life do you become aware of in this episode and how does Thomas communicate them? What kind of positive values does Thomas find as he recalls a harsh moment in his childhood?

4. Examine any page of the selection and analyze how the details of people's speeches and gestures help to characterize them and the situation.

5. Part of the effect of this selection depends on Thomas's ear for language as it is actually spoken in his world. Choose two or three passages and discuss how they demonstrate the writer's skill in using colloquial or profane language in expressive ways.

∽ Frederick Douglass ∽

(1817-1895)

*Frederick Douglass was born a slave in Maryland. He worked
as both a house servant and a field hand until he was able to
escape to the North, where he became an important figure in
the Abolitionist movement. He published the first version of
his autobiography, from which the following selection is taken,
in 1845 at the urging of antislavery leaders. Douglass was active in recruiting black troops for the North during the Civil
War, and for thirty years after the war he held various federal
appointments, including positions as U.S. representative in
Haiti and Santo Domingo. He was an advocate for a wide
range of social reforms, but above all else, his name and career are identified with the cause of equal rights for black
Americans.*

[BECOMING A MAN]

I have already intimated that my condition was much worse,
during the first six months of my stay at Mr. Covey's, than in
the last six. The circumstances leading to the change in Mr.
Covey's course toward me form an epoch in my humble history. You have seen how a man was made a slave; you shall see
how a slave was made a man. On one of the hottest days of the
month of August, 1833, Bill Smith, William Hughes, a slave
named Eli, and myself, were engaged in fanning wheat.
Hughes was clearing the fanned wheat from before the fan,

From Frederick Douglass: *Narrative of the Life of Frederick Douglass: An
American Slave, Written by Himself,* ed. Benjamin Quarles. Copyright © 1960
by the President and Fellows of Harvard College. Reprinted by permission of the
publisher, The Belknap Press of Harvard University Press, Cambridge.

Eli was turning, Smith was feeding, and I was carrying wheat to the fan. The work was simple, requiring strength rather than intellect; yet, to one entirely unused to such work, it came very hard. About three o'clock of that day, I broke down; my strength failed me; I was seized with a violent aching of the head, attended with extreme dizziness; I trembled in every limb. Finding what was coming, I nerved myself up, feeling it would never do to stop work. I stood as long as I could stagger to the hopper with grain. When I could stand no longer, I fell, and felt as if held down by an immense weight. The fan of course stopped; every one had his own work to do; and no one could do the work of the other, and have his own go on at the same time.

Mr. Covey was at the house, about one hundred yards from the treading-yard where we were fanning. On hearing the fan stop, he left immediately, and came to the spot where we were. He hastily inquired what the matter was. Bill answered that I was sick, and there was no one to bring wheat to the fan. I had by this time crawled away under the side of the post and rail-fence by which the yard was enclosed, hoping to find relief by getting out of the sun. He then asked where I was. He was told by one of the hands. He came to the spot, and, after looking at me awhile, asked me what was the matter. I told him as well as I could, for I scarce had strength to speak. He then gave me a savage kick in the side, and told me to get up. I tried to do so, but fell back in the attempt. He gave me another kick, and again told me to rise. I again tried, and succeeded in gaining my feet; but, stooping to get the tub with which I was feeding the fan, I again staggered and fell. While down in this situation, Mr. Covey took up the hickory slat with which Hughes had been striking off the half-bushel measure, and with it gave me a heavy blow upon the head, making a large wound, and the blood ran freely; and with this again told me to get up. I made no effort to comply, having now made up my mind to let him do his worst. In a short time after receiving this blow, my head grew better. Mr. Covey had now left me to my fate. At this moment I resolved, for the first time, to go to my master, enter a complaint, and ask his protection. In order to [do] this, I must that afternoon walk seven miles; and this, under the circumstances, was truly a severe undertaking. I was exceedingly feeble; made so as much by the kicks and blows which I received, as by the severe fit of sickness to which I had been subjected. I, however, watched my chance, while Covey was looking in an opposite direction, and started for St. Michael's. I succeeded in getting a considerable distance on my way to the woods, when Covey discovered me, and called after me to come back, threatening what he would do if I did not come. I disregarded both his calls and his threats, and made my way to the woods as fast as my feeble state would allow; and thinking I might be overhauled by him if I kept the road, I walked through the woods, keeping far enough from the road to avoid detection, and near enough to prevent losing my way. I had not gone far before my little strength again failed me. I could go no farther. I fell down, and lay for a considerable time. The blood was yet oozing from the wound on my head. For a time I thought I should bleed to death; and think now that I should have done so, but that the blood so matted my hair as to stop the wound. After lying there about three quarters of an hour, I nerved myself up again, and started on my way, through bogs and briers, barefooted and bareheaded, tearing my feet sometimes at nearly every step; and after a journey of about seven miles, occupying some five hours to perform it, I arrived at master's store. I then presented an appearance enough to affect any but a heart of iron. From the crown of my head to my feet, I was covered with blood. My hair was all clotted with dust and blood; my shirt was stiff with blood. My legs and feet were torn in sundry places with briers and thorns, and were also covered with blood. I suppose I looked like a man who had escaped a den of wild beasts, and barely escaped them. In this state I appeared before my master, humbly entreating him to interpose his authority for my protection. I told him all the circumstances as well as I could, and it seemed, as I spoke, at times to affect him. He would then walk the floor, and seek to justify Covey by saying he expected I deserved it. He asked me what I wanted. I told him, to let me get a new home; that as sure as I lived with Mr. Covey again, I should live with but to die with him; that Covey would surely kill me; he was in a fair way for it. Master Thomas ridiculed the idea that there was any danger of Mr. Covey's killing me, and said that he knew Mr. Covey; that he was a good man, and that he could not think of taking me from him; that, should he do so, he would lose the whole year's wages; that I belonged to Mr. Covey for one year, and that I must go back to him, come what might; and that I must not trouble him with any more stories, or that he would himself *get hold of me*. After threatening me thus, he gave me a very large dose of salts, telling me that I might remain in St. Michael's that night, (it being quite late,) but that I must be off back to Mr. Covey's early in the morning; and that if I did not, he would *get hold of me*, which meant that he would whip me. I remained all night, and, according to his orders, I started off to Covey's in the morning, (Saturday morning,) wearied in body and broken in spirit. I got no supper that night, or breakfast that morning. I reached Covey's about nine o'clock; and just as I was getting over the fence that divided Mrs. Kemp's fields from ours, out ran Covey with his cowskin, to give me another whipping. Before he could reach me, I succeeded in getting to the cornfield; and as the corn was very high, it afforded me the means of hiding. He seemed very angry, and searched for me a long time. My behavior was altogether unaccountable. He finally gave up the chase, thinking, I suppose, that I must come home for something to eat; he would give himself no further trouble in looking for me. I spent that day mostly in the woods, having the alternative before me,—to go home and be whipped to death, or stay in the woods and be starved to death. That night, I fell in with Sandy Jenkins, a slave with whom I was somewhat acquainted. Sandy had a free wife who lived about four miles from Mr. Covey's; and it being Saturday, he was on his way to see her. I told him my circumstances, and he very kindly invited me to go home with him. I went home with him, and talked this whole matter over, and got his advice as to what course it was best for me to pursue. I found Sandy an old adviser. He told me, with great solemnity, I must go back to Covey; but that before I went, I must go with him into another part of the woods, where there was a certain *root*, which, if I would take some of it with me, carrying it *always on my right side*, would render it impossible for Mr. Covey, or any other white man, to whip me. He said he had carried it for years; and since he had done so, he had never received a blow, and never expected to while he carried it. I at first rejected the idea, that the simple carrying of a root in my pocket would have any such effect as he had said, and was not disposed to take it; but Sandy impressed the necessity with much earnestness, telling me it could do no harm, if it did no good. To please him, I at length took the root, and, according to his direction, carried it upon my right side. This was Sunday morning. I immediately started for home; and upon entering the yard gate, out come Mr. Covey on his way to meeting. He spoke to me very kindly, made me drive the pigs from a lot near by, and passed on towards the church. Now, this singular conduct of Mr. Covey really made me begin to think that there was something in the *root* which Sandy had given me; and had it been on any other day than Sunday, I could have attributed the conduct to no other cause than the influence of that root; and as it was, I was half inclined to think the *root* to be something more than I at first had taken it to be. All went well till Monday morning. On this morning, the virtue of the *root* was fully tested. Long before daylight, I was called to go and rub, curry, and feed, the horses. I obeyed, and was glad to obey. But whilst thus engaged, whilst in the act of throwing down some blades from the loft, Mr. Covey entered the stable with a long rope; and just as I was half out of the loft, he caught hold of my legs, and was about tying me. As soon as I found what he was up to, I gave a sudden spring, and as I did so, he holding to my legs, I was brought sprawling on the stable floor. Mr. Covey seemed now to think he had me, and could do what he pleased; but at this moment—from whence came the spirit I don't know—I resolved to fight; and, suiting my action to the resolution, I seized Covey hard by the throat; and as I did so, I rose. He held on to me, and I to him. My resistance was so entirely unexpected, that Covey seemed taken all aback. He trembled like a leaf. This gave me assurance, and I held him uneasy, causing the blood to run where I touched him with the ends of my fingers. Mr. Covey soon called out to Hughes for help. Hughes came, and, while Covey held me, attempted to tie my right hand. While he was in the act of doing so, I watched my chance, and gave him a heavy kick close under the ribs. This kick fairly sickened Hughes, so that he left me in the hands of Mr. Covey. This kick had the effect of not only weakening Hughes, but Covey also. When he saw Hughes bending over with pain, his courage quailed. He asked me if I meant to persist in my resistance. I told him I did, come what might; that he had used me like a brute for six months, and that I was determined to be used so no longer. With that, he strove to drag me to a stick that was lying just out of the stable door. He meant to knock me down. But just as he was leaning over to get the stick, I seized him with both hands by his collar, and brought him by a sudden snatch to the ground. By this time, Bill came. Covey called upon him for assistance. Bill wanted to know what he could do. Covey said, "Take hold of him, take hold of him!" Bill said his master hired him out to work, and not to help to whip me; so he left Covey and myself to fight our own battle out. We were at it for nearly two hours. Covey at length let me go, puffing and blowing at a great rate, saying that if I had not resisted, he would not have whipped me half so much. The truth was, that he had not whipped me at all. I considered him as getting entirely the worst end of the bargain; for he had drawn no blood from me, but I had from him. The whole six months afterwards, that I spent with Mr. Covey, he never laid the weight of his finger upon me in anger. He would occasionally say, he didn't want to get hold of me again. "No," thought I, "you need not; for you will come off worse than you did before."

This battle with Mr. Covey was the turning-point in my career as a slave. It rekindled the few expiring embers of freedom, and revived within me a sense of my own manhood. It recalled the departed self-confidence, and inspired me again with a determination to be free. The gratification afforded by the triumph was a full compensation for whatever else might follow, even death itself. He only can understand the deep satisfaction which I experienced, who has himself repelled by force the bloody arm of slavery. I felt as I never felt before. It was a glorious resurrection, from the tomb of slavery, to the heaven of freedom. My long-crushed spirit rose, cowardice departed, bold defiance took its place; and I now resolved that, however long I might remain a slave in form, the day had passed forever when I could be a slave in fact. I did not hesitate to let it be known of me, that the white man who expected to succeed in whipping, must also succeed in killing me.

From this time I was never again what might be called fairly whipped, though I remained a slave four years afterwards. I had several fights, but was never whipped.

It was for a long time a matter of surprise to me why Mr. Covey did not immediately have me taken by the constable to the whipping-post, and there regularly whipped for the crime of raising my hand against a white man in defence of myself. And the only explanation I can now think of does not entirely satisfy me; but such as it is, I will give it. Mr. Covey enjoyed the most unbounded reputation for being a first-rate overseer and negro-breaker. It was of considerable importance to him. That reputation was at stake; and had he sent me—a boy about sixteen years old—to the public whipping-post, his reputation would have been lost; so, to save his reputation, he suffered me to go unpunished.

1. *Unlike Thomas or Conroy, Douglass uses almost no dialogue at all in his account. How does he give the reader a sense of a dramatic event?*

2. *Douglass wrote this account of his experiences as a slave*

after he had escaped to the North and was living as a free man. How does his situation when he writes his autobiography influence the way in which he recalls his past experience?

3. What qualities of character does Douglass emphasize in his account of himself? Do you think Douglass is interested in making his life experience representative of the experience of black people in slavery? What aspects of the slave experience do you become most aware of in this episode?

4. Compare Douglass's account of personal violence with that of Piri Thomas. What are some of the distinctive qualities of Douglass's style of narration? In what ways is it more formal than that of Thomas? Can you see some advantages in Douglass's method?

5. Why do you think Douglass includes a fairly detailed account of his trip home to Master Thomas, his actual owner who had leased Douglass's services to Mr. Covey? Why does he include an account of the time spent with Sandy Jenkins?

∽ George Orwell ∽

(1903-1950)

See the biographical note on page 61. "Shooting An Elephant"
was written in 1936, but it recalls an incident during Orwell's
service with the Indian Imperial Police in Moulmien, Burma
(1926–27). Orwell went home to England on leave in August,
1927 and never returned.

SHOOTING AN ELEPHANT

In Moulmein, in Lower Burma, I was hated by large numbers
of people—the only time in my life that I have been important
enough for this to happen to me. I was sub-divisional police officer of the town, and in an aimless, petty kind of way anti-
European feeling was very bitter. No one had the guts to raise
a riot, but if a European woman went through the bazaars
alone somebody would probably spit betel juice over her dress.
As a police officer I was an obvious target and was baited whenever it seemed safe to do so. When a nimble Burman tripped
me up on the football field and the referee (another Burman)
looked the other way, the crowd yelled with hideous laughter.
This happened more than once. In the end the sneering yellow
faces of young men that met me everywhere, the insults hooted
after me when I was at a safe distance, got badly on my nerves.
The young Buddhist priests were the worst of all. There were
several thousands of them in the town and none of them seemed
to have anything to do except stand on street corners and jeer
at Europeans.

All this was perplexing and upsetting. For at that time I had already made up my mind that imperialism was an evil thing and the sooner I chucked up my job and got out of it the better. Theoretically—and secretly, of course—I was all for the Burmese and all against their oppressors, the British. As for the job I was doing I hated it more bitterly than I can perhaps make clear. In a job like that you see the dirty work of Empire at close quarters. The wretched prisoners huddling in the stinking cages of the lock-ups, the grey, cowed faces of the long-term convicts, the scarred buttocks of the men who had been flogged with bamboos—all these oppressed me with an intolerable sense of guilt. But I could get nothing into perspective. I was young and ill-educated and I had had to think out my problems in the utter silence that is imposed on every Englishman in the East. I did not even know that the British Empire is dying, still less did I know that it is a great deal better than the younger empires that are going to supplant it. All I knew was that I was stuck between my hatred of the empire I served and my rage against the evil-spirited little beasts who tried to make my job impossible. With one part of my mind I thought of the British Raj as an unbreakable tyranny, as something clamped down, in *sæcula sæculorum*, upon the will of prostrate peoples; with another part I thought that the greatest joy in the world would be to drive a bayonet into a Buddhist priest's guts. Feelings like these are the normal by-products of imperialism; ask any Anglo-Indian official, if you can catch him off duty.

One day something happened which in a roundabout way was enlightening. It was a tiny incident in itself, but it gave me a better glimpse than I had had before of the real nature of imperialism—the real motives for which despotic governments act. Early one morning the sub-inspector at a police station the other end of the town rang me up on the 'phone and said that an elephant was ravaging the bazaar. Would I please come and do something about it? I did not know what I could do, but I wanted to see what was happening and I got on to a pony and started out. I took my rifle, an old .44 Winchester and much too small to kill an elephant, but I thought the noise might be useful *in terrorem*. Various Burmans stopped me on the way and told me about the elephant's doings. It was not, of course, a wild elephant, but a tame one which had gone "must." It had been chained up, as tame elephants always are when their attack of "must" is due, but on the previous night it had broken its chain and escaped. Its mahout, the only person who could manage it when was in that state, had set out in pursuit, but had taken the wrong direction and was now twelve hours' journey away, and in the morning the elephant had suddenly reappeared in the town. The Burmese population had no weapons and were quite helpless against it. It had already destroyed somebody's bamboo hut, killed a cow and raided some fruit-stalls and devoured the stock; also it had met the municipal rubbish van, and, when the driver jumped out and took to his heels, had turned the van over and inflicted violences upon it.

The Burmese sub-inspector and some Indian constables were waiting for me in the quarter where the elephant had been seen. It was a very poor quarter, a labyrinth of squalid bamboo huts, thatched with palm-leaf, winding all over a steep hillside. I remember that it was a cloudy, stuffy morning at the beginning of the rains. We began questioning the people as to where the elephant had gone, and, as usual, failed to get any definite information. That is invariably the case in the East; a story always sounds clear enough at a distance, but the nearer you get to the scene of events the vaguer it becomes. Some of the people said that the elephant had gone in one direction, some said that he had gone in another, some professed not even to have heard of any elephant. I had almost made up my mind that the whole story was a pack of lies, when we heard yells a little distance away. There was a loud, scandalized cry of "Go away, child! Go away this instant!" and an old woman with a switch in her hand came round the corner of a hut, violently shooing away a crowd of naked children. Some more women followed, clicking their tongues and exclaiming; evidently there was something that the children ought not to have seen. I rounded the hut and saw a man's dead body sprawling in the mud. He was an Indian, a black Dravidian coolie, almost naked, and he could not have been dead many minutes. The people said that the elephant had come suddenly upon him round the corner of the hut, caught him with its trunk, put its foot on his back and ground him into the earth. This was the rainy season and the ground was soft, and his face had scored a trench a foot deep and a couple of yards long. He was lying on his belly with arms crucified and head sharply twisted to one side. His face was coated with mud, the eyes wide open, the teeth bared and grinning with an expression of unendurable agony. (Never tell me, by the way, that the dead looked peaceful. Most of the corpses I have seen look devilish.) The friction of the great beast's foot had stripped the skin from his back as neatly as one skins a rabbit. As soon as I saw the dead man I sent an orderly to a friend's house nearby to borrow an elephant rifle. I had already sent back the pony, not wanting it to go mad with fright and throw me if it smelt the elephant.

The orderly came back in a few minutes with a rifle and five cartridges, and meanwhile some Burmans had arrived and told us that the elephant was in the paddy fields below, only a few hundred yards away. As I started forward practically the whole population of the quarter flocked out of the houses and followed me. They had seen the rifle and were all shouting excitedly that I was going to shoot the elephant. They had not shown much interest in the elephant when he was merely ravaging their homes, but it was different now that he was going to be shot. It was a bit of fun to them, as it would be to an English crowd; besides they wanted the meat. It made me vaguely uneasy. I had no intention of shooting the elephant—I had merely sent for the rifle to defend myself if necessary—and it is always unnerving to have a crowd following you. I marched down the hill, looking and feeling a fool, with the rifle over my shoulder and an ever-growing army of people jostling at my heels. At the bottom, when you got away from the huts, there was a metalled road and beyond that a miry waste of paddy fields a thousand yards across, not yet ploughed but soggy from the first rains and dotted with coarse grass. The elephant was standing eight yards from the road, his left side towards us. He took not the slightest notice of the crowd's approach. He was tearing up bunches of grass, beating them against his knees to clean them and stuffing them into his mouth.

I had halted on the road. As soon as I saw the elephant I knew with perfect certainty that I ought not to shoot him. It is a serious matter to shoot a working elephant—it is comparable to destroying a huge and costly piece of machinery—and obviously one ought not to do it if it can possibly be avoided. And at that distance, peacefully eating, the elephant looked no more dangerous than a cow. I thought then and I think now that his attack of "must" was already passing off; in which case he would merely wander harmlessly about until the mahout came back and caught him. Moreover, I did not in the least want to shoot him. I decided that I would watch him for a little while to make sure that he did not turn savage again, and then go home.

But at that moment I glanced round at the crowd that had followed me. It was an immense crowd, two thousand at the least and growing every minute. It blocked the road for a long distance on either side. I looked at the sea of yellow faces above the garish clothes—faces all happy and excited over this bit of fun, all certain that the elephant was going to be shot. They were watching me as they would watch a conjurer about to perform a trick. They did not like me, but with the magical rifle in my hands I was momentarily worth watching. And suddenly I realized that I should have to shoot the elephant after all. The people expected it of me and I had got to do it; I could feel their two thousand wills pressing me forward, irresistibly. And it was at this moment, as I stood there with the rifle in my hands, that I first grasped the hollowness, the futility of the white man's dominion in the East. Here was I, the white man with his gun, standing in front of the unarmed native crowd—seemingly the leading actor of the piece; but in reality I was only an absurd puppet pushed to and fro by the will of those yellow faces behind. I perceived in this moment that when the white man turns tyrant it is his own freedom that he destroys. He becomes a sort of hollow, posing dummy, the conventionalized figure of a sahib. For it is the condition of his rule that he shall spend his life in trying to impress the "natives," and so in every crisis he has got to do what the "natives" expect of him. He wears a mask, and his face grows to fit it. I had got to shoot the elephant. I had committed myself to doing it when I sent for the rifle. A sahib has got to act like a sahib; he has got to appear resolute, to know his own mind and do definite things. To come all that way, rifle in hand, with two thousand people marching at my heels, and then to trail feebly away, having done nothing—no, that was impossible. The crowd would laugh at me. And my whole life, every white man's life in the East, was one long struggle not to be laughed at.

But I did not want to shoot the elephant. I watched him beating his bunch of grass against his knees, with that preoccupied grandmotherly air that elephants have. It seemed to me that it would be murder to shoot him. At that age I was not squeamish about killing animals, but I had never shot an elephant and never wanted to. (Somehow it always seems worse to kill a *large* animal.) Besides, there was the beast's owner to be considered. Alive, the elephant was worth at least a hundred pounds; dead, he would only be worth the value of his tusks, five pounds, possibly. But I had got to act quickly. I turned to some experienced-looking Burmans who had been there when we arrived, and asked them how the elephant had been behaving. They all said the same thing: he took no notice of you if you left him alone, but he might charge if you went too close to him.

It was perfectly clear to me what I ought to do. I ought to walk up to within, say, twenty-five yards of the elephant and test his behaviour. If he charged I could shoot, if he took no notice of me it would be safe to leave him until the mahout came back. But also I knew that I was going to do no such thing. I was a poor shot with a rifle and the ground was soft mud into which one would sink at every step. If the elephant charged and I missed him, I should have about as much chance as a toad under a steam-roller. But even then I was not thinking particularly of my own skin, only of the watchful yellow faces behind. For at that moment, with the crowd watching me, I was not afraid in the ordinary sense, as I would have been if I had been alone. A white man mustn't be frightened in front of "natives"; and so, in general, he isn't frightened. The sole thought in my mind was that if anything went wrong those two thousand Burmans would see me pursued, caught, trampled on and reduced to a grinning corpse like that Indian up the hill. And if that happened it was quite probable that some of them would laugh. That would never do. There was only one alternative. I shoved the cartridges into the magazine and lay down on the road to get a better aim.

The crowd grew very still, and a deep, low, happy sigh, as of people who see the theatre curtain go up at last, breathed from innumerable throats. They were going to have their bit of fun after all. The rifle was a beautiful German thing with cross-hair sights. I did not then know that in shooting an elephant one would shoot to cut an imaginary bar running from ear-hole to ear-hole. I ought, therefore, as the elephant was sideways on, to have aimed straight at his ear-hole; actually I aimed several inches in front of this, thinking the brain would be farther forward.

When I pulled the trigger I did not hear the bang or feel the kick—one never does when a shot goes home—but I heard the devilish roar of glee that went up from the crowd. In that instant, in too short a time, one would have thought, even for the bullet to get there, a mysterious, terrible change had come over the elephant. He neither stirred nor fell, but every line of his body had altered. He looked suddenly stricken, shrunken, immensely old, as though the frightful impact of the bullet had paralysed him without knocking him down. At last, after what seemed a long time—it might have been five seconds, I dare say—he sagged flabbily to his knees. His mouth slobbered. An enormous senility seemed to have settled upon him. One could have imagined him thousands of years old. I fired again into the same spot. At the second shot he did not collapse but climbed with desperate slowness to his feet and stood weakly upright, with legs sagging and head drooping. I fired a third time. That was the shot that did for him. You could see the agony of it jolt his whole body and knock the last remnant of strength from his legs. But in falling he seemed for a moment to rise, for as his hind legs collapsed beneath him he seemed to tower upwards like a huge rock toppling, his trunk reaching skywards like a tree. He trumpeted, for the first and only time. And then down he came, his belly towards me, with a crash that seemed to shake the ground even where I lay.

I got up. The Burmans were already racing past me across the mud. It was obvious that the elephant would never rise again, but he was not dead. He was breathing very rhythmically with long rattling gasps, his great mound of a side painfully rising and falling. His mouth was wide open—I could see far down into caverns of pale pink throat. I waited a long time for him to die, but his breathing did not weaken. Finally I fired my two remaining shots into the spot where I thought his heart must be. The thick blood welled out of him like red velvet, but still he did not die. His body did not even jerk when the shots hit him, the tortured breathing continued without a pause. He was dying, very slowly and in great agony, but in some world remote from me where not even a bullet could damage him further. I felt that I had got to put an end to that dreadful noise. It seemed dreadful to see the great beast lying there, powerless to move and yet powerless to die, and not even be able to finish him. I sent back for my small rifle and poured shot after shot into his heart and down his throat. They seemed to make no impression. The tortured gasps continued as steadily as the ticking of a clock.

In the end I could not stand it any longer and went away. I heard later that it took him half an hour to die. Burmans were bringing dahs and baskets even before I left, and I was told they had stripped his body almost to the bones by the afternoon.

Afterwards, of course, there were endless discussions about the shooting of the elephant. The owner was furious, but he was only an Indian and could do nothing. Besides, legally I had done the right thing, for a mad elephant has to be killed, like a mad dog, if its owner fails to control it. Among the Europeans opinion was divided. The older men said I was right, the younger men said it was a damn shame to shoot an elephant for killing a coolie, because an elephant was worth more than any damn Coringhee coolie. And afterwards I was very glad that the coolie had been killed; it put me legally in the right and it gave me a sufficient pretext for shooting the elephant. I often wondered whether any of the others grasped that I had done it solely to avoid looking a fool.

1. What kind of perspective does Orwell presently have that makes the story of shooting an elephant important to him? How much of what he tells you is what he knew then and how much is what he knows now?
2. Do you think Orwell is interested in having his readers see him as a representative man? Representative of what and in what way?
3. How does Orwell develop his account of the event up to the point where he confronts the elephant? Does he tend to emphasize the drama and potential danger involved? Why or why not? Why does he describe the death of the elephant in such detail? Comment specifically on the language Orwell uses in those paragraphs.
4. How does Orwell characterize himself as an officer? In what ways does the characterization influence our understanding of the climax of the episode when Orwell shoots the elephant?
5. What is the purpose of the final paragraph of the essay, describing the aftermath of the shooting? How does it help you to understand the colonial world in which the shooting takes place?

Possibilities for Writing

1. Develop an autobiographical narrative that depends to some extent upon dialogue to recreate the incident. Try to make the dialogue differentiate the people in the scene and reveal something significant about the way they behave. You could compare your technique with that used by Frank Conroy or Piri Thomas.

2. Write about an autobiographical event in which you have had to face someone in authority in a situation where you were at a disadvantage. After you have finished, compare the kind of situation you have chosen and your method of presenting it with what Frank Conroy or Frederick Douglass has written.

3. Narrate an event in which you played a very prominent role and then retell the same event, this time assuming that you have become an onlooker rather than a participant. Try to make each narration consistent with what you would be likely to see and feel; then examine your two versions and note the differences.

4. Choose one of the autobiographical selections in this chapter and retell the event, using the perspective of some person other than the autobiographer. For example, you could retell Maya Angelou's story from the point of view of the black principal or the white guest speaker or James Herndon's story from the point of view of Maurice.

CHAPTER FOUR

PLACES

Introduction: Description and the Organization of Detail

If autobiography is essentially the story of the writer's life as he has acted it, it is also the story of the world in which those actions take place. We write about what happened to us, but often the context of where it happened makes what we think, feel, and do comprehensible. As we try to evoke for the reader our world in all its concrete detail, we depend upon our descriptive powers to document direct sensory impressions with accuracy and discrimination.

Most often, writers rely on visual perceptions, since the eye, as the primary recorder of our impressions, takes in many qualities of objects in the external world, such as size, dimension, color, and design. But at times other sense impressions may dominate, as when Catherine Drinker Bowen begins her reminiscence: "There was a special smell to the cottage at Beach Haven," and goes on to try to capture its components. On other occasions, a writer may feel that all his senses were engaged at some particular moment and his autobiographical description will interweave a record of the various elements which combined to create this total impression. In his account of hiking as a boy in the foothills near his home, William Douglas tells of hearing the grass in the breeze, smelling the delicate odor of sage, and feeling the cold and piercing mountain winds.

Obviously Douglas's account of his hike is not effective simply because he draws upon all of his senses in remembering the event. However, a situation of unusual drama or anxiety (visiting some great natural wonder, like the Grand Canyon; thinking there is a burglar in the house) often makes our senses especially alert, and these impressions can be made to reemerge and give immediacy to our writing. A writer is particularly likely to mix sensory impressions when he wishes to convey intimacy, since visual memory alone suggests greater detachment. Significantly, Catherine Drinker Bowen refers to the smell of the summer cottage as she remembers a childhood in a closely knit and happy family. What should influence a writer is not some arbitrary rule about including varied sense impressions, but only the awareness that visual impressions usually come readily to mind and are easiest to verbalize. Therefore, the resources of other senses may be neglected in describing the world (even though they are not neglected in experiencing it), unless the writer makes some conscious effort to reflect on nonvisual sense impressions as part of autobiographical memory.

In recording our sense impressions, we may tend to think of nouns and adjectives as our primary tools, as Alfred Kazin does in his description of life as a boy in Brooklyn:

> Our life every day was fought out on the pavement and in the gutter, up against the walls of the houses and the glass fronts of the drugstore and the grocery, in and out of the fresh steaming piles of horse manure, the wheels of passing carts and automobiles, along the spikes of the stairway to the cellar, the jagged edge of the open garbage cans, the crumbly steps of the old farmhouses still left on one side of the street.

But writers have many verbal resources with which to communicate their sense of the physical world. Here, for example, is Henry Thoreau's description of waterbugs and skater insects at Walden Pond:

> You can even detect a water-bug (Gyrinus) ceaselessly progressing over the smooth surface a quarter of a mile off; for they furrow the water slightly, making a conspicuous ripple bounded by two diverging lines, but the skaters glide over it without rippling it percepti-

bly. When the surface is considerably agitated there are no skaters nor water-bugs on it, but apparently, in calm days, they leave their havens and adventurously glide forth from the shore by short impulses till they completely cover it.

This passage depends as much on verbs (furrow, glide) and adverbs (ceaselessly, adventurously) as on any adjective to register the impression made by the insects. Thoreau's passage, as distinguished from Kazin's, reminds us that description can often be more than a record of the static qualities in our surroundings. We can describe a scene by rendering such qualities precisely (Kazin's "jagged edge of the garbage cans"), but we can also describe a scene by capturing the activities and the interrelationships of things in it, as Thoreau does with his insects "adventurously gliding" and rippling the water with their movements.

Thoreau's word "adventurously" (which suggests a comparison of insects to people) shows that another way of describing our world can be to juxtapose it with another world: that is, to convey our perceptions by analogy. An analogy explains our impressions by comparison, and the degree to which analogies are bound to our senses can be measured by how often such phrases as "looks like" and "sounds like" crop up in our speech. Sometimes analogies are submerged in a single word, barely noticeable, as when Thoreau uses "furrow," a word associated with the surface of the land, to describe how insects affect the surface of Walden Pond. At times, analogies are more explicit—George Orwell conveys the exotic setting of a Moroccan burial ground by noting "a huge waste of hummocky earth, like a derelict building-lot." At other times, analogies are developed more elaborately, as when Thoreau describes the surface of the pond: "It is like molten glass cooled but not congealed, and the few motes in it are pure and beautiful like the imperfection in glass."

The last two quotations from Orwell and Thoreau show in miniature what a writer seeks to do with description. Two different processes may be involved. The writer may try to make the unfamiliar familiar, in order to bring it within his reader's range of experience, as Orwell illustrates. Conversely, he may try to create a fresh perception of anything his reader would customarily regard as trite or conventional, as Thoreau does when he makes us look again at the surface of a pond. Of course, what is familiar or unfamiliar depends upon the writer and his sense of his audience—a Moroccan writing for his countrymen about Marrakech would not proceed in the same way that Orwell does. Writers find many different ways to bring their sense of the world freshly before the reader: often by striking analogy, as in the likeness of the pond's surface to a special state of molten glass, or by unusually attentive scrutiny, as in the description of the insects on the pond's surface, or by recording a highly subjective response, as in Thoreau's "In such transparent and seemingly bottomless water, I seemed to be floating through the air as in a balloon." Whatever techniques they choose, autobiographical writers, especially, strive to communicate how the world in which they live affects them personally.

We have seen how description originates in sense impressions, and have pointed to some ways these impressions are conveyed in language. The question remains: what should the writer do with these accumulated details once he has made them the touchstones of his world? In other words, how are they organized and made to contribute to the writer's larger purposes? It should already be clear that description is not merely the accumulation of details, any more than narrative is an accumulation of events. Description is as much an arrangement in space as we found narrative to be in time. For example, Henry Thoreau and Michael Collins both focus on single places—that is, despite their great difference in size, the pond and the moon are both regarded by the writers as single objects in their vision. Thoreau lives close to Walden Pond and occasionally even sails on it or immerses himself in it, while Collins sees the moon from a great distance away through the windows of a speeding space rocket. What both writers rely on is the variety created by their own changing vantage points, as well as the changes in the object itself. As they move, they see different facets of the pond or of the moon, and their writing expresses the complexity of their vision.

Not only does the writer place himself in relation to whatever he is describing, but he also places the various elements in his description in relation to one another. Malcolm X and Alfred Kazin both describe sections of New York by gathering together an enormous number of different details, but the details do not simply accumulate at random, Malcolm X creates a marvelous panorama of the kinds of excitement in the night life of Harlem that dazzled a young black seeing it all for the first time. The music, the crowds, the clubs, the dancing tumble over one another to create the same rush of impressions that would have engulfed the young Malcolm. Kazin's memory produces a similar quantity of detail, but it emerges in a different way. He is a youngster wanting gradually to go beyond the boundaries of his familiar neighborhood, and so his details are usually organized geographically in sequences that move out from the block to the less familiar world beyond, a series of forays into new territory which the boy associates with freedom. In other cases, descriptive detail may cluster around specific dramatic moments: Catherine Drinker Bowen's Beach Haven, for example, emerges as a series of varied settings (the dining room, the dock, the dunes) for family activities.

Whatever way the writer chooses to organize these details in space, he also needs to unify them through a consistent point of view. Malcolm X not only links the various details in his panorama of Harlem by grouping them according to the sources of excitement the city offers, but he also conveys his own sense of wonder at all of this energy, color, and life. Michael Collins surprises us by *not* being full of wonder at coming so close to the moon. He sees it as a "withered, sunseared peach pit" and shows his lack of awe by including casual humor in his description—"Hello, moon, how's the old back side." That kind of informality, in turn, contrasts with Alfred Kazin's highly dramatic way of describing a commonplace of city life, neighborhood boys playing handball. He seeks to re-create their passion through his emotional language: "Every day we smashed a small black viciously hard regulation handball against it with fanatical cuts and drives and slams, beating and slashing at it almost in hatred for the blind strength of the wall itself."

As descriptive details are brought within the compass of the writer's attitude, they show us the kind of bargain the writer has made with the world he lives in, the way he explores it or adapts to it. Description, then, enters into all autobiographical writing; we cannot feel we know the writer's life until we know something of the external conditions of that life. At the same time, those conditions are only a part of the ongoing process of a life, and so description remains only a part, subordinate to the narrative pattern of autobiography. Although we have been discussing description as if it had some independent existence within the selections in this chapter, we have done so primarily to isolate the techniques of description and to get a clearer view of their functions. What we find when we read the selections, however, is that description is often the bass line in a complex orchestration. If we look back to the end of the last paragraph, we can see that Kazin's sentence about the handball game describes, but it also narrates action in time, and it also registers the strong emotional involvement of the writer. Clearly, in putting that experience into words, Kazin, like any good writer, is not thinking about such abstract categories as narration and description. But he is aware of the need to ground his account in the concrete record of what his senses have told him. Our consciousness of descriptive writing should be this same awareness of the look and feel of the world we live in and of the need to place the events we narrate firmly in a recognizable place and time. Description may be subordinate but it is irreplaceable, testifying to the writer's alertness and sensitivity and leading his readers to trust his accuracy in larger matters.

∽ Michael Collins ∽

(1930-   )

Michael Collins is a graduate of the United States Military Academy. He was commissioned by the Air Force and served as an experimental flight test pilot. Becoming an astronaut in 1963, he piloted the Gemini X mission in 1966, and was the pilot of the Apollo XI for the first moon landing in July, 1969. Carrying the Fire (1974) *is his account of his life as an astronaut, and this selection describes the spaceship's approach to the moon. Collins is currently Director of the Smithsonian Institution's National Air and Space Museum.*

[APPROACHING THE MOON]

Day 4 has a decidedly different feel to it. Instead of nine hours' sleep, I get seven—and fitful ones at that. Despite our concentrated attempt to conserve our energy on the way to the moon, the pressure is overtaking us (or me at least), and I feel that all of us are aware that the honeymoon is over and we are about to lay our little pink bodies on the line. Our first shock comes as we stop our spinning motion and swing ourselves around so as to bring the moon into view. We have not been able to see the moon for nearly a day now, and the change in its appearance is dramatic, spectacular, and electrifying. The moon I have known all my life, that two-dimensional, small yellow disk in the sky, has gone away somewhere, to be replaced by the most awesome sphere I have ever seen. To begin with, it is *huge*, completely filling our window. Second, it is three-dimensional. The belly of it bulges out toward us in such a pronounced fashion that I almost feel I can reach out and touch it, while its surface obviously recedes toward the edges. It is between us and the sun, creating the most splendid lighting conditions imaginable. The sun casts a halo around it, shining on its rear surface, and the sunlight which comes cascading around its rim serves mainly to make the moon itself seem mysterious and subtle by comparison, emphasizing the size and texture of its dimly lit and pockmarked surface.

To add to the dramatic effect, we find we can see the stars again. We are in the shadow of the moon now, in darkness for the first time in three days, and the elusive stars have reappeared as if called especially for this occasion. The 360-degree disk of the moon, brilliantly illuminated around its rim by the hidden rays of the sun, divides itself into two distinct central regions. One is nearly black, while the other basks in a whitish light reflected from the surface of the earth. Earthshine, as it's called, is sunlight which has traveled from the sun to the earth and bounced off it back to the moon. Earthshine on the moon is considerably brighter than moonshine on the earth. The vague reddish-yellow of the sun's corona, the blanched white of earthshine, and the pure black of the star-studded surrounding sky all combine to cast a bluish glow over the moon. This cool, magnificent sphere hangs there ominously, a formidable presence without sound or motion, issuing us no invitation to invade its domain. Neil sums it up: "It's a view worth the price of the trip." And somewhat scary too, although no one says that.

Before we become too engrossed in the mystery of the moon, however, Houston restores some of our perspective with an earful of terrestrial chatter. We must check the flow of fluid through our secondary coolant system by bringing a second radiator onto the line. This is a test I have long opposed ("If the goddamned primary system is working O.K., why screw around with testing the secondary?"), but I have been overruled in a series of meetings. After I have successfully put the system through its paces, I guess I grump a little bit and tell

Houston, "Well at least we don't have to have any more meetings on the subject." "The flight director says 'Ouch,' " replies the CAPCOM. Have I offended Cliff Charlesworth. "No, no 'ouch' intended. I enjoyed every one of those meetings," I lie. Houston rewards us with the day's news, mostly baseball and other trivia. They do mention that Pravda has referred to Neil as the "Czar of the Ship," which title I heartily endorse for the remainder of the flight, and there is one amusing (at least to me) story about my son Michael. "What do you think," Michael is asked, "about your father going down in history," "Fine," says Michael; and after considerable pause, "What *is* history, anyway."

Houston is on to bigger things now, pumping us up with all the last-minute information we require before disappearing out of sight around the left-hand side of the moon. We have to know how to get into lunar orbit, and if trouble develops, how to get out of it—all without help from the ground. Our line-of-sight radio dictates that we can talk only to those people we can see; behind the moon, we will see no one. For the last fourteen hours we have been in the lunar sphere of influence, and our velocity has gradually picked up from a low of three thousand feet per second to its present seventy-six hundred feet per second. To be captured by the moon's gravity, we must slow down, by 2,917 feet per second to be exact, and we do this by burning our service module engine for six minutes and two seconds. Known as LOI₁, or the first lunar orbit insertion, this burn will put us in an elliptical orbit around the moon. Four hours later, we will attempt LOI₂, which should achieve a sixty-mile circular orbit.

As we ease on around the left side of the moon, I marvel again at the precision of our path. We have missed hitting the moon by a paltry three hundred nautical miles, at a distance of nearly a quarter of a million miles from earth, and don't forget that the moon is a moving target and that we are racing through the sky just ahead of its leading edge. When we launched the other day, the moon was nowhere near where it is now; it was some 40 degrees of arc, or nearly 200,000 miles behind where it is now, and yet those big computers in the basement in Houston didn't even whimper but belched out super-accurate predictions. I hope. As we pass behind the moon, finally, we have just over eight minutes to go before the burn. We are super-careful now, checking and rechecking each step several times. It is very much like the de-orbit burn of Gemini 10, when John Young and I must have checked our directions thirty times. If only one digit got slipped in our computer, the worst possible digit, we could be turned around backward and be about to blast ourselves into an orbit around the sun, instead of the moon, thereby becoming a planet the next generation might discover as the last one has discovered Pluto. No thanks.

When the moment finally arrives, the big engine instantly springs into action and reassuringly plasters us back in our seats. The acceleration is only a fraction of one G, but it feels good nonetheless. For six minutes we sit there peering intent as hawks at our instrument panel, scanning the important dials and gauges, making sure that the proper thing is being done to us. When the engine shuts down, we discuss the matter with our computer and I read out the results: "Minus one, minus one, plus one. Jesus! I take back any bad things I ever said about M.I.T." What I mean is that the accuracy of the overall system is phenomenal: out of a total of nearly three thousand feet per second, we have velocity errors in our body axis co-ordinate system of only one tenth of one foot per second in each of three directions. That is one accurate burn, and even Neil acknowledges the fact. "That was a beautiful burn," he says, and I echo, "Goddamn, I guess! . . . I don't know if we're at sixty miles or not, but at least we haven't hit that mother." Buzz queries the computer as to our orbit. "Look at that, 169.6 by 60.9," and I reply, "Beautiful, beautiful, beautiful, beautiful!" "You want to write that down or something," Buzz wants to know. Why not? "Write it down just for the hell of it; 170 by 60, like gangbusters." Buzz is precise. "We only missed by a couple of tenths of a mile." I am elated. "Hello, moon, how's the old back side?" We have arrived.

Once LOI₂ has passed, and established us in a near-circular orbit, averaging sixty miles altitude above the surface, we have a chance to examine the old back side, the front side, and parts in between. We are especially keen to study the landing site, the actual spot, just as we have been studying the photos of it for the last few months. Neil sums it up for Houston. "It looks very much like the pictures, but like the difference between watching a real football game and watching it on TV. There's no substitute for actually being here." Neil and Buzz also call out the familiar features along tomorrow's landing approach path: Mount Marilyn (named after Jim Lovell's wife), Boot Hill, Duke Island (named after Charlie Duke), Diamondback and Sidewinder (two sinuous rills etched in the Sea of Tranquility which look exactly like rattlesnakes), and so on, right up to the landing site itself. The Sea of Tranquility is just past dawn, and the sun's rays are intersecting its surface at a mere 1 degree angle. Under these lighting conditions, craters cast extremely long shadows, and to me the entire region looks distinctly forbidding, with no evidence that any part of its surface is smooth enough to park a baby buggy, never mind a lunar module. I can't resist commenting on it ("rough as a cob"), but all three of us know (we do?) that it will look a lot smoother tomorrow as the sun angle climbs toward the 10 degrees it will reach by the time of landing.

If anything, the rear side of the moon looks even rougher than the front. It doesn't have any "flat" *maria*, or seas, as the front does, but is a continuous region of "highlands," an uninterrupted jumble of tortured hills, cratered and recratered by 5 billion years of meteorite bombardment. There is no atmosphere surrounding the moon to produce clouds or smog or otherwise obscure the surface, so the details are uniformly clear. CAVU, as pilots describe a perfect day on earth: clear and visibility unlimited. The only thing that changes is the lighting, as our spacecraft passes from sunshine into earthshine, that eerie region of reflected sunlight, and then into total darkness. The feeling is more like circling in earth orbit than hanging suspended in cislunar space, as the past three days have been spent, but there are marked differences as well. First, we are traveling only one fifth as fast as we would in earth orbit, because the moon has much less mass than the earth and therefore produces a weaker gravitational pull, which, in turn, means that we require a slower orbital velocity to counterbalance this gravitational force with our own centrifugal force. However, since the moon is much smaller (2,160-mile diameter vs. the earth's 7,927), we get around it almost as fast, taking two hours for one orbit instead of ninety minutes. Also, because we are in a lower orbit (you can't orbit the earth at sixty miles because of its atmosphere), we get a noticeable sensation of speed. It's not quite as exhilarating a feeling as orbiting the earth, but it's close. In addition, it has an exotic, bizarre quality due entirely to the nature of the surface below. The earth from orbit is a delight—alive, inviting, enchanting—offering visual variety and an emotional feeling of belonging "down there." Not so with this withered, sun-seared peach pit out my window. There is no comfort to it; it is too stark and barren; its invitation is monotonous and meant for geologists only. Look at this crater, look at that one, are they the result of impacts, or volcanism, or a mixture of both?

As three amateur geologists, it doesn't take us long to get caught up with the mystery of the place and the fascination of discovering new craters on the back side. "What a spectacular view!" exclaims Neil. I agree. "Fantastic. Look back there behind us, sure looks like a gigantic crater; look at the mountains going around it. My gosh, they're monsters." Neil points out another one, even larger, and I'm even more impressed by it. "God, it's huge! It is enormous! It's so big I can't even get it in the window. That's the biggest one you have ever seen in your life. Neil, God, look at this central mountain peak. Isn't that a huge one? . . . You could spend a lifetime just geologizing that one crater alone, you know that?" Neil doesn't sound taken with *that* idea. "You could," he grunts. I hasten to add, "That's not how I'd like to spend my lifetime, but—picture that. Beautiful!" Buzz pipes up. "Yes, there's a big mother over here, too!" "Come on now, Buzz, don't refer to them as big mothers; give them some scientific name." Buzz ignores me and goes on. "It looks like a lot of them have slumped down." "A slumping big mother? Well, you see those every once in a while." Buzz decides to descend to my level. "Most of them are slumping. The bigger they are, the more they slump—that's a truism, isn't it? That is, the older they get." This conversation is taking a turn for the worse, and it will only be another few minutes until the earth pops up over the moon's rugged rim, so I drop the subject and start talking about camera and gimbal angles, as we all wait for our old friend to reappear. Still . . . the possibilities of weightlessness are there for the ingenious to exploit. No need to carry bras into space, that's for sure. Imagine a spacecraft of the future, with a crew of a thousand ladies, off for Alpha Centauri, with two thousand breasts bobbing beautifully and quivering delightfully in response to their every weightless movement . . . and I am the commander of the craft, and it is Saturday morning and time for inspection, naturally . . .

I am wrenched back to reality by the sudden appearance of the earth, a truly dramatic moment or two that we all scramble to record with our cameras. It pokes its little blue bonnet up over the craggy rim and then, not having been shot at, surges up over the horizon with a rush of unexpected color and motion. It is a welcome sight for several reasons: it is intrinsically beautiful, it contrasts sharply with the smallpox below, and it is home and voice for us. This is not at all like sunrise on earth, whose brilliance commands one's attention; it is easily missed, and therefore all the more precious to us, as we have anticipated its appearance and prepared for it. As it bursts into view, Houston starts talking, and we are back to business as usual.

1. What are some of the ways Collins's story reflects the fact that he is describing something no human has seen in this way before? How does his description of the moon help you to com-prehend the unfamiliarity of the experience?

2. *Can you think of an alternative description of the moon, one that Collins does not use? How does your description help you to understand the distinctive qualities of Collins's account?*

3. *What distinguishes Collins's way of writing about activities inside the spaceship from his descriptions of what he sees out-side the spaceship?*

4. *What are the reactions of the astronauts as they approach the moon? Does Collins's own narration reflect the same reac-tions or are his responses more complex? Does the fact that he is recollecting the experience alter his sense of it?*

5. *Collins, like the other astronauts, is a highly trained and technologically sophisticated individual. To what extent are the details of his story those that might be provided by an un-trained observer and to what extent do they reflect his special background? How is he able to integrate the two kinds of de-tails in his account?*

❦ Henry Thoreau ❧

((1817-1862)

See the biographical note on page 46. Thoreau published
Walden *in 1854. It is his masterpiece, an account of the time he*
spent in a small cabin at the shore of Concord's Walden Pond,
confronting nature and discovering her universal laws.

THE PONDS

[THE WATERS OF WALDEN]

A lake is the landscape's most beautiful and expressive feature.
It is earth's eye; looking into which the beholder measures the
depth of his own nature. The fluviatile trees next the shore are
the slender eyelashes which fringe it, and the wooded hills and
cliffs around are its overhanging brows.

Standing on the smooth sandy beach at the east end of the
pond, in a calm September afternoon, when a slight haze
makes the opposite shore line indistinct, I have seen whence
came the expression, "the glassy surface of a lake." When you
invert your head, it looks like a thread of finest gossamer
stretched across the valley, and gleaming against the distant
pine woods, separating one stratum of the atmosphere from another. You would think that you could walk dry under it to the
opposite hills, and that the swallows which skim over might
perch on it. Indeed, they sometimes dive below the line, as it
were by mistake, and are undeceived. As you look over the
pond westward you are obliged to employ both your hands to

From Henry Thoreau: *Walden (The Variorum Walden)*, ed. Walter Harding.
Reprinted by permission of Twayne Publishers.

defend your eyes against the reflected as well as the true sun, for they are equally bright; and if, between the two, you survey its surface critically, it is literally as smooth as glass, except where the skater insects, at equal intervals scattered over its whole extent, by their motions in the sun produce the finest imaginable sparkle on it, or, perchance, a duck plumes itself, or, as I have said, a swallow skims so low as to touch it. It may be that in the distance a fish describes an arc of three or four feet in the air, and there is one bright flash where it emerges, and another where it strikes the water; sometimes the whole silvery arc is revealed; or here and there, perhaps, is a thistle-down floating on its surface, which the fishes dart at and so dimple it again. It is like molten glass cooled but not congealed, and the few motes in it are pure and beautiful like the imperfections in glass. You may often detect a yet smoother and darker water, separated from the rest as if by an invisible cobweb, boom of the water nymphs, resting on it. From a hilltop you can see a fish leap in almost any part; for not a pickerel or shiner picks an insect from this smooth surface but it manifestly disturbs the equilibrium of the whole lake. It is wonderful with what elaborateness this simple fact is advertised,—this piscine murder will out,—and from my distant perch I distinguish the circling undulations when they are half a dozen rods in diameter. You can even detect a water-bug (*Gyrinus*) ceaselessly progressing over the smooth surface a quarter of a mile off; for they furrow the water slightly, making a conspicuous ripple bounded by two diverging lines, but the skaters glide over it without rippling it perceptibly. When the surface is considerably agitated there are no skaters nor water-bugs on it, but apparently, in calm days, they leave their havens and adventurously glide forth from the shore by short impulses till they completely cover it. It is a soothing employment, on one of those fine days in the fall when all the warmth of the sun is fully appreciated, to sit on a stump on such a height as this, overlooking the pond, and study the dimpling circles which are incessantly inscribed on its otherwise invisible surface amid the reflected skies and trees. Over this great expanse there is no disturbance but it is thus at once gently smoothed away and assuaged, as, when a vase of water is jarred, the trembling circles seek the shore and all is smooth again. Not a fish can leap or an insect fall on the pond but it is thus reported in circling dimples, in lines of beauty, as it were the constant welling up of its fountain, the gentle pulsing of its life, the heaving of its breast. The thrills of joy and thrills of pain are undistinguishable. How peaceful the phenomena of the lake. Again the works of man shine as in the spring. Ay, every leaf and twig and stone and cobweb sparkles now at mid-afternoon as when covered with dew in a spring morning. Every motion of an oar or an insect produces a flash of light; and if an oar falls, how sweet the echo!

In such a day, in September or October, Walden is a perfect forest mirror, set round with stones as precious to my eye as if fewer or rarer. Nothing so fair, so pure, and at the same time so large, as a lake, perchance, lies on the surface of the earth. Sky water. It needs no fence. Nations come and go without defiling it. It is a mirror which no stone can crack, whose quicksilver will never wear off, whose gilding Nature continually repairs; no storms, no dust, can dim its surface ever fresh;—a mirror in which all impurity presented to it sinks, swept and dusted by the sun's hazy brush,—this the light dust-cloth,—which retains no breath that is breathed on it, but sends its own to float as clouds high above its surface, and be reflected in its bosom still.

A field of water betrays the spirit that is in the air. It is continually receiving new life and motion from above. It is intermediate in its nature between land and sky. On land only the grass and trees wave, but the water itself is rippled by the wind. I see where the breeze dashes across it by the streaks or flakes of light. It is remarkable that we can look down on its surface. We shall, perhaps, look down thus on the surface of air at length, and mark where a still subtler spirit sweeps over it.

The skaters and water-bugs finally disappear in the latter part of October, when the severe frosts have come; and then and in November, usually, in a calm day, there is absolutely nothing to ripple the surface. One November afternoon, in the calm at the end of a rain storm of several days' duration, when the sky was still completely overcast and the air was full of mist, I observed that the pond was remarkably smooth, so that it was difficult to distinguish its surface; though it no longer reflected the bright tints of October, but the sombre November colors of the surrounding hills. Though I passed over it as gently as possible, the slight undulations produced by my boat extended almost as far as I could see, and gave a ribbed appearance to the reflections. But, as I was looking over the surface, I saw here and there at a distance a faint glimmer, as if some skater insects which had escaped the frosts might be collected there, or, perchance, the surface, being so smooth, betrayed where a spring welled up from the bottom. Paddling gently to one of these places, I was surprised to find myself surrounded by myriads of small perch, about five inches long, of a rich bronze color in the green water, sporting there and constantly rising to the surface and dimpling it, sometimes leaving bubbles on it. In such transparent and seemingly bottomless water, reflecting the clouds, I seemed to be floating through the air as in a balloon, and their swimming impressed me as a kind of flight or hovering, as if they were a compact flock of birds passing just beneath my level on the right or left, their fins, like sails, set all around them. There were many such schools in the pond, apparently improving the short season before winter would draw an icy shutter over their broad skylight, sometimes giving to the surface an appearance as if a slight breeze struck it, or a few rain-drops fell there. When I approached carelessly and alarmed them, they made a sudden plash and rippling with their tails, as if one had struck the water with a brushy bough, and instantly took refuge in the depths. At length the wind rose, the mist increased, and the waves began to run, and the perch leaped much higher than before, half out of water, a hundred black points, three inches long, at once above the surface. Even as late as the fifth of December, one year, I saw some dimples on the surface, and thinking it was going to rain hard immediately, the air being full of mist, I made haste to take my place at the oars and row homeward; already the rain seemed rapidly increasing, though I felt none on my cheek, and I anticipated a thorough soaking. But suddenly the dimples ceased, for they were produced by the perch, which the noise of my oars had scared into the depths, and I saw their schools dimly disappearing; so I spent a dry afternoon after all.

An old man who used to frequent this pond nearly sixty years ago, when it was dark with surrounding forests, tells me that in those days he sometimes saw it all alive with ducks and other water fowl, and that there were many eagles about it. He came here a-fishing, and used an old log canoe which he found on the shore. It was made of two white-pine logs dug out and pinned together, and was cut off square at the ends. It was very clumsy, but lasted a great many years before it became waterlogged and perhaps sank to the bottom. He did not know whose it was; it belonged to the pond. He used to make a cable for his anchor of strips of hickory bark tied together. An old man, a potter, who lived by the pond before the Revolution, told him once that there was an iron chest at the bottom, and that he had seen it. Sometimes it would come floating up to the shore; but when you went toward it, it would go back into deep water and disappear. I was pleased to hear of the old log canoe, which took the place of an Indian one of the same material but more graceful construction, which perchance had first been a tree on the bank, and then, as it were, fell into the water, to float there for a generation, the most proper vessel for the lake. I remember that when I first looked into these depths there were many large trunks to be seen indistinctly lying on the bottom, which had either been blown over formerly, or left on the ice at the last cutting, when wood was cheaper; but now they have mostly disappeared.

When I first paddled a boat on Walden, it was completely surrounded by thick and lofty pine and oak woods, and in some of its coves grape vines had run over the trees next the water and formed bowers under which a boat could pass. The hills which form its shores are so steep, and the woods on them were then so high, that, as you looked down from the west end, it had the appearance of an amphitheatre for some kind of sylvan spectacle. I have spent many an hour, when I was younger, floating over its surface as the zephyr willed, having paddled my boat to the middle, and lying on my back across the seats, in a summer forenoon, dreaming awake, until I was aroused by the boat touching the sand, and I arose to see what shore my fates had impelled me to; days when idleness was the most attractive and productive industry. Many a forenoon have I stolen away, preferring to spend thus the most valued part of the day; for I was rich, if not in money, in sunny hours and summer days, and spent them lavishly; nor do I regret that I did not waste more of them in the workshop or the teacher's desk. But since I left those shores the woodchoppers have still further laid them waste, and now for many a year there will be no more rambling through the aisles of the wood, with occasional vistas through which you see the water. My Muse may be excused if she is silent henceforth. How can you expect the birds to sing when their groves are cut down?

Now the trunks of trees on the bottom, and the old log canoe, and the dark surrounding woods, are gone, and the villagers, who scarcely know where it lies, instead of going to the pond to bathe or drink, are thinking to bring its water, which should be as sacred as the Ganges at least, to the village in a pipe, to wash their dishes with!—to earn their Walden by the turning of a cock or drawing of a plug! That devilish Iron Horse, whose ear-rending neigh is heard throughout the town, has muddied the Boiling Spring with his foot, and he it is that has browsed off all the woods on Walden shore; that Trojan horse, with a thousand men in his belly, introduced by mercenary Greeks! Where is the country's champion, the Moore of Moore Hall, to meet him at the Deep Cut and thrust an avenging lance between the ribs of the bloated pest?

Nevertheless, of all the characters I have known, perhaps Walden wears best, and best preserves its purity. Many men have been likened to it, but few deserve that honor. Though the woodchoppers have laid bare first this shore and then that, and the Irish have built their sties by it, and the railroad has infringed on its border, and the ice-men have skimmed it once, it is itself unchanged, the same water which my youthful eyes fell on; all the change is in me. It has not acquired one permanent wrinkle after all its ripples. It is perennially young, and I may stand and see a swallow dip apparently to pick an insect from its surface as of yore. It struck me again tonight, as if I had not seen it almost daily for more than twenty years,—Why, here is Walden, the same woodland lake that I discovered so many years ago; where a forest was cut down last winter another is springing up by its shore as lustily as ever; the same thought is welling up to its surface that was then; it is the same liquid joy and happiness to itself and its Maker, ay, and it *may* be to me. It is the work of a brave man surely, in whom there was no guile! He rounded this water with his hand, deepened and clarified it in his thought, and in his will bequeathed it to Concord. I see by its face that it is visited by the same reflection; and I can almost say, Walden, is it you?

> It is no dream of mine,
> To ornament a line;
> I cannot come nearer to God and Heaven
> Than I live to Walden even.
> I am its stony shore,
> And the breeze that passes o'er;
> In the hollow of my hand
> Are its water and its sand,
> And its deepest resort
> Lies high in my thought.

The cars never pause to look at it; yet I fancy that the engineers and firemen and brakemen, and those passengers who have a season ticket and see it often, are better men for the sight. The engineer does not forget at night, or his nature does not, that he has beheld this vision of serenity and purity once at least during the day. Though seen but once, it helps to wash out State-street and the engine's soot. One proposes that it be called "God's Drop."

I have said that Walden has no visible inlet nor outlet, but it is on the one hand distantly and indirectly related to Flint's Pond, which is more elevated, by a chain of small ponds coming from that quarter, and on the other directly and manifestly to Concord River, which is lower, by a similar chain of ponds through which in some other geological period it may have flowed, and by a little digging, which God forbid, it can be made to flow thither again. If by living thus reserved and austere, like a hermit in the woods, so long, it has acquired such wonderful purity, who would not regret that the comparatively impure waters of Flint's Pond should be mingled with it, or itself should ever go to waste its sweetness in the ocean wave?

1. *How does Thoreau support his statement that "a lake is the landscape's most beautiful and expressive feature"? Does his account make you understand what he means by "expressive"?*
2. *Much of what Thoreau describes involves activities characteristic of virtually any pond—for example, in the second paragraph he writes of the surface of the pond and the insects and fish that disturb it, and in the fifth paragraph he describes fish swimming in the pond. Reread these paragraphs and explain how Thoreau can write about such commonplace incidents and make them represent his distinctive perceptions of the pond.*
3. *Thoreau was a trained surveyor and a skilled amateur botanist as well as a poet and philosopher. To what extent do you find the different facets of his background reflected in the way he describes the pond? Where is he highly detailed and factually precise? Where is he metaphorical and poetic? How are the two strains related?*

4. Try to decide how often Thoreau changes his vantage point—in time or in place—as he describes the pond. After you have identified such shifts, explain how some kind of unity or progression still remains in the description.

5. In the next to last paragraph, Thoreau says that all those who see Walden Pond while riding past on the train "are better men for the sight." Has his description of the pond given you any understanding of how he could make this statement?

∽ Alfred Kazin ∽

(1915-   )

Alfred Kazin was born, brought up, and educated in New York City. His influential study of modern American prose, On Native Grounds *(1942), published while still in his twenties, began his career as a critic, editor, and teacher. Much of his writing has been concerned with American life and with its literary and social traditions. He now teaches at the City University of New York. He has published two volumes of autobiography:* A Walker in the City *(1951), dealing with his boyhood in the Jewish immigrant neighborhood of Brownsville in east Brooklyn, and* Starting Out in the Thirties *(1965).*

THE BLOCK AND BEYOND

The block: *my* block. It was on the Chester Street side of our house, between the grocery and the back wall of the old drugstore, that I was hammered into the shape of the streets. Everything beginning at Blake Avenue would always wear for me some delightful strangeness and mildness, simply because it was not of my block, *the* block, where the clang of your head sounded against the pavement when you fell in a fist fight, and the rows of storelights on each side were pitiless, watching you. Anything away from the block was good: even a school you never went to, two blocks away: there were vegetable gardens in the park across the street. Returning from "New York," I would take the longest routes home from the subway, get off a station ahead of our own, only for the unexpectedness of walk-

ing through Betsy Head Park and hearing the gravel crunch
under my feet as I went beyond the vegetable gardens, smelling the sweaty sweet dampness from the pool in summer and
the dust on the leaves as I passed under the ailanthus trees. On
the block itself everything rose up only to test me.

We worked every inch of it, from the cellars and the back-
yards to the sickening space between the roofs. Any wall, any
stoop, any curving metal edge on a billboard sign made a place
against which to knock a ball; any bottom rung of a fire escape
ladder a goal in basketball; any sewer cover a base; any crack
in the pavement a "net" for the tense sharp tennis that we
played by beating a soft ball back and forth with our hands
between the squares. Betsy Head Park two blocks away would
always feel slightly foreign, for it belonged to the Amboys and
the Bristols and the Hopkinsons as much as it did to us. *Our* life
every day was fought out on the pavement and in the gutter,
up against the walls of the houses and the glass fronts of the
drugstore and the grocery, in and out of the fresh steaming
piles of horse manure, the wheels of passing carts and automobiles, along the iron spikes of the stairway to the cellar, the
jagged edge of the open garbage cans, the crumbly steps of the
old farmhouses still left on one side of the street.

As I go back to the block now, and for a moment fold my
body up again in its narrow arena—there, just there, between
the black of the asphalt and the old women in their kerchiefs
and flowered housedresses sitting on the tawny kitchen chairs—
the back wall of the drugstore still rises up to test me. Every
day we smashed a small black viciously hard regulation handball against it with fanatical cuts and drives and slams, beating
and slashing at it almost in hatred for the blind strength of the
wall itself. I was never good enough at handball, was always
practicing some trick shot that might earn me esteem, and
when I was weary of trying, would often bat a ball down
Chester Street just to get myself to Blake Avenue. I have this
memory of playing one-o'-cat by myself in the sleepy twilight,
at a moment when everyone else had left the block. The spar-

rows floated down from the telephone wires to peck at every fresh pile of horse manure, and there was a smell of brine from the delicatessen store, of egg crates and of the milk scum left in the great metal cans outside the grocery, of the thick white paste oozing out from behind the fresh Hecker's Flour ad on the metal signboard. I would throw the ball in the air, hit it with my bat, then with perfect satisfaction drop the bat to the ground and run to the next sewer cover. Over and over I did this, from sewer cover to sewer cover, until I had worked my way to Blake Avenue and could see the park.

With each clean triumphant ring of my bat against the gutter leading me on, I did the whole length of our block up and down, and never knew how happy I was just watching the asphalt rise and fall, the curve of the steps up to an old farm-house. The farmhouses themselves were streaked red on one side, brown on the other, but the steps themselves were always gray. There was a tremor of pleasure at one place; I held my breath in nausea at another. As I ran after my ball with the bat heavy in my hand, the odd successiveness of things in my-self almost choked me, the world was so full as I ran—past the cobblestoned yards into the old farmhouses, where stray chick-ens still waddled along the stones; past the little candy store where we went only if the big one on our side of the block was out of Eskimo Pies; past the three neighboring tenements where the last of the old women sat on their kitchen chairs yawning before they went up to make supper. Then came Mrs. Rosenwasser's house, the place on the block I first identified with what was farthest from home, and strangest, because it was a "private" house; then the fences around the monument works, where black cranes rose up above the yard and you could see the smooth gray slabs that would be cut and carved into tombstones, some of them already engraved with the names and dates and family virtues of the dead.

Beyond Blake Avenue was the pool parlor outside which we waited all through the tense September afternoons of the World's Series to hear the latest scores called off the ticker tape—and where as we waited, banging a ball against the bottom of the wall and drinking water out of empty coke bottles, I breathed the chalk off the cues and listened to the clocks ringing in the fire station across the street. There was an old warehouse next to the pool parlor; the oil on the barrels and the iron staves had the same rusty smell. A block away was the park, thick with the dusty gravel I liked to hear my shoes crunch in as I ran round and round the track; then a great open pavilion, the inside mysteriously dark, chill even in summer; there I would wait in the sweaty coolness before pushing on to the wading ring where they put up a shower on the hottest days.

Beyond the park the "fields" began, all those still unused lots where we could still play hard ball in perfect peace—first shooing away the goats and then tearing up goldenrod before laying our bases. The smell and touch of those "fields," with their wild compost under the billboards of weeds, goldenrod, bricks, goat droppings, rusty cans, empty beer bottles, fresh new lumber, and damp cement, lives in my mind as Brownsville's great open door, the wastes that took us through to the west. I used to go round them in summer with my cousins selling near-beer to the carpenters, but always in a daze, would stare so long at the fibrous stalks of the goldenrod as I felt their harshness in my hand that I would forget to make a sale, and usually go off sick on the beer I drank up myself. Beyond! Beyond! Only to see something new, to get away from each day's narrow battleground between the grocery and the back wall of the drugstore! Even the other end of our block, when you got to Mrs. Rosenwasser's house and the monument works, was dear to me for the contrast. On summer nights, when we played Indian trail, running away from each other on prearranged signals, the greatest moment came when I could plunge into the darkness down the block for myself and hide behind the slabs in the monument works. I remember the air whistling around me as I ran, the panicky thud of my bones in my sneakers, and then the slabs rising in the light from the street lamps as I sped past the little candy store and crept under the fence.

In the darkness you could never see where the crane began.

We liked to trap the enemy between the slabs and sometimes jumped them from great mounds of rock just in from the quarry. A boy once fell to his death that way, and they put a watchman there to keep us out. This made the slabs all the more impressive to me, and I always aimed first for that yard whenever we played follow-the-leader. Day after day the monument works became oppressively more mysterious and remote, though it was only just down the block; I stood in front of it every afternoon on my way back from school, filling it with my fears. It was not death I felt there—the slabs were usually faceless. It was the darkness itself, and the wind howling around me whenever I stood poised on the edge of a high slab waiting to jump. Then I would take in, along with the fear, some amazement of joy that I had found my way out that far.

1. *Can you categorize the kinds of details that Kazin uses most often in portraying his neighborhood? How frequently does Kazin use details other than those supplied by visual memories? What do these other details contribute to your sense of his experience?*

2. *What sense of Kazin as a boy do you get from his account? Do you think that he is trying to emphasize his uniqueness as a child or his representativeness? Explain how you arrived at your judgment.*

3. *What attitude does Kazin take toward his past as he tells you about it? Does he seem detached from it or immersed in it? Nostalgic for it or relieved to be free of it? How does his attitude express itself in the details he uses and the way he presents them?*

4. *Since Kazin does not use any strict chronological order in writing about his experiences, what kind of order does he provide? How are his memories related to one another?*

5. *Kazin rarely describes incidents that happened once and once only. Why not? How does he create the impression of recurring experiences? What does that contribute to his autobiography?*

～ Malcolm X ～

(1925-1965)

*Born Malcolm Little in Omaha, Malcolm X spent his ado-
lescence in the black communities of Roxbury, Massachusetts,
and Harlem. He soon became involved with the underworld
life of the ghetto, first as a drug seller, then as a burglar. Convicted of burglary in 1946, he was sentenced to ten years in
prison. There he was converted to the Black Muslim religion.
After his parole in 1952, he became an outspoken and controversial minister for the Muslim leader, Elijah Muhammad,
and he lectured widely in behalf of black separatism. Later,
disagreements with Elijah Muhammad led Malcolm to form
his own group, The Organization of African Unity. He was
murdered while addressing one of its meetings in Harlem in
1965. His* Autobiography *(1964) recounts his turbulent past,
his conversion, and his rise to leadership in the black nation-
alist movement.*

HARLEMITE

The cooks took me up to Harlem in a cab. White New York
passed by like a movie set, then abruptly, when we left Central
Park at the upper end, at 110th Street, the people's complexion
began to change.

Busy Seventh Avenue ran along in front of a place called
Small's Paradise. The crew had told me before we left Boston
that it was their favorite night spot in Harlem, and not to miss
it. No Negro place of business had ever impressed me so much.

From Malcolm X (with the assistance of Alex Haley): *The Autobiography of
Malcolm X*. Copyright © 1964 by Alex Haley and Malcolm X, © 1965 by Alex
Haley and Betty Shabazz. Reprinted by permission of Grove Press, Inc.

Around the big, luxurious-looking, circular bar were thirty or forty Negroes, mostly men, drinking and talking.

I was hit first, I think, by their conservative clothes and manners. Wherever I'd seen as many as ten Boston Negroes— let alone Lansing Negroes—drinking, there had been a big noise. But with all of these Harlemites drinking and talking, there was just a low murmur of sound. Customers came and went. The bartenders knew what most of them drank and automatically fixed it. A bottle was set on the bar before some.

Every Negro I'd ever known had made a point of flashing whatever money he had. But these Harlem Negroes quietly laid a bill on the bar. They drank. They nonchalantly nodded to the bartender to pour a drink for some friend, while the bartenders, smooth as any of the customers, kept making change from the money on the bar.

Their manners seemed natural; they were not putting on any airs. I was awed. Within the first five minutes in Small's, I had left Boston and Roxbury forever.

I didn't yet know that these weren't what you might call everyday or average Harlem Negroes. Later on, even later that night, I would find out that Harlem contained hundreds of thousands of my people who were just as loud and gaudy as Negroes anywhere else. But these were the cream of the older, more mature operators in Harlem. The day's "numbers" business was done. The night's gambling and other forms of hustling hadn't yet begun. The usual night-life crowd, who worked on regular jobs all day, were at home eating their dinners. The hustlers at this time were in the daily six o'clock congregation, their favorite bars all over Harlem largely to themselves.

From Small's, I taxied over to the Apollo Theater. (I remember so well that Jay McShann's band was playing, because his vocalist was later my close friend, Walter Brown, the one who used to sing "Hooty Hooty Blues.") From there, on the other side of 125th Street, at Seventh Avenue, I saw the big, tall, gray Theresa Hotel. It was the finest in New York

City where Negroes could then stay, years before the down-town hotels would accept the black man. (The Theresa is now best known as the place where Fidel Castro went during his U.N. visit, and achieved a psychological coup over the U.S. State Department when it confined him to Manhattan, never dreaming that he'd stay uptown in Harlem and make such an impression among the Negroes.)

The Braddock Hotel was just up 126th Street, near the Apol-lo's backstage entrance. I knew its bar was famous as a Negro celebrity hang-out. I walked in and saw, along that jam-packed bar, such famous stars as Dizzy Gillespie, Billy Eck-stine, Billie Holiday, Ella Fitzgerald, and Dinah Washington.

As Dinah Washington was leaving with some friends, I overheard someone say she was on her way to the Savoy Ball-room where Lionel Hampton was appearing that night—she was then Hamp's vocalist. The ballroom made the Roseland in Boston look small and shabby by comparison. And the lindy-hopping there matched the size and elegance of the place. Hampton's hard-driving outfit kept a red-hot pace with his greats such as Arnett Cobb, Illinois Jacquet, Dexter Gordon, Alvin Hayse, Joe Newman, and George Jenkins. I went a couple of rounds on the floor with girls from the sidelines.

Probably a third of the sideline booths were filled with white people, mostly just watching the Negroes dance; but some of them danced together, and, as in Boston, a few white women were with Negroes. The people kept shouting for Hamp's "Flyin' Home," and finally he did it. (I could believe the story I'd heard in Boston about this number—that once in the Apollo, Hamp's "Flyin' Home" had made some reefer-smoking Negro in the second balcony believe he could fly, so he tried—and jumped—and broke his leg, an event later im-mortalized in song when Earl Hines wrote a hit tune called "Second Balcony Jump.") I had never seen such fever-heat dancing. After a couple of slow numbers cooled the place off, they brought on Dinah Washington. When she did her "Salty Papa Blues," those people just about tore the Savoy roof off.

(Poor Dinah's funeral was held not long ago in Chicago. I read that over 20,000 people viewed her body, and I should have been there myself. Poor Dinah! We became great friends, back in those days.)

But this night of my first visit was Kitchen Mechanics' Night at the Savoy, the traditional Thursday night off for domestics. I'd say there were twice as many women as men in there, not only kitchen workers and maids, but also war wives and defense-worker women, lonely and looking. Out in the street, when I left the ballroom, I heard a prostitute cursing bitterly that the professionals couldn't do any business because of the amateurs.

Up and down along and between Lenox and Seventh and Eighth Avenues, Harelm was like some technicolor bazaar. Hundreds of Negro soldiers and sailors, gawking and young like me, passed by. Harlem by now was officially off limits to white servicemen. There had already been some muggings and robberies, and several white servicemen had even been found murdered. The police were also trying to discourage white civilians from coming uptown, but those who wanted to still did. Every man without a woman on his arm was being "worked" by the prostitutes. "Baby, wanna have some fun?" The pimps would sidle up close, stage-whispering, "All kinds of women, Jack—want a white woman?" And the hustlers were merchandising: "Hundred dollar ring, man, diamond; ninety-dollar watch, too—look at 'em. Take 'em both for twenty-five."

In another two years, I could have given them all lessons. But that night, I was mesmerized. This world was where I belonged. On that night I had started on my way to becoming a Harlemite. I was going to become one of the most depraved parasitical hustlers among New York's eight million people— four million of whom work, and the other four million of whom live off them.

I couldn't quite believe all that I'd heard and seen that night as I lugged my shoulder-strap sandwich box and that heavy five-gallon aluminum coffee pot up and down the aisles of the "Yankee Clipper" back to Boston. I wished that Ella and I had been on better terms so that I could try to describe to her how I felt. But I did talk to Shorty, urging him to at least go to see the Big Apple music world. Sophia listened to me, too. She told me that I'd never be satisfied anywhere but New York. She was so right. In one night, New York—Harlem—had just about narcotized me.

That sandwich man I'd replaced had little chance of getting his job back. I went bellowing up and down those train aisles. I sold sandwiches, coffee, candy, cake, and ice cream as fast as the railroad's commissary department could supply them. It didn't take me a week to learn that all you had to do was give white people a show and they'd buy anything you offered them. It was like popping your shoeshine rag. The dining car waiters and Pullman porters knew it too, and they faked their Uncle Tomming to get bigger tips. We were in that world of Negroes who are both servants and psychologists, aware that white people are so obsessed with their own importance that they will pay liberally, even dearly, for the impression of being catered to and entertained.

Every layover night in Harlem, I ran and explored new places. I first got a room at the Harlem YMCA, because it was less than a block from Small's Paradise. Then, I got a cheaper room at Mrs. Fisher's rooming house which was close to the YMCA. Most of the railroad men stayed at Mrs. Fisher's. I combed not only the bright-light areas, but Harlem's residential areas from best to worst, from Sugar Hill up near the Polo Grounds, where many famous celebrities lived, down to the slum blocks of old rat-trap apartment houses, just crawling with everything you could mention that was illegal and immoral. Dirt, garbage cans overflowing or kicked over; drunks, dope addicts, beggars. Sleazy bars, storefront churches with gospels being shouted inside, "bargain" stores, hockshops, undertaking parlors. Greasy "home-cooking" restaurants, beauty shops smoky inside from Negro women's hair getting fried, barbershops advertising cong experts. Cadillacs, second-hand and new, conspicuous among the cars on the streets.

All of it was Lansing's West Side or Roxbury's South End magnified a thousand times. Little basement dance halls with "For Rent" signs on them. People offering you little cards advertising "rent-raising parties." I went to one of these—thirty or forty Negroes sweating, eating, drinking, dancing, and gambling in a jammed, beat-up apartment, the record player going full blast, the fried chicken or chitlins with potato salad and collard greens for a dollar a plate, and cans of beer or shots of liquor for fifty cents. Negro and white canvassers sidled up alongside you, talking fast as they tried to get you to buy a copy of the *Daily Worker:* "This paper's trying to keep your rent controlled . . . Make that greedy landlord kill them rats in your apartment . . . This paper represents the only political party that ever ran a black man for the Vice Presidency of the United States . . . Just want you to read, won't take but a little of your time . . . Who do you think fought the hardest to help free those Scottsboro boys?" Things I overheard among Negroes when the salesmen were around let me know that the paper somehow was tied in with the Russians, but to my sterile mind in those early days, it didn't mean much; the radio broadcasts and the newspapers were then full of our-ally-Russia, a strong, muscular people, peasants, with their backs to the wall helping America to fight Hitler and Mussolini.

But New York was heaven to me. And Harlem was Seventh Heaven! I hung around in Small's and the Braddock bar so much that the bartenders began to pour a shot of bourbon, my favorite brand of it, when they saw me walk in the door. And the steady customers in both places, the hustlers in Small's and the entertainers in the Braddock, began to call me "Red," a natural enough nickname in view of my bright red conk. I now had my conk done in Boston at the shop of Abbott and Fogey; it was the best conk shop on the East Coast, according to the musical greats who had recommended it to me.

1. *How does Malcolm create the sense that Harlem is a very special and distinctive community? How does he make it reflect some of the life styles of black Americans?*

2. *Malcolm is describing Harlem as he saw it for the first time as a young and inexperienced teenager. In what ways does he suggest his youthful point of view in presenting his description of Harlem?*

3. *Malcolm is writing his autobiography at a time when he has been converted to the Muslim religion and is committed to black nationalism and to a strict code of moral conduct. Does this viewpoint of the older Malcolm find some expression in the selection?*

4. *What happens to Malcolm himself after he first arrives in Harlem? Do the descriptions of Harlem provide a setting that helps to explain the young Malcolm's actions? How does he establish himself as a "Harlemite"?*

5. *Characterize Malcolm's use of specific details in describing Harlem. Does he use many or few? Are they closely or loosely related? What effect do they have on you as a reader?*

⌒ Willie Morris ⌒

(1934-   )

Willie Morris was raised in Mississippi and educated at the University of Texas and at Oxford University. His interest in journalism began when he worked for the school newspaper at Texas and resulted in his later becoming editor-in-chief of The Texas Observer *and then an editor of* Harper's Magazine *in the 1960s. He has since devoted himself to his own writing, publishing among other books the autobiographical volumes* Good Old Boy *(1971) and* North Toward Home *(1967).*

NEW YORK

The apartment I found was in the east twenties, between Madison and Park. The other places that I had seen and liked, airy places with parks nearby, never rented for less than $250 or $300 a month, for rents in the city were criminal. This one rented at $125, and it occupied the third floor of a narrow gray building next to a parking lot. The exposed side was pocked with holes and ridges, and someone had written on it in white enamel: "The Dukes." Looking at this unusual structure from a block down the street, one was struck by its lean-to quality; it seemed to have no business existing at all. It rose from the west side of the parking lot, gaunt and improvised. Someone walking down the street with the address almost always walked right past it, thinking that the place might not be inhabited. One reason may have been that there was a red canopy over the sidewalk at the front door advertising the short-

212

order take-home service which shared the entrance off to the left.

One walked up the three flights through several padlocked doors, often past the garbage which the landlords had neglected to remove for two or three days. Once inside our place, things were not bad at all. There was a big front room with an old floor, a little alcove for a study, and to the back a short corridor opening up into a tiny bedroom for my son and a larger bedroom in the back. The kitchen was in the back bedroom. I had not been able to find a view of an extensive body of water at popular prices, but from the back window, about forty yards out, there *was* a vista of a big tank, part of some manufacturing installation in the building under it, and the tank constantly bubbled with some unidentified greenish substance. From this window one could also see the tarred rooftops of the surrounding buildings, and off to the right a quiet stretch of God's earth, this being the parking lot next door.

From the front room the view of the street was more animated. Across the street there was a large bar which seemed to remain open twenty-four hours a day, and in front of this, on the corner, one could look down at any hour and see the little circles of people, just standing, watching the mad traffic on lower Madison. We were without sunlight, which was unable to penetrate down from the tall office building across the street; and when it rained, which was often that first year, I remembered the hard cold rainfalls in the Mississippi delta of my childhood, and how they encompassed the green earth and fields and trees in such a torrent that one seemed at the mercy of nature itself; here, from the front window, the rain merely kicked up little pools of dirt and debris on East 26th, and sent people under the canopy of the bar. One oppressive Saturday afternoon, our old Texas friends Ronnie Dugger and Larry Goodwyn sat here in our front room with us; our separate work had all brought us briefly together in New York City. We sat here talking of old times and places; then, out of a gray sky, there came a blizzard. We watched the big flakes come down for a while, a little depressed and intimidated. Suddenly Good-wyn opened the window, stuck his head out, and gazed down at the scene on East 26th. Then he put his head back in, turned around, and said, "Well, boys, they got us all up here together . . . and then they *snowed* on us." The subway was also diffi-cult to get used to. There was a station twenty yards from the building; every five minutes the building rocked and groaned at its very foundations.

I was only seven blocks from my office at *Harper's*, and in the mornings I could walk up Madison to work. On a fine day, carrying my black briefcase with poems from housewives in the Midwest, or stream-of-consciousness prose from the gradu-ate schools, I enjoyed making my way up the avenue through the bustling crowds on the sidewalks, feeling very much the cosmopolite. But on some grim foggy morning, when the steam came out of the sewers in the streets as if the earth be-neath were on fire, the city had a dreadful claustrophobic qual-ity, like death itself: closed-in, blind, and airless, compressed by the endless concrete and asphalt exteriors. The horns from the cabs, the cursing of the drivers, the harsh violence of the streetworkers dodging the already clogged traffic, caused a new arrival to feel that humanity here was always at war with its machines and with itself. In the course of a year, walking seven blocks to work and back over the same route, I saw three people killed by cars and four others badly hurt. The most likely place for this mayhem was the curious intersection of Park and 33rd. Here there was a tunnel which came suddenly out of nowhere. Cars whipped out of it at terrific speeds, catch-ing pedestrians crossing against the red light on Park. There was no sign suggesting the existence of this tunnel, which added somewhat to the spirit of adventure. At first it would be disrupting to see the white sheet covering an unfortunate pe-destrian caught by surprise by some taxicab coming out of the tunnel, the crowds milling around with that sullen big-city curiosity looking at the blood, the cop or two waiting perfunc-torily for the ambulance to arrive. After a time I grew used to the spectacle, however, and would walk gingerly past the broken body and its spectators as if it were all in the morning's walk.

Many times, walking home from work, I would see some unknowing soul venture across that intersection against the light and then freeze in horror when he saw the cars ripping out of the tunnel toward him. For a brief instant the immobile human would stand there, transfixed by the vehicle bearing down upon him, the contrast of desperate vulnerable flesh and hard chrome never failing to send a horrible tremor through an onlooker's being. Then, suddenly, the human reflex would take over, and the pedestrian would jackknife first one way, then another, arms flaying the empty air, and often the car would literally *skim* the man, brushing by him so close it would touch his coat or his tie. If another car coming behind did not nail him then, much the way a linebacker moves in for the kill after the tackle or end merely slows down a ball-carrier, the pedestrian would stand there briefly, all the blood drained from his face, oblivious to the curses from the driver of the car which had just missed him. If there was a cop on the corner he would wait while the man staggered in his shock to the sidewalk beyond, there to accost him: "Ya crazy, hah? Ya stupid? Walkin' against the light! Hah! Ya almost got killed, ya know it? Ya *know* it?" I saw this ritual several times; on one occasion, feeling sorry for the person who had brushed against the speeding car, I hurried across the intersection after him to cheer him up a little. Catching up with him down by 32nd I said, "That was good legwork, sir. Excellent moves for a big man!" but the man looked at me with an empty expression in his eyes, and then moved away mechanically and trancelike, heading for the nearest bar.

On a number of occasions on my peregrinations from 33rd to 26th there would be some bum sprawled out on the sidewalk, and the people would walk right past him, or sometimes step over him, glancing back a little nervously, usually saying to their companions, "Somebody should call a cop." The first time I saw a man lying prone on the concrete, blood trickling slightly from his nose, I bent over and asked him if he was all right, and he moaned a little, and I went into a restaurant and phoned the police to report his distress. But after a while, like the others when confronted with such a sight, I would keep going too, though always a little guiltily; wishing a cop would come by soon. Why should people in such a city be *expected* to stop and do something about their fallen wounded, not knowing them nor caring? The existence involved in moving daily to and from work in the immense and faceless crowds inevitably hardens one's senses to violence and despair. I came to feel it perfectly natural, this isolated callousness of the city-dweller. Anyone who expected valor or compassion in everyday acts in a monstrous American city in these times expected too much of human nature, and would sooner or later be disappointed. The cops became the guardians of benevolence; they were our salaried Samaritans.

Along the sidewalks in our neighborhood roamed two old walkers who made their mark on the area. One was a bent-over old man who wore pince-nez; he carried an American flag, a Bible, and a megaphone. At almost any hour of the day you could hear him, standing on some street corner nearby, delivering a feverish sermon on sin, redemption, and patriotism, or moving along the sidewalk with his dragging gait shouting vengeance on every moving object in the vicinity, animal or vegetable. He was just as content trying to convert a Chevrolet pick-up truck as he was in shouting his evangelical threats to the little Italian boys who congregated at the fruit stand on Lexington. There was a horror to this old man, to the echo of his grating voice coming down the narrow streets between the big buildings. Thin trickles of saliva would form on his mouth and drip to the pavement; his moist insane proselytizing seemed as inexorable and illogical as the city itself, as its insane flow of vehicles and people. One Christmas morning, as my son played with his toys in the front room of our apartment, I heard him from down the block, and through a drab

December mist I saw him shuffling along on 26th street, solitary and mad; suddenly I felt sorry for him, alone on this Christmas day. I picked up a couple of cans of fancy sardines and rushed down the stairs, catching up with him on the sidewalk. "Merry Christmas," I said, the first words I had ever spoken to him, and handed him the sardines. A puffed-up smile creased his face. He took the gift and said, "What is your religion, young man?" "I'm an old Mississippi Methodist," I replied. "Ah . . . Methodist," he said. "Then you don't believe in Jesus. Pity on you, young man." And he walked away, gingerly putting the sardines in his coat pocket.

The other neighborhood apparition was a woman of about sixty, a gaunt old specter who worked regularly as clockwork. She was a junkie, and every afternoon from three to five she roamed the streets shouting some demented gibberish, a considerable tumult for such a scrawny old woman. Once I saw the evangelist and the drug addict meet by chance in front of a shabby building on Lexington with a plaque explaining that Chester A. Arthur had been sworn in here as President of the USA after Garfield was assassinated, and they shouted at one another as if mortal enemies, and the old man walked away, whispering through his megaphone, *Doomed. Doomed!*" The woman's shouts were even more disrupting than the man's, however, because they were self-inflicted, and because she worked on a schedule, coming out of God knows what place every day to exercise her private perspectives. Both were always alone and always ignored. Except when taunted by the neighborhood kids they seemed quite self-sufficient.

In our apartment my son walked and crawled around the front room, exploring the edges of his new existence. There was nowhere to take him to run. Running him down the sidewalks of Madison or Park or Lexington in early evening was like taking a nighttime trot in the Carlsbad Caverns. Once the traffic had thinned out at night, traffic lights for the taxis were as physically efficacious as a resolution of the UN General Assembly; I had never seen red lights ignored with such disdain.

Madison Park, the closest piece of earth in the vicinity, was a good place to watch the drunks and the old men sleeping under shrubs, but no likely retreat for a three-year-old child. Finally I took to playing with him in the parking lot next door, throwing a tennis ball against our apartment house and letting him retrieve it, until the man who owned the lot came by one bright fall evening and said, "Cancha see that *sign:* it says *private property.* If ya can't read, mistuh, go back to trainin' school."

We missed the easy, open life of Texas, the impromptu beer parties in our house on Bridle Path, the casual way people had of dropping by on friends, the old German beer hall and the tables under the trees in back. The only person we knew in the neighborhood was Nick, who sold newspapers at a little stand on Madison. I could leave my son with him for half an hour or so while I went off on an errand, and come back and find the child behind the counter, helping sell the *Journal-American* and the *World-Telegram.* Returning to the newsstand one night, I sidled up to the papers and saw my son selling a *Post* to a cabdriver, who gave him a nickel tip; the Harpers of Mississippi seemed far, far away.

1. What kind of details does Morris present as characteristic of big-city life? How are they different from the kind of description of New York that Malcolm X provides?
2. Morris was raised in the South. How does he create an impression of the city as seen by someone familiar with another way of life? What can you infer are the characteristics of that other way of life? What are some of the qualities of city life he emphasizes that a long-time resident might ignore?
3. Do the details Morris uses suggest the variety of city life or do they reinforce one another to emphasize only one aspect of the city?
4. What is Morris's attitude when he describes the dangers to pedestrians at the intersection of Park Avenue and 33rd Street? In the fourth paragraph, why does he call it a "curious inter-

*section"? In the next paragraph, how does he make you see the
meeting of car and pedestrian? How would you explain his
behavior to the pedestrian afterwards?*
5. *When Morris describes the apartment he has rented, what
aspects of it does he concentrate on and what does he ignore?
How does his choice of details fit his general portrait of city
life?*

⟳ Catherine Drinker Bowen ⟳

(1897-1973)

Catherine Drinker Bowen was a member of a distinguished Pennsylvania family. Her father was President of Lehigh University and many of her relatives had notable public careers. She herself was a gifted and successful biographer, whose subjects included John Adams, Francis Bacon, and Oliver Wendell Holmes. She also wrote and lectured on the craft of writing biography. As its title implies, her Family Portrait *(1970) is as much a biography of her family as it is her own autobiography. "Beach Haven" concerns the family's annual summer holiday at their cottage on the New Jersey shore during the years just before the First World War.*

BEACH HAVEN

There was a special smell to the cottage at Beach Haven, indigenous, I think, to the Jersey shore. The minute one opened the front door one met it—a combination of dampness, beach sand, old wicker furniture, oil from the guns that stood racked with the fishing rods in the little west room off the hall. Whatever the mixture, to my nostrils it was very sweet. This whiff, this musty breath meant running barefoot on the beach, bathing in the foam of the breakers. It meant sailing on the bay, crabbing from the dock, riding one's bicycle on the wide yellow-pebbled streets, easy and free.

Yet there was more to these summer months than a vacation. We worked hard at what we did. Both parents saw to that, whether it was learning to shoot or swim or manage a sailboat or even to clean fish before we brought them to Bridget at the back door. It was here also that the family came together and stayed together; when my brothers were in college and graduate school they spent much time at Beach Haven, studying, working on a thesis or a projected book such as Harry's volumes on the Interstate Commerce Act.

As years passed the cottage became for us a kind of homestead. Our parents might move from Philadelphia to Haverford to Bethlehem and back again. But always that creaky cottage door with the painted glass panels opened to home. . . . The stuffed curlew over the mantel spread its gray-brown wings, the mounted drumfish stared blindly from its board above the sofa. Upstairs the painted iron beds waited with their hard hair mattresses, and in a corner of the dining room the wooden water cooler dribbled from its spigot.

Beach Haven lies at the south end of Long Beach Island, twenty-five miles above Atlantic City. My father bought the cottage in 1888. Before that he had belonged to a gun and fishing club which kept an old schooner, the *Novelette*, as headquarters in Barnegat Bay. Harry was nine when he boarded the *Novelette* on his first trip for ducks. Already he owned a gun; by the time he was twelve Papa let him go alone up the beach for shore birds, though Mamma strongly disapproved. All four brothers possessed guns at an early age and were trained to look on their weapons with respect. Oddly enough Papa never let let them go gunning with a friend or even a brother. He said when two boys got together they began fooling and there might be an accident. Harry told me that when he wanted to get up at 2:30 to shoot reedbirds Ma restricted him to three mornings a week; he would wear himself out, she said. Downstairs in the dark kitchen he used to cook six eggs for breakfast and be at the inlet, three miles away, by sunrise. The boys shot plover, snipe, willet, curlew. Yellowlegs flew over the dunes with their clear strong cry; we used it as a family whistle: phew-hew; phew-hew-hew-hew.

Today the whole gunning program seems wicked—and it

was wicked, none the less so because of our bland innocence. To no one of our acquaintance did it occur that we were in a way of ruining and rifling our domain, nor that America's pioneer days were gone forever and with them the philosophy of natural abundance. Theodore Roosevelt, one of the first public conservationists, himself was celebrated as a big game hunter. All over America, game still abounded; if there existed wildlife preserves or sanctuaries we did not know it. And there was no limit on the shoot. A man could bring home a bag of ninety birds—and this at a time when Europe had long cared for its game by breeding and replacement. At Beach Haven Inlet the snipe flew in close white formations, swerving and skimming the water. They would come in for clamshells on sticks, no decoys needed.

Paradoxically, my father was to be a founder of the national conservation movement, working with Gifford Pinchot in Pennsylvania and elsewhere. But in these early days, before the First World War, the sky indeed remained the limit, though Pa would not permit a bigger bag than we could eat at table, and to shoot at any but a game bird partook of serious offense.

. . .

The memories of Beach Haven run all to smells and sounds and sights; they are physical, of the blood and appetite, as is natural to summertime. At the west end of Coral Street the marshes began, turning soft with color at sunset, pink and lilac and golden green. The ocean beach at low tide lay hard underfoot, wet sand dark below the waterline. On the dunes—we called them sandhills—we played King of the Castle or slid down on our bloomer seats, yelling with triumph and pure joy. The floors of Curlew Cottage, the chairs, even the beds were sandy. Always a lone sneaker sat beneath the hall sofa; by August our city shoes were mildewed in the closets, and towels were forever damp.

Behind our house in the laundry, Mary and Tessie spent

their Mondays on two sides of a big ironing table, passing over the sheets an iron heated by a little coal stove. Outside the laundry in a small mosquitoey backyard, bathing suits hung eternally on the line; there was a big coal bin by the fence. One day a black snake was discovered amid a general hubbub and upheaval of coal. Cecil went after him with a club, but Tessie said Cecil could save his trouble, the snake wouldn't die before sundown. Impressed, I noted this bit of natural philosophy in my diary.

At mid-afternoon the maids went bathing with their friends, wading through the surf in full-skirted black suits, joining hands in a row and screaming as they jumped the waves. I never saw one of them go beyond the breakers; Philly told me Irish people couldn't swim and I believed him. It would be hard to exaggerate the meaning these maids had for the family; it went far beyond the services for which they were paid. In Mamma's old age Mary McClafferty was to be her friend and confidant; Mary could make her laugh and forget pain. Mary stayed with us, as I have said, for fifty years; she died in Harry's house. She was a big woman, handsome, and bore herself well. She always had followers; I used to hear their deep laugh in the back sitting room on Saturday evenings, but she refused to marry. Mary knew the name of every Irish prizefighter from John L. Sullivan down, but her great hero when he came on the scene was John L. Lewis. Mary said you had to be born in Mauch Chunk to know what John L. had done for the miners, and that of all them loud talkers in Washington he was the one who got things done. The Big Boy, she called him; she has his picture stuck in her mirror, with his hat on, looking fierce.

Bridget stayed with us nearly as long, a tiny woman, first-generation Irish; she told me she never growed beyond four feet because there wasn't enough potatoes in County Clare. Bridget had a quick temper and we were careful not to try it; she used to swear that if I left the pan dirty after making fudge I'd find it clammy cold in my bed some night, and that I was more trouble to her than all her money. She also told my fortune by tea leaves. I would marry a poor man with brains in his head, not a millionaire like my sister. When I asked how she knew Ernesta would marry a rich man, Bridget said, "Did ye ever see her walkin' out with a poor one?"

In Beach Haven I was always hungry. We all were, though we remained thin as rails. I remember the food vividly, though I cannot recall a single meal in Bethlehem. On Sundays we often had boiled bluefish for dinner, so big the fish's tail reached over the edge of the Ivanhoe platter; Bridget came ceremoniously from the kitchen and passed her egg sauce in a china boat. I don't know where my mother got the Ivanhoe china, of which we owned a full set, bowls and pitchers included. Perhaps it came with the cottage, like the twin paintings of the boy and the lobster that hung in the dining room. In the first picture the boy has caught the lobster and is gloating; in the second the lobster has him by the thumb. But the Ivanhoe plates each carried a story from the novel, boldly etched in black and white, with the legend underneath. The one I liked best was *Rebecca Repulsing the Templar*. Rebecca had long black hair, a sweeping medieval gown, and one bare arm outstretched in horror. I gazed long at this scene over the years, but early concluded that Rebecca was making a mistake; the Templar in his armor looked very fierce and taking.

For dessert on Sundays there would be a huge cold watermelon which my father stood up to carve as if it were a turkey. I remember the reedbirds for supper, tiny and buttery, and Pa saying it was all right to gnaw the bones but for heaven's sake, Mamma, tell that child to wipe her mouth. In August came lima beans, and fresh corn piled steaming on the dish, one's eye hopefully on a certain piece. At table I could have eaten every dinner plateful three times over; if Mamma called a halt I sulked. I sat at her left. When the hot covered dishes were handed through the pantry window, Mary carried them around counterclockwise, which meant I came last. Once—I must have been about ten—I was sent from the table for shrieking when Philly got the part of the roast beef I wanted, the crackly outside piece. I swore at him. My mother left me upstairs to kick the bedroom door till dinner was over, when she appeared and spanked me with the back of her old wire hairbrush.

When my brothers married and brought in turn their wives to Beach Haven, there was apprehension as to how the wives would react. People not accustomed to the island, like New Englanders, were apt to scoff, complaining that they missed the trees and green grass. They asked how we could endure all this sun and sand and didn't we think keels on boats were really superior to centerboards? Sophie however liked it from the first. She went fishing with Harry in her old sneakers and dark blue skirt. She cruised with him on the *Gee Whiz*, which at best offered crowded quarters; she followed him up the beach when the bluefish "came ashore." About once every five years this happened, the most exciting episode in Beach Haven sporting life. Suddenly the waves would sparkle with hundreds of shiners, driven inshore by the big fish; above them gulls hovered thick. The boys would telegraph their father in Bethlehem, then dash for their rods and stand all day in the surf, running as the schools moved, and reeling in the magnificent catch.

At one period my brothers took to shark fishing at the inlet or somewhere outside, with heavy rods. It was a bloody, awful sport. They baited with fresh dogfish; when the shark struck they pulled up anchor and sailed after him until the beast, exhausted, could be drawn alongside, when he was whacked on the head and speared with a lance. Harry killed thirty-six sharks, all over six feet long, duly weighed and measured. The only way to prove the size of the catch was to dissect out the jaw and bring it home. Harry presented one such trophy to a friend at the Philadelphia Academy of Sciences—the jaw of a brown shark, eight feet six inches and weighing three hundred pounds. The other thirty-five jaws hung on the side porch wall at Curlew Cottage, cleaned, polished and grinning. Papa would have nothing to do with any of it, but Sophie showed no distaste. She said shark fishing was a good way to keep the Drinker males busy and she could think of lots worse diversions. Often enough she went with Harry on these expeditions.

Ernesta was not in Beach Haven more than half the time. She spent her summers at Gloucester with Aunt Beaux, or in Northeast Harbor, visiting what Cecil called her fancy friends. But it was Ernesta who taught me to sail; the boys of course had taught her. I was late learning for the reason that I could not swim and we weren't allowed to take our boats out alone until we could do twenty yards. Our family fleet consisted of the *Gee Whiz*, which remained altogether the boys' territory, an eighteen-foot catboat we called the skiff, and two sneak boxes. By the time I inherited the skiff she was old and heavy and came about slowly. But I loved her and spent hours on the bay with my friends, fishing or crabbing at some cove or just drifting peacefully along. Sailing was taken seriously by the family. You didn't make mistakes like jibing in a heavy wind; you were supposed to know the tides and the weather and come in fast when a squall blew up. To do anything silly on a boat was a mortal disgrace.

The great trick lay in making the dock at the day's end. The *Gee Whiz* sat at a mooring, but the little boats tied up every night. The professional yacht captains who took the summer people sailing kept their big catboats at the main dock; we juniors were down on the attached wooden jetty. When not out sailing the captains sat in rows on their clubhouse porch, smoking their pipes and talking about fish. Sailing in, one faced this formidable audience, which watched one's performance closely, saving its comments until one stepped ashore. "Keep a-goin', young lady, and you may learn somethin'. Ought to have come about sooner though, off that last channel marker. . . . I never seed a girl yet could throw a proper half hitch. Here, let me show you. And didn't Cecil teach you to shake your reefs out before furlin'? If he didn't he shoulda. Go on back now and unfurl."

There must have been fifteen or twenty of these captains. In winter they lived on the mainland, at Huckertown or West Creek. Every summer my father gave a dinner for them in our house. They trooped up the porch steps, impressive in their dark blue coats and hats with gold anchors above the visors. The dining room could not hold them, and tables were set up in the hall. At each plate was a present of a seaman's penknife. The captains knew bribery when they saw it: they were to keep an eye out should any of us get in trouble on the bay. Yet they plainly liked to come, and enjoyed the party; there was deep laughter and reminiscence about the old days on the *Novelette*. Phil and I used to listen, crouched on the staircase.

Saturday was race day on the bay; I acted as crew for Phil when he couldn't get anyone better. Beforehand we trudged back and forth to the dunes, filling sandbags, then sewed them tight, lugged them to the dock and deposited them forward or astern as commanded. The channels and coves at Beach Haven were tricky, a sailor had indeed to know his tides. For myself I think I spent as much time aground on some reef as I did on blue water. The reason our boats had centerboards became evident almost as soon as one left the dock. Shallows appeared unexpectedly and the sand forever shifted; the charts could not keep up with it.

I have often thought that my father, as his children grew to their teens, considered Beach Haven less as a refuge, where "days drift on with those I love," than as a training ground and education for the young. He had always looked seriously on sports, though never as spectator; I doubt if he ever bought a ticket to a "big game" in his life. Nor did he go sailing with me in the skiff, though my mother did. The notion of myself at the helm of any vehicle, a-sea or ashore, in which my father sat passive would have seemed impossible, a contradiction in terms. Papa left "the girls," as I have said, to Mamma; it was she who kept Ernesta and me in order and wielded the hairbrush when needed. In my entire youth I can remember only one occasion when Papa disciplined me, and that occurred at

Beach Haven. So greatly did it impress me that even today I cannot recall the scene without discomfort.

I was fifteen, and due to leave next day for a girls' camp in Maine. I suffered from hay fever, and August saw me shipped off above the ragweed line. That summer I had a heavy crush on the boy across the street; Win Allen, his name was. My train was to leave early in the morning. The night before, we planned to picnic up the beach. I suspect that Win was not nearly so taken with me as I with him. At any rate he never told me so or even said he liked me, though there had been much tennis and sailing together and dancing at the Engleside Hotel on Saturday nights. Perhaps Win was as shy as I. Anyway I counted on the evening picnic, the influence of the moon and my imminent departure to induce some kind of declaration. I wanted it badly.

Up the beach we built a bonfire and sat round it after supper, laughing and talking in the dark. Ernesta was along but she had Hervey, Win's older brother, so I didn't have to worry about *that*. Win remained jolly, attentive but entirely impersonal. In desperation I told myself I could not leave Beach Haven unless this boy said something. I didn't quite know what. I began to figure it so that on the way home we two would walk apart from the others. This would give Win the chance to say he was sorry I was going away, put his arm around me and maybe kiss me goodby. With the trembling passion of fifteen I sat by the embers and laid my plans. . . .

From the darkness beyond the fire I heard my name called, and not in the tones of love. My father's figure loomed out, I remember he had on his old panama hat. "Kitty!" he said. "Come home with me. Now, at once!" I saw that he was angry and I asked no questions but rose and followed him in silence, a full half mile down the beach to the boardwalk lights and home. He led me to the room I shared with Ernesta. "Pack that trunk," he said, pointing to where it gaped open by the window, empty except for a few things at the bottom marked for camp. "Pack it *now!* Your mother has gone to bed, she is tired.

It is not your mother's business to pack the trunks of fifteen-year-old girls."

I was so scared I took all the things from the beds, including two dresses of Ernesta's, swept them into the trunk, put the first tray in and emptied my top bureau drawer over all. Set in the top tray were compartments for hats; in panic I took two hats from the closet shelf. One was Ernesta's; we wore them to church on Sundays, mine had red poppies round the brim. I packed them in tissue paper while my father watched. Then I closed the trunk and he locked it. When I got to Camp Wahgash and unpacked the hats they asked me where I thought I was headed for, Newport or Narragansett?

1. How does Bowen use details of the life in the summer cottage to create a portrait of family relationships? What characteristics of the family members strike you as most important and how are they brought out in this summer setting?

2. Bowen is writing about events in her life that happened well over fifty years before. How does she create the image of a different world and how does she suggest its differences from life today?

3. What are some of the differences you can find between the way Bowen describes her childhood, its setting and its activities, and the way Kazin describes his?

4. Look more closely at the two paragraphs describing meals at Beàch Haven. How does Bowen interweave different kinds of details and what overall impression does she create?

5. Why does Bowen end her story of Beach Haven with the scene where her father makes her pack for camp? What function does the scene have in enabling you to understand Bowen or the life of the family at Beach Haven?

∽ William O. Douglas ∽

(1898-   )

William O. Douglas was born in Minnesota, raised in Washington, and received his law degree from Columbia University in 1925. He taught law at Columbia and Yale and was active in the federal government until 1939, when Franklin Roosevelt appointed him to the Supreme Court. His resignation in 1975 terminated the longest service on the court of any judge in its history and concluded a judicial career notable for its commitment to the cause of civil liberties. While still a boy, Douglas was stricken with polio and regained his health by strengthening his legs through hiking. Those experiences led him to a lifelong passion for the outdoors and a lifelong interest in conservation. He remembers his hikes in the Cascade Mountains in this selection from his autobiography, Go East, Young Man *(1974).*

POLIO

[HIKING IN THE MOUNTAINS]

I took my early hikes into the hills to try to strengthen my legs, but they were to strengthen me in subtler ways. As I came to be on intimate terms with the hills, I learned something of their geology and botany. I heard the Indian legends associated with them. I discovered many of their secrets. I learned that they were always clothed in garments of delicate hues, though they seemed to be barren; though they looked dead and monotonous, they teemed with life and had many moods.

It was a real ordeal for me to walk the hills in the dead of summer, for then they were parched and dry and offered no shade from the hot sun and no springs or creeks where thirst could be quenched. Then the rattlesnake seemed to thrive. But in the spring, fall, and winter, there were interesting places to explore; my walks then were more fun than ordeal.

When I tramped the foothills in dead of winter, the pulse of life on the ridges was slow. The wind swept down from Mount Adams and Mount Rainier, cold and piercing, and I would find some black rimrock where I could sit, my back to the rock, protected from the wind, hoping the warmth of my sagebrush fire would not awaken a den of rattlers with the false message that spring had arrived. And when I turned around and started home, the same strong wind at my back made me feel as if the strength of giants was in me. I strode along the barren ridge with ease, commanding the city that lay at my feet.

Sometimes the chinook, the soft and balmy breeze from the west side of the Cascade Mountains, would blow. With the chinook came a light and gentle rain; and as it swept across this desert area it always carried the refreshing smell of dampened dust and the pungent but delicate odor of sage. Often I walked at night, when the chinook blew hardest and the outdoors always seemed most alive.

When I stretched out on the ground and listened, I could hear the cheatgrass singing softly in the wind. The sage, too, would join the symphony. The legend is that as the wind goes softly through the sage, it sings in memory of the Idaho Indians whose plains it covered as far as the eye could see and whose mountains it decorated far above the deep-snow line. And the verse of its song is always the same, "Shoshone, Shoshone."

I discovered, too, that if I looked carefully I could find a variety of wildflowers surprising in so arid an environment. I remember looking down one spring afternoon, fresh from the man-made gardens of the valley, and seeing at my feet among the sagebrush a scattering of delicate pink. It was the rock rose, or bitterroot, a gentle membrane that the Creator seemed to have fashioned from bare rock-dust simply to decorate desolate places. A low plant, with waxy pale-pink flowers ribbed in a darker hue, the bitterroot has a translucent quality that makes it look as fragile to the touch as the gossamer wings of a tropical butterfly. Its leaves, I later learned, dry and vanish when the flowers appear, and its blossoms open with the sun and close with the darkness.

But the bitterroot is sturdier than it looks, and useful as well as decorative. The plant was collected by Lewis at the mouth of the Lou Lou Fork of the Bitterroot River in Montana. Its roots are the spatlum known to Indians, explorers, and early settlers as valued food. They contain a rich supply of starch, slightly bitter, thence its name. I never see the bitterroot blooming among the sage without feeling that I should take off my hat and stand in adoration at the wondrous skill of the Creator. I'll always remember the words of the artist who said, "I have grown to feel that there is nothing more amazing about a personal God than there is about the blossoming of the gorgeous little bitterroot."

I do not envy those whose introduction to nature was lush meadows, lakes, and swamps where life abounds. The desert hills of Yakima had a poverty that sharpened perception. Even a minute violet quickens the heart when one has walked far or climbed high to find it. Where nature is more bountiful, even the tender bitterroot might go unnoticed. Yet when a lone plant is seen in bloom on scabland between batches of bunch grass and sage, it can transform the spot as completely as only a whole bank of flowers could do in a more lush environment. It is the old relationship between scarcity and value, one of the lessons which the foothills of Yakima taught me.

There are two early trips that stand out especially in my memory. One was in the coolness of early spring. I left town before dusk and climbed the barren ridge west of Selah Gap. On the way up I had crossed a draw and caught the sweet odor of the mock orange. In the darkness I could vaguely see the lone shrub that filled this draw with the fragrance of its blossoms. It stood six feet high, and in this barren ravine the delicacy of its fragrance seemed strangely out of place.

The night was clear and the moon had just reached this horizon. Mount Adams loomed in the west, "high-humped," as Lewis and Clark aptly described it when they saw it on April 2, 1806. Along the ridge of the Cascades to the north was Mount Rainier, cold, aloof, and forbidding. Below at my feet the lights of the town had come on, blinking like stars of a minor firmament. A faint streak of light, sparkling in the moonlight, marked the course of the Yakima River as it wound its way across the valley, through dark splotches of sumac, cottonwood, and willow.

Above the dark rim of the foothills were the stars of the universe. They were the same stars that saw these valleys and hills and mountains rise from the murk of the ocean, reaching for the sun. They saw the Columbia lava, hot and steaming, pour in molten form across this land again and again, scorching to cinders everything it touched, burying great ponderosa pine four and five feet thick under its deep folds, and filling the sky with smoke that finally drew a curtain over the sun. They saw a subtropical land touched by the chill of the Arctic and rimmed with ice and snow. They saw the mighty Columbia and the Yakima grow from driblets to minor drainage canals to great rivers. They saw the glaciers recede and floods come. After the floods they saw the emergence of a desert that some unseen hand had sown with fragrant sage and populated with coyotes, rabbits, kangaroo rats, sage hens, sage sparrows, desert sparrows, bluebirds, and doves. They saw the Indians first appear on the horizon to the north, spreading out to all parts of the continent in their long trek from Asia. And thousands of years later they saw some newcomers arrive, the ones that fought, quarreled, and loved, the ones that built houses and roads and planted orchards, the ones that erected spires and lifted their eyes to the sky in prayer.

I think it was that night that I got my first sense of Time. I began to appreciate some of the lessons that geology taught. In the great parade of events that this region unfolded, man was indeed insignificant. He appeared under this firmament only briefly and then disappeared. His transit was too short for geological time to measure.

As I walked the ridge that evening, I could hear the chinook on distant ridges before it reached me. Then it touched the sage at my feet and made it sing. It brushed my cheek, warm and soft. It ran its fingers through my hair and rippled away in the darkness. It was a friendly wind, friendly to man throughout time. It was beneficent, carrying rain to the desert. It was soft, bringing warmth to the body. It had almost magical qualities, for it need touch the snow only lightly to melt it.

It became for me that night a measure of the kindliness of the universe to man, a token of the hospitality that awaits man when he puts foot on this earth. It became for me a promise of the fullness of life to him who, instead of shaking his fist at the sky, looks to it for health and strength and courage.

That night I felt at peace. I felt that I was a part of the universe, a companion to the friendly chinook that brought the promise of life and adventure. That night, I think, there first came to me the germ of a philosophy of life: that man's best measure of the universe is in his hopes and his dreams, not his fears, that man is a part of a plan, only a fraction of which he, perhaps, can ever comprehend.

Another trip into those hills marked a turning point in my life. It was April and the valley below was in bloom, lush and content with fruit blossoms. Then came a sudden storm, splattering rain in the lower valley and shooting tongues of lightning along the ridges across from me. As the weather cleared, Adams and Rainier stood forth in power and beauty, monarchs to every peak in their range.

Away from town, in the opposite direction from its comforts, the backbone of the Cascades was clear against the western sky, the slopes and ravines dark blue in the afternoon sun.

The distant ridges and canyons seemed soft and friendly. They appeared to hold untold mysteries and to contain solitude many times more profound than that of the barren ridge on which I stood. They offered streams and valleys and peaks to explore, snow fields and glaciers to conquer, wild animals to know. That afternoon I felt that the high mountains in the distance were extending to me an invitation to get acquainted with them, to tramp their trails and sleep in their high basins.

My heart filled with joy, for I knew I could accept the invitation. I would have legs and lungs equal to it.

1. Douglas begins by saying that his mountain hikes strengthened his legs, but also strengthened him "in subtler ways." How does the selection make you understand what these "subtler ways" are?

2. What kind of information is Douglas most interested in giving you about his environment? What does he particularly value in the natural world?

3. Note the places in this selection where Douglas's response to nature depends on other senses besides his sight. How do those moments alter your understanding of Douglas and his relation to his environment?

4. Douglas concludes by recalling two early trips to the Yakima foothills. Why does he find them especially memorable? Do the two trips have similar significance for him or does each fulfill a different function?

5. Douglas and Thoreau are the two writers in this chapter who are on the most intimate terms with nature. Compare their methods of describing the natural world and their reasons for finding it significant.

∼ George Orwell ∼

(1903-1950)

See the biographical note on page 61. Orwell spent several months in Morocco (September, 1938–March, 1939) while working on the manuscript of a novel, Coming Up for Air; *it was his first visit to the country. He wrote "Marrakech" in the spring of 1939.*

MARRAKECH

As the corpse went past the flies left the restaurant table in a cloud and rushed after it, but they came back a few minutes later.

The little crowd of mourners—all men and boys, no women —threaded their way across the market-place between the piles of pomegranates and the taxis and the camels, wailing a short chant over and over again. What really appeals to the flies is that the corpses here are never put into coffins, they are merely wrapped in a piece of rag and carried on a rough wooden bier on the shoulders of four friends. When the friends get to the burying-ground they hack an oblong hole a foot or two deep, dump the body in it and fling over it a little of the dried-up, lumpy earth, which is like broken brick. No gravestone, no name, no identifying mark of any kind. The burying-ground is merely a huge waste of hummocky earth, like a derelict building-lot. After a month or two no one can even be certain where his own relatives are buried.

When you walk through a town like this—two hundred thousand inhabitants, of whom at least twenty thousand own literally nothing except the rags they stand up in—when you see how the people live, and still more how easily they die, it is always difficult to believe that you are walking among human beings. All colonial empires are in reality founded upon that fact. The people have brown faces—besides, there are so many of them! Are they really the same flesh as yourself? Do they even have names? Or are they merely a kind of undifferentiated brown stuff, about as individual as bees or coral insects? They rise out of the earth, they sweat and starve for a few years, and then they sink back into the nameless mounds of the graveyard and nobody notices that they are gone. And even the graves themselves soon fade back into the soil. Sometimes, out for a walk, as you break your way through the prickly pear, you notice that it is rather bumpy underfoot, and only a certain regularity in the bumps tells you that you are walking over skeletons.

I was feeding one of the gazelles in the public gardens.

Gazelles are almost the only animals that look good to eat when they are still alive, in fact, one can hardly look at their hindquarters without thinking of mint sauce. The gazelle I was feeding seemed to know that this thought was in my mind, for though it took the piece of bread I was holding out it obviously did not like me. It nibbled rapidly at the bread, then lowered its head and tried to butt me, then took another nibble and then butted again. Probably its idea was that if it could drive me away the bread would somehow remain hanging in mid-air.

An Arab navvy working on the path nearby lowered his heavy hoe and sidled slowly towards us. He looked from the gazelle to the bread and from the bread to the gazelle, with a sort of quiet amazement, as though he had never seen anything quite like this before. Finally he said shyly in French:

"*I* could eat some of that bread."

I tore off a piece and he stowed it gratefully in some secret place under his rags. This man is an employee of the Municipality.

When you go through the Jewish quarters you gather some idea of what the medieval ghettoes were probably like. Under their Moorish rulers the Jews were only allowed to own land in certain restricted areas, and after centuries of this kind of treatment they have ceased to bother about overcrowding. Many of the streets are a good deal less than six feet wide, the houses are completely windowless, and sore-eyed children cluster everywhere in unbelievable numbers, like clouds of flies. Down the centre of the street there is generally running a little river of urine.

In the bazaar huge families of Jews, all dressed in the long black robe and little black skull-cap, are working in dark fly-infested booths that look like caves. A carpenter sits cross-legged at a prehistoric lathe, turning chair-legs at lightning speed. He works the lathe with a bow in his right hand and guides the chisel with his left foot, and thanks to a lifetime of sitting in this position his left leg is warped out of shape. At his side his grandson, aged six, is already starting on the simpler parts of the job.

I was just passing the coppersmiths' booths when somebody noticed that I was lighting a cigarette. Instantly, from the dark holes all round, there was a frenzied rush of Jews, many of them old grandfathers with flowing grey beards, all clamouring for a cigarette. Even a blind man somewhere at the back of one of the booths heard a rumour of cigarettes and came crawling out, groping in the air with his hand. In about a minute I had used up the whole packet. None of these people, I suppose, works less than twelve hours a day, and every one of them looks on a cigarette as a more or less impossible luxury.

As the Jews live in self-contained communities they follow the same trades as the Arabs, except for agriculture. Fruit-sellers, potters, silversmiths, blacksmiths, butchers, leather-workers, tailors, water-carriers, beggars, porters—whichever way you look you see nothing but Jews. As a matter of fact there are thirteen thousand of them, all living in the space of a few acres. A good job Hitler wasn't here. Perhaps he was on his way, however. You hear the usual dark rumours about the Jews, not only from the Arabs but from the poorer Europeans.

"Yes, mon vieux, they took my job away from me and gave it to a Jew. The Jews! They're the real rulers of this country, you know. They've got all the money. They control the banks, finance—everything."

"But," I said, "isn't it a fact that the average Jew is a labourer working for about a penny an hour?"

"Ah, that's only for show! They're all moneylenders really. They're cunning, the Jews."

In just the same way, a couple of hundred years ago, poor old women used to be burned for witchcraft when they could not even work enough magic to get themselves a square meal.

All people who work with their hands are partly invisible, and the more important the work they do, the less visible they are. Still, a white skin is always fairly conspicuous. In northern Europe, when you see a labourer ploughing a field, you probably give him a second glance. In a hot country, anywhere south of Gibraltar or east of Suez, the chances are that you don't even see him. I have noticed this again and again. In a tropical landscape one's eye takes in everything except the human beings. It takes in the dried-up soil, the prickly pear, the palm tree and the distant mountain, but it always misses the peasant hoeing at his patch. He is the same colour as the earth, and a great deal less interesting to look at.

It is only because of this that the starved countries of Asia and Africa are accepted as tourist resorts. No one would think of running cheap trips to the Distressed Areas. But where the human beings have brown skins their poverty is simply not noticed. What does Morocco mean to a Frenchman? An orange-grove or a job in Government service. Or to an Englishman? Camels, castles, palm trees, Foreign Legionnaires, brass trays, and bandits. One could probably live there for years without noticing that for nine-tenths of the people the reality of life is an endless, back-breaking struggle to wring a little food out of an eroded soil.

Most of Morocco is so desolate that no wild animal bigger than a hare can live on it. Huge areas which were once covered with forest have turned into a treeless waste where the soil is exactly like broken-up brick. Nevertheless a good deal of it is cultivated, with frightful labour. Everything is done by hand. Long lines of women, bent double like inverted capital L's, work their way slowly across the fields, tearing up the prickly weeds with their hands, and the peasant gathering lucerne for fodder pulls it up stalk by stalk instead of reaping it, thus saving an inch or two on each stalk. The plough is a wretched wooden thing, so frail that one can easily carry it on one's shoulder, and fitted underneath with a rough iron spike which stirs the soil to a depth of about four inches. This is as much as the strength of the animals is equal to. It is usual to plough with a cow and a donkey yoked together. Two donkeys would not be quite strong enough, but on the other hand two cows would cost a little more to feed. The peasants possess no harrows, they merely plough the soil several times over in different directions, finally leaving it in rough furrows, after which the whole field has to be shaped with hoes into small oblong patches to conserve water. Except for a day or two after the rare rainstorms there is never enough water. Along the edges of the fields channels are hacked out to a depth of thirty or forty feet to get at the tiny trickles which run through the subsoil.

Every afternoon a file of very old women passes down the road outside my house, each carrying a load of firewood. All of them are mummified with age and the sun, and all of them are tiny. It seems to be generally the case in primitive communities that the women, when they get beyond a certain age, shrink to the size of children. One day a poor old creature who could not have been more than four feet tall crept past me under a vast load of wood. I stopped her and put a five-sou piece (a little more than a farthing) into her hand. She answered with a shrill wail, almost a scream, which was partly gratitude but mainly surprise. I suppose that from her point of view, by taking any notice of her, I seemed almost to be violating a law of nature. She accepted her status as an old woman, that is to say as a beast of burden. When a family is travelling it is quite usual to see a father and a grown-up son riding ahead on donkeys, and an old woman following on foot, carrying the baggage.

But what is strange about these people is their invisibility. For several weeks, always at about the same time of day, the file of old women had hobbled past the house with their firewood, and though they had registered themselves on my eyeballs I cannot truly say that I had seen them. Firewood was passing—that was how I saw it. It was only that one day I happened to be walking behind them, and the curious up-and-down motion of a load of wood drew my attention to the human being beneath it. Then for the first time I noticed the poor old earth-coloured bodies, bodies reduced to bones and leathery skin, bent double under the crushing weight. Yet I suppose I had not been five minutes on Moroccan soil before I noticed the overloading of the donkeys and was infuriated by it. There is no question that the donkeys are damnably treated. The Moroccan donkey is hardly bigger than a St. Bernard dog, it carries a load which in the British Army would be considered too much for a fifteen-hands mule, and very often its pack-saddle is not taken off its back for weeks together. But what is peculiarly pitiful is that it is the most willing creature on earth, it follows its master like a dog and does not need either bridle or halter. After a dozen years of devoted work it suddenly drops dead, whereupon its master tips it into the ditch and the village dogs have torn its guts out before it is cold.

This kind of thing makes one's blood boil, whereas—on the whole—the plight of the human beings does not. I am not commenting, merely pointing to a fact. People with brown skins are next door to invisible. Anyone can be sorry for the donkey with its galled back, but it is generally owing to some kind of accident if one even notices the old woman under her load of sticks.

As the storks flew northward the Negroes were marching southward—a long, dusty column, infantry, screw-gun batteries, and then more infantry, four or five thousand men in all, winding up the road with a clumping of boots and a clatter of iron wheels.

They were Senegalese, the blackest Negroes in Africa, so black that sometimes it is difficult to see whereabouts on their necks the hair begins. Their splendid bodies were hidden in reach-me-down khaki uniforms, their feet squashed into boots that looked like blocks of wood, and every tin hat seemed to be a couple of sizes too small. It was very hot and the men had marched a long way. They slumped under the weight of their packs and the curiously sensitive black faces were glistening with sweat.

As they went past a tall, very young Negro turned and caught my eye. But the look he gave me was not in the least the kind of look you might expect. Not hostile, not contemptuous, not sullen, not even inquisitive. It was the shy, wide-eyed Negro look, which actually is a look of profound respect. I saw how it was. This wretched boy, who is a French citizen and has therefore been dragged from the forest to scrub floors and catch syphilis in garrison towns, actually has feelings of reverence before a white skin. He has been taught that the white race are his masters, and he still believes it.

But there is one thought which every white man (and in this connection it doesn't matter twopence if he calls himself a socialist) thinks when he sees a black army marching past. "How much longer can we go on kidding these people? How long before they turn their guns in the other direction?"

It was curious, really. Every white man there had this

thought stowed somewhere or other in his mind. I had it, so had the other onlookers, so had the officers on their sweating chargers and the white N.C.O.'s marching in the ranks. It was a kind of secret which we all knew and were too clever to tell; only the Negroes didn't know it. And really it was like watching a flock of cattle to see the long column, a mile or two miles of armed men, flowing peacefully up the road, while the great white birds drifted over them in the opposite direction, glittering like scraps of paper.

1. Why do you think Orwell begins his essay with the account of the funeral and burial? After reading the entire essay, do you think it is a good introduction to Orwell's view of Marrakech? What difference would it make if he added more specific details—for example, gave the name of the dead man and the site of the burial ground, or described the faces of the friends?
2. Whom do you think Orwell sees as his audience? For example, do you think he is addressing natives of Morocco or people who are deciding on their next vacation trip? Explain what details in the description help you define the audience.
3. Orwell relies on a series of scenes to create his view of Marrakech—the zoo, the ghetto, the women carrying firewood, the Senegalese troops. Why does he include each of these scenes and how are they related to one another?
4. What is Orwell's own role in his account? What is the vantage point from which he describes the scenes in Marrakech? To what kinds of details does Orwell as an observer seem particularly sensitive. Do you think his primary interest is in describing Marrakech itself?
5. Why do you think Orwell concludes with the scene involving the Senegalese troops? How would it change his account if he had concluded a page earlier with the scene involving the old women?

Possibilities for Writing

1. Accumulate a list of details describing a place that you remember vividly, then go over the list and decide how all of these details might best fit together. See also if there might be any opportunity for something other than visual memory to play a part in your description. When you have finished the description, exchange your essay with someone else in the class and compare what you were attempting to convey with what your reader finds memorable.
2. Write a description of a place you remember that has now changed in very noticeable ways. Concentrate on trying to capture the difference between what it was and what it is and on trying to convey whatever shifts in your feelings and your interest have occurred as a result.
3. Write a description of a reasonably large geographical area —for example, a city block, a particular district in a town— any place that would include a considerable variety of people and activities and sights. Make your description express a significant pattern within all this variety, one that would express what you feel is the essence of this particular place.
4. Write an analysis of the kind of community Alfred Kazin grew up in, and the attitude he had toward that community, based on the specific details he uses in his description of "the block and beyond."

CHAPTER FIVE

PEOPLE

Introduction: Concreteness and Generalization

An autobiographical record invariably tells not only what happened and where, but with whom. In most accounts of personal experience much of what a writer has to say about himself emerges through what he says about his relationships with other people. An autobiographer introduces other characters in order to create a context for his own life, since his role as principal actor would make very little sense if the rest of the stage always remained empty. But any revelations about other people also constitute a form of self-revelation. When we characterize a friend, an enemy, even some slight acquaintance, there is always an implicit element of self-characterization, for we are revealing what we value in another person, what we distrust or even abhor, whom we depend upon and why.

Characterization also introduces a new dimension in the autobiographical writer's method of organizing his experience. Narration leads us immediately to think about time, description about space. But characterization depends much more upon the isolation of qualities that strike us through recurrence; it requires us to sort out the habitual from the occasional as a way of identifying who we think another person really is. Of course we often rely on narration or description to create the portrait of a particular human being. We may dramatize a moment of generosity or heroism or affection as a vivid illustration of character, or we may provide a detailed description of someone's face or style of dress as a significant confirmation of their basic qualities. But each time we do, we are usually calling upon our memories of other particular occasions as well, using them as a basis for judging the representativeness of the moment we are dramatizing or describing.

Our sense of what characterization is may be warped by memories of articles about "The Most Unforgettable Person I Ever Met," articles that relied on the drama of single chance meetings or sudden unexpected revelations. In such accounts, a vivid character stands out, like The Lone Ranger, as someone who does his impressive deed and then disappears into the sunset. It is much more likely, however, that the persons who get considerable attention in our autobiographies will be those about whom we feel deeply and with whom we have relations of long standing, not someone who reveals himself in a single moment of dramatic crisis. Personal memories usually involve parents, relatives, lovers, husbands or wives, close friends, professional associates—a whole range of people whose characters emerge for us through a long cumulative experience. As a result many writers tend to emphasize recurrent events and habitual conduct. Compare, for example, the methods used in the selections that follow when a writer is remembering his or her own father. The writers may begin in their own minds with memories of specific moments, but they select those memories that they identify as part of a persistent pattern in their father's behavior.

The selection by Frank O'Connor illustrates the writer's use of representative conduct as a basis for characterization. O'Connor provides a series of sketches of his father's activities at home—reading the paper after work, writing letters about his pension, fixing his pipe, making fumbling attempts to do repair work. In every instance, O'Connor stresses how he is telling us of things his father did habitually, actions that the writer can visualize in great detail but that he refuses to locate at a specific moment. O'Connor never says "One morning in May" or "On the day of my sixth birthday"; he prefers "often" or "usually" or "whenever." He will frequently introduce an account of his father's behavior with a sentence establishing a general trait of his father's character; then whatever follows gives us details that are specific examples and yet not single instances of that trait.

> Nothing could ever persuade Father that he was anything but a naturally home-loving body—which, indeed, for a great part of the time, he was. Nobody but himself could lock up the house for the night, and he had a big bolt for the back door and two bolts for the front, and only he could properly check the catch on the window, wind the alarm on the clock, and see that the lamp was out before we retired.

The process by which an autobiographical writer characterizes another person, then, is often similar to the one used by O'Connor. The writer sifts the random memories of his relations with someone in order to find some pattern of recurrence that leads him to make generalizations. In effect, he uses a cluster of narrations and descriptions and begins to bind them together into analogous groupings. O'Connor, for example, may have begun with mental images of his father doing a whole series of commonplace tasks. These memories all showed the father taking comfort and pleasure in being at home and willingly performing a number of household chores. As a result, O'Connor creates a generalization, a statement that expresses the common ground shared by these memories. The generalization establishes the father as a "naturally home-loving body" (we will discuss the qualifications in O'Connor's sentence a bit later) and provides a focus for specific memories that serve in the quoted passage to substantiate the father's characteristic of being home-loving. The passage also illustrates how, although we organize our experiences by moving from a particular impression to a larger generalization, we are likely to reverse this movement in our written account. We can usually see our own way more clearly and direct the reader more forcefully if, like O'Connor, we begin with a statement general enough to include the more particular impressions that follow: "any project of Father's . . . involved preparation on a major scale"; "he was one of the most awkward men who ever handled a tool."

Whether generalizations precede or follow the specific memories that foster them is not especially significant, but the interrelationship of the two determines the effectiveness of the writer's characterization. Any generalization represents a conclusion based on some evidence, and if it is an important conclusion—one the writer wishes his readers to take note of and agree with—he must be careful to include some of the evidence that led to it. His task is to be both convincing and economical; not all of the evidence is required, only the most compelling. O'Connor might have decided to narrate a single dramatic event to "prove" his father a homebody or to present a single detailed description of his father comfortably settled in his chair next to the hearth with his pipe and paper. Instead he provides several brief examples, all of which contribute to the cumulative impression of his father that fits the general term O'Connor introduced at the start.

Although as writers we frequently rely on narration and description to give body to more general statements we wish to make, we are not restricted only to these two methods. We may find we can communicate our sense of someone's character more clearly by thinking of him in relation to someone else (father as a homebody in contrast to his well-traveled brother). Again, our memories can shift away from the immediate subject to focus on our associations with it (O'Connor's characterization of his father going through his discharge papers: "he would be moved like an old novelist re-reading a review of his first talented book"). In such cases we would still be making our generalizations clearer by particularizing them, but we would be moving away from memories of a specific moment or scene from the past and instead making use of comparison or analogy to create images that indirectly illuminate our subject. Whatever kind of particularization we choose—narrative illustration, descriptive illustration, a sequence of examples, comparison, analogy, or some combination among them—we are reassuring the reader that our generalizations are based on actual experience.

Our generalizations themselves then provide the basis for the overall shape of our biographical account. In other words, the general terms that we have used in naming the qualities of a person's character become in their turn the bases for developing a larger pattern of organization. We can see that O'Connor has such a larger pattern firmly in mind when he begins by first saying, not that his father was a "naturally home-loving body," but rather that nobody could persuade his father he wasn't this type of person. After we have read the entire selection, we realize that O'Connor qualifies the generalization about his father as home-loving because he will later show us how his father, when out of control on an alcoholic binge, will quite literally strip the house bare, pawning everything saleable in order to pay for his drinks. O'Connor wants to begin his portrait with an account of his father's domestic feelings partially to create a sense of ironic contrast with what he later reveals, partially to introduce a more winning and kindly side of his father's character before he tells of the destructive side. If we learned of the father's drinking and its impact on the home at the outset of O'Connor's characterization, we might refuse any sympathetic attention to the Father's more attractive human qualities.

Studying the examples of characterization in this section shows us how autobiographical writing can remain autobiographical and yet move away from the temporal organization of narrative and the spatial organization of description (forms of organization that dominated the two preceding chapters). As we have seen, narration and description often contribute to characterization, but they are subordinated to a pattern of ideas about general qualities that reveal the nature of the character. We may think of a person as energetic, friendly, hard-working, ambitious, quick-tempered, efficient; then we must decide which of these impressions should be used in our characterization and in what order and relationship they should be introduced. We obviously would not adopt a simple narrative organization, telling of each quality as it first manifested itself in the character's actions, nor would we rely only on describing the character at home, at work, at the beach, on the tennis court. What we do instead is to establish a sequence of relationships among the concepts that we have associated with the other person, a sequence that makes us feel we have communicated something significant about the other person's nature as it touched our own. The result may be a classification of features in the order of their importance, or a division into public and private, or a contrast between the life-enhancing and the self-destructive. We may define the person the way N. Scott Momaday presents his grandmother, placing her within the traditions of American Indian experience and making her represent an entire cultural tradition. Or we may create another kind of comparison by using another person's attitudes and characteristics as a way of revealing our own values, as Lillian Hellman does in her memoir of Dashiell Hammett. Another possibility is to select one or two extraordinary traits and to emphasize their persistence in a range of situations, as James Thurber does, with wonderful comic effect, in telling the story of Doc Marlowe.

Since characterization involves the writer in a search for patterns of recurrence and relationship, it makes him particularly aware of the need for some kind of general organization that would govern the account of his life. Because it can follow whatever direction an individual life may take, autobiography is an especially permissive form, and a writer may feel a sense of relief that with autobiography he does not have to maintain the rigorous logic demanded by an argumentative or expository essay. But the autobiographer cannot simply reproduce on paper the random images of an evening's reverie; although he may begin with disconnected memories, he must discover some comprehensible shape that will make these memories communicable to others. For example, Joan Baez decides to organize her memories of her father around his ethical character and, although she touches on many aspects of her father's life, she keeps returning to ways in which he provided her with valuable moral counsel and example. Studying such characterizations created by other writers can help us with the problem of self-characterization, the ultimate goal of autobiography, and can prepare us to search for an appropriate design within the rich tangle of our memories.

⌐ Frank O'Connor ⌐

(1903-1966)

See the biographical note on page 26. O'Connor wrote two autobiographies, An Only Child *(1958), about his early life in Cork, from which this selection is taken, and* My Father's Son *(1968), about his emergence into the literary world and his friendships with other Irish writers.*

CHILD, I KNOW YOU'RE GOING TO MISS ME

[AN IRISH FATHER]

Father was a really fine-looking man. He was a six-footer and built to match, and years of work as a navvy had not affected the soldierly erectness of bearing he had picked up as a young man in the Army. He had a long Scandinavian head, but because of the slightly Mongolian cast of feature he had inherited from Grandmother, the lines of his face were horizontal instead of vertical. At the same time the bulge of the brows and the height of the cheekbones, instead of making his eyes seem weak, made them look as though they were twinkling. He was extraordinarily like certain photographs of the young Maxim Gorky. He dressed carefully, in the manner of an old-fashioned tradesman, in a blue serge suit with the cuffs of the trousers turned down over the heels, a bowler hat cocked a little to one side, and a starched shirt-front. Dressing him for Mass on Sunday was a serious task for any woman, for his fingers were all thumbs. He could rarely fasten his own studs,

From Frank O'Connor: *An Only Child.* Copyright © 1958, 1959, 1960, 1961 by Frank O'Connor. Reprinted by permission of Alfred A. Knopf, Inc.

and it sometimes ended with his stamping and cursing before
the big mirror, and Mother's grabbing at a stool to stand on, so
that she could reach up to him, and begging him for the Lord's
sake to keep quiet and let her do it for him. Then he put an
open white handkerchief, casually disposed, in his breast
pocket, and went down the road, graciously bowing and raising his hat to any woman he met, a fine figure of a man, and as
vain as a child in his first sailor suit. In the "tall tales" he
loved to tell of his soldiering days there was a great favourite
of his about a review held by Queen Victoria during which
she said: "And tell me, General, who is that distinguished-
looking man in the second rank?" to which the general replied: "That, Your Majesty, is Michael O'Donovan, one of the
best-looking men in your whole army."

Nothing could ever persuade Father that he was anything
but a naturally home-loving body—which, indeed, for a great
part of the time, he was. Nobody but himself could lock up the
house for the night, and he had a big bolt for the back door
and two bolts for the front, and only he could properly check
the catch on the window, wind the alarm on the clock, and see
that the lamp was out before we retired. Often he would be up
first in the morning, give Mother a cup of tea in bed, and have
a tremendous wash-up under the tap in the yard, winter and
summer. Indeed, if there was snow he rubbed himself all over
with it because it prevented chilblains. It was a bitter disappointment to him that I was a sissy, and he made angry comments when I drew a basin of water and then poured hot water
from the kettle into it. When he got in from work in the evening, he usually had a more leisurely, noisy wash, changed
into old trousers and "slippers" that were old boots cut down
and hacked in all directions so that the leather did not press
on his corns, and, with his cap on to protect his head from
drafts, sat at the head of the table by the window to read the
evening *Echo* aloud to Mother, with comments that went on
longer than the news. He began with the Police Court news to
put him into good humour, and reserved for the last the polit-

ical meetings, which made him scowl and mutter. "Oh, that unspeakable scut, George Crosbie!" I liked that till I began to read myself, but even then it did not disturb me much, for I was always too involved in what I read even to notice when neighbours dropped in.

This was just as well, because any project of Father's, from cutting his corns to writing to Whitehall about his pension, involved preparation on a major scale and something like general mobilization, and in any detail of this he could become entirely lost. For instance, when he wrote to Whitehall—this usually meant no more than filling out some form to show he was still alive—he had first of all to get the penny bottle of ink, and a new nib for the pen, and a bit of blotting-paper, and lay them all out on the table before him; then he had to get his papers, which were in a locked tin trunk in the bedroom, and he could never take one of these out without re-reading the lot: and on going through his discharge papers and discovering again what a model soldier he had been, he would be moved like an old novelist re-reading a review of his first talented book, and would have to bring them down and read them all over again to Mother, who knew them by heart. Every question on a questionnaire he read over several times before replying to it, because he knew it had been drafted by an old and cunning hand with the deliberate intention of catching him out. When he spotted the trap—and there nearly always was a trap—his whole face lit up with approval and he explained the problem carefully to Mother while he considered how best to handle it. He liked a subtle enemy because it enabled him to show how subtle he could be himself. He was a born hob-lawyer, always laying down the law about regulations, and greatly looked up to by other old soldiers, like Bill Heffernan, who were too humble even to pretend that they knew what the War Office wanted of them. When the form was filled out and in its envelope on the mantelpiece, and Mother had been warned that she must post it with her own hand and not entrust it to me, he would become emotional again about the goodness of the British Government and its consideration for its old servants—unlike the gnats of employers he worked for in Cork, who would see an old workman dying in the streets and not lift a hand to help him. The pension meant much more to him than the trifle of money it represented. It gave him a personal interest in the British Government. A Liberal Government might be good for the Irish cause, but a Conservative one would be better for the pension. It gave him wild dreams, because no quarter passed without his toying with the idea of compounding it for a capital sum, the size of which staggered imagination. It gave him the prospect of a happy old age, for when Mother died he could hand it in in return for provision in one of the military hospitals like Chelsea or Kilmainham where every day for the rest of his life he would get his pint of beer for nothing.

When the time came to cut his corns, he got a chair and rooted about on top of the wardrobe, which was his hidey-hole, well out of my reach, or intended to be; and after contemplating his many treasures, he took down his current razor, wrapped in oiled cloth, and a couple of other, older razors that he had either abandoned or picked up from those who had no further use for them but that could be trusted to do the rough work of corn-cutting. Then he got the wash-basin, and a jug of cold water, and a kettle of boiling water, and a bottle of corn cure, and a paper of some sort to read while his feet soaked, and a hand mirror to see the parts of his feet that were normally hard to see, and anything else that could conceivably be of use to him, and then, with Mother or myself lined up to hold the mirror, he was set for the evening. Not that I ever remember his doing it without cutting himself.

Or else it was an evening with his pipes. He was an inveterate magpie, and everything that anyone else threw away Father would pick up, in the full conviction that if you kept it for seven years it would be bound to come in useful, while the person who had discarded it would probably pay for his improvidence by dying in the workhouse. Old broken pipes were a tremendous temptation to him, and he had a large collection of bowls and stems, all of which needed only careful handling to turn them into brand-new pipes of the most expensive kind. This task would have been considerably easier if he had ever had anything like a gimlet handy, but as he rarely did, he had to make a tool. Usually, the treasure chest yielded some sort of blade, and some sort of handle, and the blade had to be heated and set in the handle, and then the handle usually burst and had to be bound with a bit of string or wax-end. Then the improvised tool had to be heated again, and the bowl or the stem burned till the two pieces could be joined. I can still remember the rancid smell of burned amber. The result was usually most peculiar—a delicate bowl joined to a colossal stem or a delicate stem to a rural bowl—but Father puffed it with great satisfaction, in the belief that he had cheated some ruffian of a tobacco merchant out of the price of a brand-new pipe.

Father was, I think, a naturally melancholy man; though he was always pleased when people called, he rarely called on anybody himself; and, like all melancholy men, he made his home his cave, and devoted a great deal of thought to its beauty and utility. Unfortunately, he was one of the most awkward men who ever handled a tool, and it is a subject·I can speak on with some authority, for I have inherited his awkwardness. Along with the razors, the pipe bowls and stems and the rest, he had a peculiar hoard of tools and equipment, mostly stored on top of the wardrobe. They had been lovingly accumulated over the years in the conviction that eventually they would be bound to come in useful. Prior to tackling any major job, all this had to be unloaded onto the kitchen table, and Father put on his glasses and studied it affectionately in the way in which he studied the documents in the tin trunk, forgetting whatever he was supposed to be looking for as he recited the history of hinges, bolts, screws, wooden handles, blades, clock springs, and mysterious-looking bits of machinery that had probably fallen out of a railway engine in process of dissolution, and wondered what some of them could be used for.

Finally, having selected his equipment—the nice bit of timber that would nearly do for a shelf, and the brackets that didn't quite match, and the screws or nails that were either a bit too long or a bit too short, and the old chisel that would do for a screw-driver, and the hammer with the loose head—Father set to work. He had lined up my mother and myself as builder's mates, to hold the plank and the hammer, the saw that needed setting, and the nails and screws. Before he had been at work for five minutes, the top of the hammer would have flown off and hit him in the face, or the saw would have cut the chair instead of the plank, or the nail that was to have provided the setting for the screw would have carried away inches of the plank with the unmerciful wallops he gave it. Father had the secret of making inanimate objects appear to possess a secret, malevolent life of their own, and sometimes it was hard to believe that his tools and materials were not really in a conspiracy against him.

His first reaction to this behaviour was chagrin that, for all his love and care, they were turning on him again, but this soon changed to blind rage and an autocratic determination to put them in their places. Hacking away great chunks of the plaster, he nailed in the brackets any old way, while Mother and I, our hearts in our mouths, stood by with anything we thought might come in handy. He swore bloody murder, exactly as he did when the studs in his shirt-front turned against him before Mass on Sunday and it became a toss-up whether, to spite them, he might not go to Mass at all; and in the same gentle voice Mother besought him to let it alone and not to be upsetting himself like that. And when it was all over, and the kitchen a wreck, he would sit down with gloomy pride to read a paper he could not concentrate on, obsessed by the image of himself as a good man and kind father on whom everybody and everything turned.

That was why, in spite of the fact that he had a cobbler's last among his treasures, and that I was forever hacking the good boots that were bought for me with his money, he didn't often try his hand at cobbling. A man who could hardly hit a three-inch nail with a large hammer could not be expected to do much with a shoemaker's tack. Most often it was Mother who did the cobbling, buying a patch or a pair of half-soles in town and tacking them on herself. But I seem to remember that his hoarding instinct betrayed him once when he discovered a large strip of fan-belting from a factory, made of some extraordinary material which he maintained was stronger than leather and would save us a fortune, and he did cut strips off this and nail them to his working boots, on which they looked like pieces of board. On the other hand, he liked rough tailoring, and was perfectly happy sewing a patch onto his working trousers.

But I never minded Father as a handyman the way I minded him as a barber. He always had one pair of clippers, and sometimes two, wrapped in oil rags among the other treasures, and, according to him, these clippers had saved him untold expense. Given a pencil and paper, he could even work it out, as he worked out the amount he saved by being a teetotaller. He was a great man for saving. "My couple of ha'pence," he used to call it. Mother, I suspect, never knew how much he really earned, and when he was sober he usually had a substantial sum in the locked trunk in the bedroom. When he was feeling depressed, he went upstairs by way of consulting his documents and counted it softly, but not so softly that we couldn't hear the chink of the coins as he caressed them. He was a bit of a skinflint and disliked the improvident way Mother bought me sweets, biscuits, or boys' weeklies, not to mention toys at Christmas—a season that seemed to have been specially invented for his mortification. Father, of course, was only providing for the rainy day.

So, on a sunny afternoon, he would take down the clippers, pull off the oily rags, adjust the blades, set a chair in the back yard, and, with a towel round his neck, let Mother cut his hair. There was no great difficulty about this, since all Father wanted was the equivalent to a close shave. According to him, this was excellent for the growth of the hair, and one of his ambitions was to double his savings by protecting my hair as well. I didn't want my hair protected, though he assured me angrily that I would be bald before I was grown up at all; neither did Mother want it, and so, the moment it grew a bit too long and she saw Father casting brooding glances at it, she gave me tuppence to go to the barber. This made Father furious, for not only had she again demonstrated her fundamental improvidence, but Curtin, the barber, would have left me with what Father called "a most unsightly mop." It was like the business of wanting me to wash under the tap. But no matter how carefully she watched over me, he sometimes caught me with the clippers in his hand, and I had to sit on a chair in the back yard, sobbing and sniffling, while he got to work on me and turned me into a laughing-stock for the neighbourhood. He went about it in exactly the same way that he went about cutting his corns or putting up a shelf. "Wisha, is it the way you want to make the child look like a convict?" Mother would cry indignantly, and Father would stamp and curse and pull at a whole chunk of hair till I screamed, and then curse again and shout: "It's your own fault, you little puppy, you! Why can't you stop quiet?"

Then one evening Father would be late, and Mother and I would sit over the fire, half crazy with panic, and I would say prayers to the Sacred Heart and the Blessed Virgin to look after him. I can never remember that my prayers had any effect. Finally, he would come in, full of fallacious good humour, and stand at the door, rubbing his palms and puckering up his lips in a sly grin. He expressed great—indeed, undue—surprise at the lateness of the hour. He had been detained talking to a man he hadn't met for fifteen years—not since the funeral of poor Jack Murphy of the Connaught Rangers in September '98, which he remembered distinctly because Tim O'Connor, God rest him, had been there as well, and the three of them had left the funeral together and spent the evening in a pub called Keohane's that used to be at the corner of Windmill Road but had since been torn down. He would ramble on like that for half an hour, in loosely related clauses that gave the impression of coherence but were difficult to follow, and toward ten o'clock would decide to take a little stroll. That was the end of Father in his role as a home-loving body. Next evening he would slink upstairs to the locked trunk where he kept his savings, and then go out again. The rainy day had at last arrived. He would return in a state of noisy amiability that turned to sullenness when it failed to rouse a response. I was most often to blame for this because, in spite of Mother's appeals to me not to answer him back, I could not bear his maudlin attentions, which made him so like my grandmother, and, like her, he was offended, and snarled that I was "better fed than taught." The day after, he would not go to work and at twelve or one would be at the trunk again and off for a longer carouse.

The savings usually lasted him for a week or ten days. When they were exhausted, Mother had to go to the pawnshop with his best blue suit. So that the neighbours would not see what she was doing, she would put on her long black shawl. I hated the very sight of that shawl, even though I knew that it suited her long, thin, virginal face; it meant an immediate descent in the social scale from the "hatties" to the "shawlies"—the poorest of the poor. I also hated the pawning of the blue suit, because it meant that Father stopped going for walks or to Mass—especially to Mass, for he would not have dreamed of worshipping God in anything less dignified than blue serge—and it meant that we had him all day about the house, his head swollen, his eyes bloodshot, sitting by the fire and shivering in the fever of alcoholism or getting up and walking to and fro, unable to read, unable to work, unable to think of anything except drink. Home was no longer a refuge for him. It had become a prison and a cage, and the only hope of escaping from it was more money. When Mother returned from town and put the five or six shillings on the table with the pawn tickets, he sometimes turned on her with an angry "Lord God, was that all you got on it?" It was not so much that he expected more as that staging a quarrel at this point meant that she would not dare to ask him for money for food, or the rent, or the insurance, or Levin the peddler, who had sold her a suit for me.

Two days later she would be off again with one of the two clocks—her own clock from the bedroom, which did not have an alarm. After that came the clock with the alarm, which was no longer necessary as he did not go to work, and then his silver watch. "In God's name, Mick Donovan, do you want to put us on the street?" she would cry, and he would stamp and shout like a madman. He didn't know what being put on the street meant as she, the orphan, did. Then her blue costume went, and his military medals, and, lastly, his "ring paper"— so called because it was printed in a series of small circles intended for the post-office date stamp—his authority for drawing his Army pension. Though the transaction was illegal, the security was excellent. Even then he would be greedily eying the wedding ring on her finger and whining at her to pawn this as well, "just for a couple of days till I steady up," but it was only when she was really desperate that she let this go, and it took precedence of everything else when the time came to reclaim the little bits of married life. By this time all the money coming into the house would be the ninepence or shilling she earned as a charwoman, and he would be striding like a caged tiger up and down the kitchen in the dusk, waiting for her to come in from work so that he could get this from her.

"Come on!" he would say with forced joviality. "Tuppence is all I want. Me entrance fee!"

"And where am I to get the child's dinner?" she would cry in despair. "Or is it the way you want us to starve?"

"Look, it's all over now. No one is going to starve. Can't you see I'm steadying up? Come on, woman, give us the money!"

"Stay here, then, and I'll go and get it for you!"

"I don't want you to get it for me," he would say, turning nasty. "Getting it for him" was a later stage, which occurred only when he had completely exhausted his credit and old friends cleared out when he came red-eyed and fighting mad into the pub. With his "entrance fee," as he called it, he had not only the price of a drink but the chance of cadging more, either from the barmaid, if the publican was out, or from one of his old cronies.

If he did not get the money immediately, his tone would change again and he would become whining and maudlin. As night came on and his chances of a real debauch diminished, he would grow vicious. "Jesus Christ, I'll put an end to this!" he would mutter, and take down his razor. His threats were never empty, as I well knew since the night when I was an infant and he flung the two of us out into Blarney Lane in our night clothes, and we shivered there in the roadway till some neighbours took us in and let us lie in blankets before the fire. Whenever he brandished the razor at Mother, I went into hysterics, and a couple of times I threw myself on him, beating him with my fists. That drove her into hysterics, too, because she knew that at times like that he would as soon have slashed me as her. Later, in adolescence, I developed pseudo-epileptic fits that were merely an externalization of this recurring nightmare, and though I knew they were not real, and was ashamed of myself for indulging in them at all, I could not resist them when once I had yielded to the first nervous spasm.

In those days, the house would be a horror. Only when he had money for drink would we have peace for an hour, and sometimes Mother borrowed it just to get him out of the house. When I was old enough to go to school, I would come back at three o'clock and scout round to make sure that he was not at home. If he wasn't, I would sneak in and hastily make myself a cup of tea. If he was, I did without the tea and wandered round the rest of the afternoon, waiting till it was time to intercept Mother on her way home from work. I never went near my grandmother. From the moment Father began his drinking bout, you could feel her disapproval of Mother and me— the two heartless creatures who did not sympathize with her darling son. This, she seemed to say, all came of Father's mistake in marrying a woman who did not know her place, a would-be lady. When I talked of him to Mother, I always called him "he" or "him," carefully eschewing the name of "Father" which would have seemed like profanation to me. "You must not speak like that of your father, child," Mother would say severely. "Whatever he does, he's still your father." I resented her loyalty to him. I wanted her to talk to me about him the way I knew the neighbours talked. They could not understand why she did not leave him. I realize now that to do so she would have had to take a job as housekeeper and put me into an orphanage—the one thing in the world that the orphan child could not do.

It always ended in the same way—only when we were completely destitute; when the shop-keepers refused Mother even a loaf of bread, and the landlord threatened us with eviction, and Father could no longer raise the price of a single pint. At that point only did he give in—"cave in" better describes what really happened to him. Sour and savage and silent, he began to look for another job. He rarely went back to the job he had left, and in those days I believed it was because he had lost it. Now I am certain that he was far too good a workman to be put off because of a drinking bout, however prolonged, and that he was too humiliated to go back. To have done that would have been to admit his weakness and guilt. He was, as I have said, a proud man, and he would never have admitted to the other poor labourers, whom he despised, that he had sunk so low. And because something had to be done about the mass of debt that had accumulated in the meantime, he and Mother would have to go to the loan office in Paul Street, accompanied by some friend to act as guarantor. Mother had to go with him, because even at this stage he would still have taken the money and drunk it along with the rest. I was very impressed by the big interest we had to pay, and it struck me that if only I could accumulate a little capital and lend them the money myself, it would be an excellent way both of getting rich and of saving Mother anxiety—the money would, at least, be in the family. But my own savings usually evaporated in the first few days of strain, and I realized that I would need a more settled background before I could set up in business as a money-lender.

With the aid of the loan, Father would take out his "ring paper" and draw his pension, and out of that he would release his best suit, so that he could again worship God on Sundays in the Dominican Church on the Sand Quay. Then would come the clocks and the watch and chain and the military medals, and finally Mother's blue costume. It was characteristic of him that when he started to put money aside again, it was to pay the publicans. He preferred to let Mother work for a shilling a day rather than defer the payment of his drinking debts. It would seem to be obvious that he was only preparing the way for another debauch—because this, in fact, was the ultimate effect of it—and yet I should still say that this was untrue. I am sure it was pride that moved him. I don't think Mother had much pride. Gay people have no need of pride because gaiety is merely the outward sign of inward integrity, but Father had no integrity; as with all mentally sick people, the two sides of his nature hardly communicated and were held together by pins and Hail Marys, and pride was one of the ways in which he protected the false conception of his own character that was one side.

And once again the little house was reconstituted about that incomplete conception of Father as a home-loving body, and a new cycle began. Brisk and cheerful, he rose in the early morning to wash under the tap and bring Mother a cup of tea in bed, and in the evenings he read the *Echo* to her while I sat in some corner, absorbed in my own boys' weekly, and a wind blew up the river and seemed to isolate us as on a ship at sea. On such evenings, no one could doubt his love for her or hers for him, but I, who had no other security, knew better than she did what he was really like, and watched him suspiciously, in the way that only a child can watch, and felt that all authority was only a pretense and that God Himself was probably not much better, and directed my prayers not to Him, but to His mother, who had said nothing but merely suffered.

Because I was jealous of him, I knew that there was real devotion between that strangely assorted pair, and yet I often wonder what really went on in Mother's mind during those terrible years. I think when she wasn't entirely desperate, pity was what was uppermost in her mind, pity for this giant of a man who had no more self-knowledge or self-control than a baby. The least pain could bewilder and madden him and even a toothache could drive him to drink. He died as he had lived, wandering about Cork, looking for drink when he was in the last stages of pneumonia, and I, who might have controlled him, was not informed because it would upset me too much, and besides Mother felt I wouldn't understand. Even God wouldn't understand. Whenever his anniversary came round, she withdrew into herself for weeks, and, without a word to anyone, the offering for Masses was sent to the Cistercians at Mount Melleray, because God might fail to realize that poor Father really was at heart a home-loving body and a good husband and father, and might keep him too long in Purgatory, a place he would not be happy in at all because he could not stand pain, and even a toothache would drive him mad.

Once only did she say anything significant, and that was while she was raving. I was a grown man and living in Dublin, and I came back to Cork on holiday to find her desperately ill, and poor Father—the world's most hopeless man with his hands—devotedly nursing her with nothing but neat whisky. I blasted him for not wiring for me, and he snarled back: "How could I, when she wouldn't let me?" And then he sat over the fire, flapping his hands and snivelling: "What would I do without her?" When I had made her comfortable for the night, I sat with her, holding her hand, and heard her muttering about me as though I were not there.

"God! God!" she whispered. "He raised me from the gutter

where the world threw me. He raised me from the gutter where the world threw me!"

1. *What kind of household jobs does O'Connor describe his father as doing? How do they help characterize the man?*

2. *O'Connor writes at length of several of his father's habitual activities (filling out a government form, cutting his corns, mending a pipe), activities that would ordinarily strike a reader as trivial and not worth mentioning. Why do you think O'Connor presents them in detail? How does he make them of greater interest than you might expect?*

3. *When and how does O'Connor introduce the subject of his father's drinking? What sort of attitude does O'Connor have toward his father? How is his attitude toward his mother different? Do you think O'Connor seems detached or emotionally involved in the story of his family?*

4. *How does O'Connor manage to give variety and pace to his account of his father's behavior? What sustains your interest through this lengthy characterization?*

5. *Read the interview with O'Connor in the first section of this book. In what ways do his comments there about his values and his methods as a writer help you to understand what he has done here?*

∽ Joan Baez ∽

(1941-   )

Joan Baez began singing publicly in coffee shops and at folk concerts around Boston. She became nationally known during the 1960s, both because of her talents as a singer and because of her strong opposition to American military involvement in Vietnam. Today she continues a highly successful career as a songwriter, performer, and recording artist. Her autobiography, Daybreak *(1966), deals with her early life, her strong family ties, and her political, social, and musical interests.*

MY FATHER

My father is short, honest, dark, and very handsome. He's good, he's a good man. He was born in Mexico, and brought up in Brooklyn. His father was a Mexican who left the Catholic church to become a Methodist minister. My father worked hard in school. He loved God and the church and his parents. At one time in his life he was going to be a minister, but the hypocrisy of the church bothered him and he became a scientist instead. He has a vision of how science can play the major role in saving the world. This vision puts a light into his eyes. He is a compulsive worker, and I know that he will never stop his work long enough to have a look at some of the things in his life which are blind and tragic. But it's not my business to print. About me and my father I don't know. I keep thinking of how hard it was for him to say anything nice about me to my face. Maybe he favored me and felt guilty about it, but he couldn't say anything nice. A lot of times I thought he would break my heart. Once he complimented me for something I was wearing. "You ought to wear that kind of thing more often," he said, and I looked into the mirror and I was wearing a black dress which I hated. I was fourteen then and I remember thinking, "Hah. I remind him of his mother in this thing."

My father is the saint of the family. You work at something until you exhaust yourself, so that you can be good at it, and with it you try to improve the lot of the sad ones, the hungry ones, the sick ones. You raise your children trying to teach them decency and respect for human life. Once when I was about thirteen he asked me if I would accept a large sum of money for the death of a man who was going to die anyway. I didn't quite understand. If I was off the hook, and just standing by, and then the man was killed by someone else, why shouldn't I take a couple of million? I told him sure, I'd take the money, and he laughed his head off. "That's immoral," he said. I didn't know what immoral meant, but I knew something was definitely wrong taking money for a man's life.

Once in my life I spent a month alone with my father. In 1950, when he was assigned to a project in Baghdad, Iraq, for UNESCO, my sisters got jaundice, and couldn't leave the States. My father left on schedule, for a month of briefing in Paris before going to Baghdad. I had jaundice too, but I didn't tell anyone. I wanted very badly to go to Paris. So despite bad pains in my stomach and black urine which I flushed in a hurry so he wouldn't see, and a general yellow hue which was creeping over my skin, and sometimes seemed to be tinting everything I looked at, I took full advantage of that time with my old man in Gay Paree. We bicycled everywhere, and bought long fresh bread and cheese and milk. We sat in outdoor cafés and had tea, and while he was busy at UNESCO house, I would run the elevators and visit secretaries and draw pictures of everyone and go off to feed pigeons in the park. Neither of us spoke French, but we faked it. One night in a restaurant, we couldn't understand anything on the dessert menu, so my father took a gamble and said, *"Ça, s'il vous plaît,"* pointing to the word *"Confiture,"* and they brought him a dish of strawberry jam, which he ate.

Once the family was together in Baghdad, I developed a terrible fear that my father was going to die. The fact is he almost killed himself tampering with the stupid brick oven which had to be lit in order to get hot bath water. He was "experimenting" with it—trying to determine how fast he could get the fire going by increasing the flow of kerosene into the oven. It exploded in his face, setting his clothes on fire and giving him third degree burns on his hands and face. He covered his eyes instinctively, or he would probably have been blinded, but his eyelashes and eyebrows were burned off anyway. Pauline passed out after telling Mother that "Popsy is on fire," and Mother wrapped him up in a sheet and called the English hospital for an ambulance. While we waited for the ambulance, my father tapped his feet in rhythm on the kitchen tiles, and cleared his throat every four or five seconds. He smelled terrible, and except for Mother, we just stood there. I was probably praying. Mother took me to the hospital to see him once, and I felt bad because I got dizzy when I saw his hands. They had big pussy blisters on them, and his face looked like a Rice Krispie, and I wanted to make him feel better, but I also wanted to go stick my head out the window and get some fresh air. When he came home from the hospital he was bandaged so that all you could see were his eyes and his ears. He held classes for his students at home. He is a brilliant teacher, and they loved him. I know they loved him, because the room smelled so awful from burnt flesh and Middle East medication that I felt sick every time I passed his door. And they came every day to learn and to see him.

My father teaches physics. He is a Ph.D. in physics, and we all wish he'd had just one boy who wasn't so opposed to school, to degrees, to formal education of any kind. One child to show some interest when he does physics experiments at the dinner table. But then it must be partly because we felt obligated to

271

be student-types that we have all rebelled so completely. I can barely read. That is to say, I would rather do a thousand things before sitting down to read.

He used to tell us we should read the dictionary. He said it was fun and very educational. I've never gotten into it.

When we lived in Clarence Center, New York (it was a town of eight hundred people, and as far as they knew, we were niggers; Mother says that someone yelled out the window to me, "Hey, nigger!" and I said, "You ought to see me in the summertime!"), my father had a job working in Buffalo. It was some kind of armaments work. I just knew that it was secret, or part of it was secret, and that we began to get new things like a vacuum cleaner, a refrigerator, a fancy coffee pot, and one day my father came home with a little Crosley car. We were so excited about it that we drove it all over the front lawn, around the trees and through the piles of leaves. He was driving, Mother was in the front seat, and we three kids were in the back. The neighbors knew we were odd to begin with, but this confirmed it. Mother was embarrassed and she kept clutching my father's arm and saying, "Oh, Abo!" but he would take a quick corner around a tree and we'd all scream with laughter and Mother gave up and had hysterics.

Then something started my father going to Quaker meetings. We all had to go. It meant we had to sit and squelch giggles for about twenty minutes, and then go off with some kind old lady who planted each of us a bean in a tin can, and told us it was a miracle that it would push its little head up above the damp earth and grow into a plant. We knew it was a miracle, and we knew she was kind, but we made terrible fun of her the entire time and felt guilty about it afterwards.

While we were in the side room with the kind old lady, watching our beans perform miracles, my father was in the grown-up room, the room where they observe silence for a whole hour, and he was having a fight with his conscience. It took him less than a year of those confrontations with himself in that once a week silence to realize that he would have to give up either the silences or his job. Next thing I knew we were packing up and moving across the country. My father had taken a job as a professor of physics at the University of Redlands for about one-half the pay, and one-tenth the prestige—against the advice of everyone he knew except my mother. Since leaving Buffalo in 1947, he's never accepted a job that had anything to do with armaments, offense, defense, or whatever they prefer to call it. Last night I had a dream about him. I dreamed he was sitting next to himself in a theater. One of him was as he is now, and the other was the man of thirty years ago. I kept trying to get him to look at himself and say hello. Both faces smiled very understandingly, but neither would turn to greet the other.

I don't think he's ever understood me very well. He's never understood my compulsiveness, my brashness, my neuroses, my fears, my antinationalism (though he's changing on that), my sex habits, my loose way of handling money. I think often I startle him, and many times I please him. Sometimes I have put him through hell, like when I decided to live with Michael when I was twenty. "You mean you're going to . . . *live* with him?" "Yes," I said, and my father took a sleeping bag and went to the beach for two days, because Michael was staying in the house. Years later he sent me an article by Bertrand Russell, whom he respects very much, underlining the part which said that if young people could have a chance at "experimental marriages" while they were in college, they might know more about what it's all about before they actually got married. My father wrote that it always amazed him how I came to conclusions intuitively which took him years to realize.

. . .

Lately my father has told me, off and on, that he is 100 percent behind me in the things I do. I think that's hard for him to say, for lots of reasons, one being the reason I mentioned earlier—that he has trouble telling me nice things about myself or what I do. Another is that he hasn't always gone along with my radical ideas of nonviolence and antinationalism, or my feelings that formal education is meaningless at best, and that universities are baby-sitting operations. Even though he was peace-marching long before I was, when I swung, I swung all the way, and left my father looking and acting, in my opinion, fairly moderate. But he has changed very much in the last five years, and I know that when my mother and Mimi and I went to jail for doing Civil Disobedience at the Army induction center, he had no doubts that we were doing the right thing, and he took over the Institute for Non-Violence for the weekend seminars. I think that all the while he was working with UNESCO in Paris, traveling around the world, trying to help find ways of teaching science in underdeveloped countries, he was more concerned than he admitted to himself about two problems: One was how he could teach people the wonders of science and at the same time keep them from simply trying to ape the powerful nations of the world and race to discover new scientific ways to destroy themselves and each other. The temptation for power is so great, and unfortunately, what power has always meant is one's ability and efficiency to murder one's neighbor. The other problem that haunted my father had to do with UNESCO itself: It was filled with power-hungry and money-hungry individuals, and he never wanted to admit it. My mother told me of a time when they were at a dinner party of UNESCO science division men and their wives. Some of the men were loosening up on wine and my father was talking about his difficulties in South America. His colleagues were not really interested in his successes or failures in teaching science to Brazilians, and that fact became more and more apparent. Finally, one of them said something to the effect of, "Aw c'mon, Baez, you don't really give a damn about science teaching methods, do you?" My mother was completely floored by this, and she said, "That's what we're here for," and asked the man why *he* was with UNESCO. He had a publishing job, the man said, and it hadn't really paid much:

UNESCO paid a hell of a lot more, plus you got to travel, so he had gone to work for UNESCO and ended up in Paris. Not a bad deal all the way around. He went on kidding my father, who was struck dumb; and Mother did something she doesn't do unless she's in a state of shock or fury—she gave something resembling a speech. "My husband was an idealist when he came to work for UNESCO. He's a pacifist. He's concerned about the fact that people are starving to death and he thought the best way he could help out would be through UNESCO, to spread the uses of science to people who need it. Maybe we're just crazy, but I never imagined anyone came to work here for any other reason."

While he was with UNESCO, he seemed to lose his sense of humor. When I would visit them in Paris, sometimes it seemed that all I ever heard him say was, "I have this deadline . . . You know I just have to keep to this schedule . . ." He was trying to finish a book, which took him eight years to write. A basic text in physics. I seriously thought he would not ever complete that book, that it was like an eternally incomplete project he had to have to keep himself worn out. And I thought he was afraid to get it printed. But it was published while he was still in Paris. It's beautiful. The introduction is preceded by a picture of a huge rock suspended over the ocean. The picture makes you want to sit down heavily on the floor, or throw a paperweight out the window and watch it hit the sidewalk. There are little bits of human philosophy preceding each chapter, over eight hundred pictures, and the book is dedicated to "my wife, Joan, and my three daughters, Pauline, Joanie, and Mimi." And on page 274 there is a drawing which illustrates how an image is projected onto a television screen, and the image being projected is of a familiar-looking girl with long black hair, who stands holding a guitar.

In my estimation, my old man got his sense of humor back when he left Paris, and returned to the States. Toward the end of a course he was teaching at Harvard, a crash summer course, based on his book, he gave what he later described to me as the "demonstration of the century." He told the class that he was going to give an example of jet propulsion. He had a little red wagon brought in, and then he took the fire extinguisher off the wall and sat down in the wagon and jet propelled himself in circles around the front of the room, explaining, at the top of his voice, exactly what was happening technically. The students stood on their chairs and gave him an ovation, and it was all so overwhelming that he repeated the experiment. He shouted halfway through it for someone to open the door, and shot himself out into the hall, and disappeared. When he came back the bell had rung and the class was still there, cheering.

Right now, in 1967, my mother has planted my father and herself in a beautiful place in Carmel Valley, about one mile from my house, and not far from Pauline. A while after they began to be settled, I asked him if he could give himself permission to enjoy the luxury of his new home, his swimming pool, the endless beauty of the hills around. He tried to avoid my question by making a joke, but I said I was serious. We were sitting on the floor on a nice carpet, and he smoothed his hands over it as he leaned back against the wall. He looked very brown and Mexican in that moment, and I watched his profile against the valley hills as he struggled with himself. He said something about other people in the world, and about hunger. Then he looked up and gave me a smile of such a combination of things. "Yes, honey," he said, "I think I can enjoy it . . . if I keep myself busy enough . . ."

1. After reading the selection, how would you explain what Baez means when she says of her father, "He's good, he's a good man"?

2. Are there incidents in the narrative that help explain why Baez says she thinks "formal education is meaningless," even though her father is a professor? Are there aspects of her style and her way of organizing her autobiography that would identify her as someone reacting against academic training?

3. *Does Baez tend to rely on telling you about things her father did habitually or about experiences that only happened once? Identify at least two or three anecdotes about unique events and show how they contribute to the portrait.*

4. *To what extent does Baez concentrate on her personal relationship with her father? How does she present that relationship to you?*

5. *How does Baez relate her interest in presenting a family portrait with her political and social concerns? Which do you think dominates the selection?*

∾ William Butler Yeats ∾

(1865-1939)

*William Butler Yeats was born in Dublin and lived most of his
life in Ireland, where he encouraged the development of a national literature, helped found a national theater, and was active in Irish politics. His greatest distinction was as a poet, and
he is generally regarded as one of the two or three most important poets writing in English in the twentieth century.
Yeats wrote a number of prose works of autobiography, including* Reveries over Childhood and Youth *(1914), which concerns his life until he published his first volume of poems in
1889. This selection describes his mother's parents, whom
Yeats often visited at Sligo, in the west of Ireland.*

[GRANDFATHER POLLEXFEN]

Some of my misery was loneliness and some of it fear of old
William Pollexfen my grandfather. He was never unkind, and
I cannot remember that he ever spoke harshly to me, but it
was the custom to fear and admire him. He had won the freedom of some Spanish city, for saving life perhaps, but was so
silent that his wife never knew it till he was near eighty, and
then from the chance visit of some old sailor. She asked him if
it was true and he said it was true, but she knew him too well
to question and his old shipmate had left the town. She too had
the habit of fear. We knew that he had been in many parts of
the world, for there was a great scar on his hand made by a

whaling-hook, and in the dining-room was a cabinet with bits of coral in it and a jar of water from the Jordan for the baptizing of his children and Chinese pictures upon rice-paper and an ivory walking-stick from India that came to me after his death. He had great physical strength and had the reputation of never ordering a man to do anything he would not do himself. He owned many sailing ships and once, when a captain just come to anchor at Rosses Point reported something wrong with the rudder, had sent a messenger to say "Send a man down to find out what's wrong." "The crew all refuse" was the answer, and to that my grandfather answered, "Go down yourself," and not being obeyed, he dived from the main deck, all the neighbourhood lined along the pebbles of the shore. He came up with his skin torn but well informed about the rudder. He had a violent temper and kept a hatchet at his bedside for burglars and would knock a man down instead of going to law, and I once saw him hunt a party of men with a horse-whip. He had no relation for he was an only child and, being solitary and silent, he had few friends. He corresponded with Campbell of Islay who had befriended him and his crew after a shipwreck, and Captain Webb, the first man who had swum the Channel and who was drowned swimming the Niagara Rapids, had been a mate in his employ and a close friend. That is all the friends I can remember and yet he was so looked up to and admired that when he returned from taking the waters at Bath his men would light bonfires along the railway line for miles; while his partner William Middleton whose father after the great famine had attended the sick for weeks, and taken cholera from a man he carried in his arms into his own house and died of it, and was himself civil to everybody and a cleverer man than my grandfather, came and went without notice. I think I confused my grandfather with God, for I remember in one of my attacks of melancholy praying that he might punish me for my sins, and I was shocked and astonished when a daring little girl—a cousin I think—having waited under a group of trees in the avenue, where she knew he would pass near four o'clock on the way to his dinner, said to him, "If I were you and you were a little girl, I would give you a doll."

Yet for all my admiration and alarm, neither I nor any one else thought it wrong to outwit his violence or his rigour; and his lack of suspicion and something helpless about him made that easy while it stirred our affection. When I must have been still a very little boy, seven or eight years old perhaps, an uncle called me out of bed one night, to ride the five or six miles to Rosses Point to borrow a railway-pass from a cousin. My grandfather had one, but thought it dishonest to let another use it, but the cousin was not so particular. I was let out through a gate that opened upon a little lane beside the garden away from earshot of the house, and rode delighted through the moonlight, and awoke my cousin in the small hours by tapping on his window with a whip. I was home again by two or three in the morning and found the coachman waiting in the little lane. My grandfather would not have thought such an adventure possible, for every night at eight he believed that the stable-yard was locked, and he knew that he was brought the key. Some servant had once got into trouble at night and so he had arranged that they should all be locked in. He never knew, what everybody else in the house knew, that for all the ceremonious bringing of the key the gate was never locked.

Even to-day when I read *King Lear* his image is always before me and I often wonder if the delight in passionate men in my plays and in my poetry is more than his memory. He must have been ignorant, though I could not judge him in my childhood, for he had run away to sea when a boy, "gone to sea through the hawsehole" as he phrased it, and I can but remember him with two books—his Bible and Falconer's *Shipwreck*, a little green-covered book that lay always upon his table; he belonged to some younger branch of an old Cornish family. His father had been in the Army, had retired to become an owner of sailing ships, and an engraving of some old family place my grandfather thought should have been his hung next a painted coat of arms in the little back parlour. His mother had been a Wexford woman, and there was a tradition that his family had been linked with Ireland for generations and once had their share in the old Spanish trade with Galway. He had a good deal of pride and disliked his neighbours, whereas his wife, a Middleton, was gentle and patient and did many charities in the little back parlour among frieze coats and shawled heads, and every night when she saw him asleep went the round of the house alone with a candle to make certain there was no burglar in danger of the hatchet. She was a true lover of her garden, and before the care of her house had grown upon her, would choose some favourite among her flowers and copy it upon rice-paper. I saw some of her handiwork the other day and I wondered at the delicacy of form and colour and at a handling that may have needed a magnifying glass it was so minute. I can remember no other pictures but the Chinese paintings, and some coloured prints of battles in the Crimea upon the wall of a passage, and the painting of a ship at the passage end darkened by time.

1. This selection is taken from a volume Yeats entitled Reveries over Childhood and Youth. *What does the word "reverie" mean? Does it fit the way in which Yeats tells us about his grandfather?*

2. How does Yeats suggest that the memories he has of his grandfather are those of a very young child? How does he indicate that his grandfather belonged to a different age and a different kind of world?

3. Look carefully at the different objects Yeats associates with his grandfather. Explain the ways in which these objects help to characterize the man.

∽ N. Scott Momaday ∽

(1934-   )

N. Scott Momaday is a Kiowa Indian raised on Indian reserva-
tions in the southwestern United States. He is now a Professor
of English and Comparative Literature at the University of
California, Berkeley. He has published essays on American
literature and was awarded the Pulitzer Prize in 1969 for his
first novel, House Made of Dawn. *The following selection is*
the autobiographical preface to his collection of Indian leg-
ends and folk tales, The Way to Rainy Mountain *(1969).*

[A KIOWA GRANDMOTHER]

A single knoll rises out of the plain in Oklahoma, north and
west of the Wichita Range. For my people, the Kiowas, it is an
old landmark, and they gave it the name Rainy Mountain.
The hardest weather in the world is there. Winter brings bliz-
zards, hot tornadic winds arise in the spring, and in summer
the prairie is an anvil's edge. The grass turns brittle and
brown, and it cracks beneath your feet. There are green belts
along the rivers and creeks, linear groves of hickory and pecan,
willow and witch hazel. At a distance in July or August the
steaming foliage seems almost to writhe in fire. Great green
and yellow grasshoppers are everywhere in the tall grass, popping up like corn to sting the flesh, and tortoises crawl about
on the red earth, going nowhere in the plenty of time. Loneliness is an aspect of the land. All things in the plain are isolate;

there is no confusion of objects in the eye, but *one* hill or *one* tree or *one* man. To look upon that landscape in the early morning, with the sun at your back, is to lose the sense of proportion. Your imagination comes to life, and this, you think, is where Creation was begun.

I returned to Rainy Mountain in July. My grandmother had died in the spring, and I wanted to be at her grave. She had lived to be very old and at last infirm. Her only living daughter was with her when she died, and I was told that in death her face was that of a child.

I like to think of her as a child. When she was born, the Kiowas were living the last great moment of their history. For more than a hundred years they had controlled the open range from the Smoky Hill River to the Red, from the headwaters of the Canadian to the fork of the Arkansas and Cimarron. In alliance with the Comanches, they had ruled the whole of the southern Plains. War was their sacred business, and they were among the finest horsemen the world has ever known. But warfare for the Kiowas was preeminently a matter of disposition rather than of survival, and they never understood the grim, unrelenting advance of the U.S. Cavalry. When at last, divided and ill-provisioned, they were driven onto the Staked Plains in the cold rains of autumn, they fell into panic. In Palo Duro Canyon they abandoned their crucial stores to pillage and had nothing then but their lives. In order to save themselves, they surrendered to the soldiers at Fort Sill and were imprisoned in the old stone corral that now stands as a military museum. My grandmother was spared the humiliation of those high gray walls by eight or ten years, but she must have known from birth the affliction of defeat, the dark brooding of old warriors.

Her name was Aho, and she belonged to the last culture to evolve in North America. Her forebears came down from the high country in western Montana nearly three centuries ago. They were a mountain people, a mysterious tribe of hunters whose language has never been positively classified in any major group. In the late seventeenth century they began a long migration to the south and east. It was a journey toward the dawn, and it led to a golden age. Along the way the Kiowas were befriended by the Crows, who gave them the culture and religion of the Plains. They acquired horses, and their ancient nomadic spirit was suddenly free of the ground. They acquired Tai-me, the sacred Sun Dance doll, from that moment the object and symbol of their worship, and so shared in the divinity of the sun. Not least, they acquired the sense of destiny, therefore courage and pride. When they entered upon the southern Plains they had been transformed. No longer were they slaves to the simple necessity of survival; they were a lordly and dangerous society of fighters and thieves, hunters and priests of the sun. According to their origin myth, they entered the world through a hollow log. From one point of view, their migration was the fruit of an old prophecy, for indeed they emerged from a sunless world.

Although my grandmother lived out her long life in the shadow of Rainy Mountain, the immense landscape of the continental interior lay like memory in her blood. She could tell of the Crows, whom she had never seen, and of the Black Hills, where she had never been. I wanted to see in reality what she had seen more perfectly in the mind's eye, and traveled fifteen hundred miles to begin my pilgrimage.

Yellowstone, it seemed to me, was the top of the world, a region of deep lakes and dark timber, canyons and waterfalls. But, beautiful as it is, one might have the sense of confinement there. The skyline in all directions is close at hand, the high wall of the woods and deep cleavages of shade. There is a perfect freedom in the mountains, but it belongs to the eagle and the elk, the badger and the bear. The Kiowas reckoned their stature by the distance they could see, and they were bent and blind in the wilderness.

Descending eastward, the highland meadows are a stairway to the plain. In July the inland slope of the Rockies is luxuriant with flax and buckwheat, stonecrop and larkspur. The earth unfolds and the limit of the land recedes. Clusters of trees, and animals grazing far in the distance, cause the vision to reach away and wonder to build upon the mind. The sun follows a longer course in the day, and the sky is immense beyond all comparison. The great billowing clouds that sail upon it are shadows that move upon the grain like water, dividing light. Farther down, in the land of the Crows and Blackfeet, the plain is yellow. Sweet clover takes hold of the hills and bends upon itself to cover and seal the soil. There the Kiowas paused on their way; they had come to the place where they must change their lives. The sun is at home on the plains. Precisely there does it have the certain character of a god. When the Kiowas came to the land of the Crows, they could see the dark lees of the hills at dawn across the Bighorn River, the profusion of light on the grain shelves, the oldest deity ranging after the solstices. Not yet would they veer southward to the caldron of the land that lay below; they must wean their blood from the northern winter and hold the mountains a while longer in their view. They bore Tai-me in procession to the east.

A dark mist lay over the Black Hills, and the land was like iron. At the top of a ridge I caught sight of Devil's Tower upthrust against the gray sky as if in the birth of time the core of the earth had broken through its crust and the motion of the world was begun. There are things in nature that engender an awful quiet in the heart of man; Devil's Tower is one of them. Two centuries ago, because they could not do otherwise, the Kiowas made a legend at the base of the rock. My grandmother said:

Eight children were there at play, seven sisters and their brother. Suddenly the boy was struck dumb; he trembled and began to run upon his hands and feet. His fingers became claws, and his body was covered with fur. Directly there was a bear where the boy had been. The sisters were terrified; they ran, and the bear after them. They came to the stump of a great tree, and the tree spoke to them. It bade them climb upon

*it, and as they did so it began to rise into the air. The bear
came to kill them, but they were just beyond its reach. It
reared against the tree and scored the bark all around with its
claws. The seven sisters were borne into the sky, and they
became the stars of the Big Dipper.*

From that moment, and so long as the legend lives, the Kiowas
have kinsmen in the night sky. Whatever they were in the
mountains, they could be no more. However tenuous their
well-being, however much they had suffered and would suffer
again, they had found a way out of the wilderness.

My grandmother had a reverence for the sun, a holy regard
that now is all but gone out of mankind. There was a wariness
in her, and an ancient awe. She was a Christian in her later
years, but she had come a long way about, and she never for-
got her birthright. As a child she had been to the Sun Dances;
she had taken part in those annual rites, and by then she had
learned the restoration of her people in the presence of Tai-me.
She was about seven when the last Kiowa Sun Dance was held
in 1887 on the Washita River above Rainy Mountain Creek.
The buffalo were gone. In order to consummate the ancient
sacrifice—to impale the head of a buffalo bull upon the medicine tree—a delegation of old men journeyed into Texas, there
to beg and barter for an animal from the Goodnight herd. She
was ten when the Kiowas came together for the last time as a
living Sun Dance culture. They could find no buffalo; they
had to hang an old hide from the sacred tree. Before the dance
could begin, a company of soldiers rode out from Fort Sill
under orders to disperse the tribe. Forbidden without cause the
essential act of their faith, having seen the wild herds slaughtered and left to rot upon the ground, the Kiowas backed away
forever from the medicine tree. That was July 20, 1890, at the
great bend of the Washita. My grandmother was there. Without bitterness, and for as long as she lived, she bore a vision
of deicide.

Now that I can have her only in memory, I see my grandmother in the several postures that were peculiar to her: stand-

ing at the wood stove on a winter morning and turning meat in a great iron skillet; sitting at the south window, bent above her beadwork, and afterwards, when her vision failed, looking down for a long time into the fold of her hands; going out upon a cane, very slowly as she did when the weight of age came upon her; praying. I remember her most often at prayer. She made long, rambling prayers out of suffering and hope, having seen many things. I was never sure that I had the right to hear, so exclusive were they of all mere custom and company. The last time I saw her she prayed standing by the side of her bed at night, naked to the waist, the light of a kerosene lamp moving upon her dark skin. Her long, black hair, always drawn and braided in the day, lay upon her shoulders and against her breasts like a shawl. I do not speak Kiowa, and I never understood her prayers, but there was something inherently sad in the sound, some merest hesitation upon the syllables of sorrow. She began in a high and descending pitch, exhausting her breath to silence; then again and again—and always the same intensity of effort, of something that is, and is not, like urgency in the human voice. Transported so in the dancing light among the shadows of her room, she seemed beyond the reach of time. But that was illusion; I think I knew then that I should not see her again.

Houses are like sentinels in the plain, old keepers of the weather watch. There, in a very little while, wood takes on the appearance of great age. All colors wear soon away in the wind and rain, and then the wood is burned gray and the grain appears and the nails turn red with rust. The window-panes are black and opaque; you imagine there is nothing within, and indeed there are many ghosts, bones given up to the land. They stand here and there against the sky, and you approach them for a longer time than you expect. They belong in the distance; it is their domain.

Once there was a lot of sound in my grandmother's house, a lot of coming and going, feasting and talk. The summers there were full of excitement and reunion. The Kiowas are a sum-

287

mer people; they abide the cold and keep to themselves, but when the season turns and the land becomes warm and vital they cannot hold still; an old love of going returns upon them. The aged visitors who came to my grandmother's house when I was a child were made of lean and leather, and they bore themselves upright. They wore great black hats and bright ample shirts that shook in the wind. They rubbed fat upon their hair and wound their braids with strips of colored cloth. Some of them painted their faces and carried the scars of old and cherished enmities. They were an old council of warlords, come to remind and be reminded of who they were. Their wives and daughters served them well. The women might indulge themselves; gossip was at once the mark and compensation of their servitude. They made loud and elaborate talk among themselves, full of jest and gesture, fright and false alarm. They went abroad in fringed and flowered shawls, bright beadwork and German silver. They were at home in the kitchen, and they prepared meals that were banquets.

There were frequent prayer meetings, and great nocturnal feasts. When I was a child I played with my cousins outside, where the lamplight fell upon the ground and the singing of the old people rose up around us and carried away into the darkness. There were a lot of good things to eat, a lot of laughter and surprise. And afterwards, when the quiet returned, I lay down with my grandmother and could hear the frogs away by the river and feel the motion of the air.

Now there is a funeral silence in the rooms, the endless wake of some final word. The walls have closed in upon my grandmother's house. When I returned to it in mourning, I saw for the first time in my life how small it was. It was late at night, and there was a white moon, nearly full. I sat for a long time on the stone steps by the kitchen door. From there I could see out across the land; I could see the long row of trees by the creek, the low light upon the rolling plains, and the stars of the Big Dipper. Once I looked at the moon and caught sight of a strange thing. A cricket had perched upon the handrail, only a few inches away from me. My line of vision was such that the creature filled the moon like a fossil. It had gone there, I thought, to live and die, for there, of all places, was its small definition made whole and eternal. A warm wind rose up and purled like the longing within me.

The next morning I awoke at dawn and went out on the dirt road to Rainy Mountain. It was already hot, and the grasshoppers began to fill the air. Still, it was early in the morning, and the birds sang out of the shadows. The long yellow grass on the mountain shone in the bright light, and a scissortail hied above the land. There, where it ought to be, at the end of a long and legendary way, was my grandmother's grave. Here and there on the dark stones were ancestral names. Looking back once, I saw the mountain and came away.

1. To what extent is Momaday interested in describing what his grandmother did or said and what she looked like? How is his method of characterization different from that of other writers represented in this chapter?

2. Identify two or three passages where Momaday writes about specific memories he has of his grandmother and explain why you think he includes these particular memories in his sketch.

3. Momaday was raised on Indian reservations in the southwestern United States. How do his concerns as a member of a distinctive culture shape his story? What attitudes does he have toward Indian people and Indian traditions? How is his portrait of his grandmother related to those attitudes?

4. The selection printed here serves as an introduction to a book in which Momaday retells the legends and stories of the Kiowa. Does the portrait of his grandmother strike you as an appropriate introduction to such a book? Why or why not?

5. Unlike most of the other selections in this chapter, Momaday's account does not begin by discussing himself or his family. How does his opening paragraph serve as an introduction to what he wants to tell his readers?

∽ Mary McCarthy ∽

(1912-   )

Orphaned at six, Mary McCarthy was raised by her paternal grandparents in Minnesota and then by her maternal grandparents in Seattle, Washington. She graduated from Vassar in 1933 and quickly established herself as a highly intelligent and acerbic literary critic and drama reviewer. Since the 1940s, she has combined work as a critic with a career as a novelist and a short-story writer. Her recent work includes the novel Birds of America *(1971), and essays on the Vietnam War and the Watergate scandals.* Memories of a Catholic Girlhood *(1948) concerns her life until she goes away to college.*

YONDER PEASANT, WHO IS HE?

[GRANDMOTHER MCCARTHY]

Whenever we children came to stay at my grandmother's house, we were put to sleep in the sewing room, a bleak, shabby, utilitarian rectangle, more office than bedroom, more attic than office, that played to the hierarchy of chambers the role of a poor relation. It was a room seldom entered by the other members of the family, seldom swept by the maid, a room without pride; the old sewing machine, some cast-off chairs, a shadeless lamp, rolls of wrapping paper, piles of cardboard boxes that might someday come in handy, papers of pins, and remnants of material united with the iron folding cots put

From Mary McCarthy: *Memories of a Catholic Girlhood.* Copyright 1948 by Mary McCarthy. First published in *The New Yorker.* Reprinted by permission of Harcourt Brace Jovanovich, Inc.

out for our use and the bare floor boards to give an impression of intense and ruthless temporality. Thin white spreads, of the kind used in hospitals and charity institutions, and naked blinds at the windows reminded us of our orphaned condition and of the ephemeral character of our visit; there was nothing here to encourage us to consider this our home.

Poor Roy's children, as commiseration damply styled us, could not afford illusions, in the family opinion. Our father had put us beyond the pale by dying suddenly of influenza and taking our young mother with him, a defection that was remarked on with horror and grief commingled, as though our mother had been a pretty secretary with whom he had wantonly absconded into the irresponsible paradise of the hereafter. Our reputation was clouded by this misfortune. There was a prevailing sense, not only in the family but among storekeepers, servants, streetcar conductors, and other satellites of our circle, that my grandfather, a rich man, had behaved with extraordinary munificence in allotting a sum of money for our support and installing us with some disagreeable middle-aged relations in a dingy house two blocks distant from his own. What alternative he had was not mentioned; presumably he could have sent us to an orphan asylum and no one would have thought the worse of him. At any rate, it was felt, even by those who sympathized with us, that we led a privileged existence, privileged because we had no rights, and the very fact that at the yearly Halloween or Christmas party given at the home of an uncle we appeared so dismal, ill clad, and unhealthy, in contrast to our rosy, exquisite cousins, confirmed the judgment that had been made on us—clearly, it was a generous impulse that kept us in the family at all. Thus, the meaner our circumstances, the greater seemed our grandfather's condescension, a view in which we ourselves shared, looking softly and shyly on this old man—with his rheumatism, his pink face and white hair, set off by the rosebuds in his Pierce-Arrow and in his buttonhole—as the font of goodness and philanthropy, and the nickel he occasionally gave us to drop into the collection plate on Sunday (two cents was our ordinary contribution) filled us not with envy but with simple admiration for his potency; this indeed was princely, *this* was the way to give. It did not occur to us to judge him for the disparity of our styles of living. Whatever bitterness we felt was kept for our actual guardians, who, we believed, must be embezzling the money set aside for us, since the standard of comfort achieved in our grandparents' house—the electric heaters, the gas logs, the lap robes, the shawls wrapped tenderly about the old knees, the white meat of chicken and red meat of beef, the silver, the white tablecloths, the maids, and the solicitous chauffeur—persuaded us that prunes and rice pudding, peeling paint and patched clothes were *hors concours* with these persons and therefore could not have been willed by them. Wealth, in our minds, was equivalent to bounty, and poverty but a sign of penuriousness of spirit.

Yet even if we had been convinced of the honesty of our guardians, we would still have clung to that beneficent image of our grandfather that the family myth proposed to us. We were too poor, spiritually speaking, to question his generosity, to ask why he allowed us to live in oppressed chill and deprivation at a long arm's length from himself and hooded his genial blue eye with a bluff, millionairish grey eyebrow whenever the evidence of our suffering presented itself at his knee. The official answer we knew: our benefactors were too old to put up with four wild young children; our grandfather was preoccupied with business matters and with his rheumatism, to which he devoted himself as though to a pious duty, taking it with him on pilgrimages to Ste. Anne de Beaupré and Miami, offering it with impartial reverence to the miracle of the Northern Mother and the Southern sun. This rheumatism hallowed my grandfather with the mark of a special vocation; he lived with it in the manner of an artist or a grizzled Galahad; it set him apart from all of us and even from my grandmother, who, lacking such an affliction, led a relatively unjustified existence and showed, in relation to us children, a sharper and more bellicose spirit. She felt, in spite of everything, that she was open to criticism, and, transposing this feeling with a practiced old hand, kept peering into our characters for symptoms of ingratitude.

We, as a matter of fact, were grateful to the point of servility. We made no demands, we had no hopes. We were content if we were permitted to enjoy the refracted rays of that solar prosperity and come sometimes in the summer afternoons to sit on the shady porch or idle through a winter morning on the wicker furniture of the sun parlor, to stare at the player piano in the music room and smell the odor of whisky in the mahogany cabinet in the library, or to climb about the dark living room examining the glassed-in paintings in their huge gilt frames, the fruits of European travel: dusky Italian devotional groupings, heavy and lustrous as grapes, Neapolitan women carrying baskets to market, views of Venetian canals, and Tuscan harvest scenes—secular themes that, to the Irish-American mind, had become tinged with Catholic feeling by a regional infusion from the Pope. We asked no more from this house than the pride of being connected with it, and this was fortunate for us, since my grandmother, a great adherent of the give-them-an-inch-and-they'll-take-a-yard theory of hospitality, never, so far as I can remember, offered any caller the slightest refreshment, regarding her own conversation as sufficiently wholesome and sustaining. An ugly, severe old woman with a monstrous balcony of a bosom, she officiated over certain set topics in a colorless singsong, like a priest intoning a Mass, topics to which repetition had lent a senseless solemnity: her audience with the Holy Father; how my own father had broken with family tradition and voted the Democratic ticket; a visit to Lourdes; the Sacred Stairs in Rome, bloodstained since the first Good Friday, which she had climbed on her knees; my crooked little fingers and how they meant I was a liar; a miracle-working bone; the importance of regular bowel movements; the wickedness of Protestants; the conversion of my mother to Catholicism; and the assertion that my other grandmother must certainly dye her hair. The most trivial reminiscences (my aunt's having hysterics in a haystack) received from her delivery and from the piety of the context a strongly monitory flavor; they inspired fear and guilt, and one searched uncomfortably for the moral in them, as in a dark and riddling fable.

Luckily, I am writing a memoir and not a work of fiction, and therefore I do not have to account for my grandmother's unpleasing character and look for the Oedipal fixation or the traumatic experience which would give her that clinical authenticity that is nowadays so desirable in portraiture. I do not know how my grandmother got the way she was; I assume, from family photographs and from the inflexibility of her habits, that she was always the same, and it seems as idle to inquire into her childhood as to ask what was ailing Iago or look for the error in toilet-training that was responsible for Lady Macbeth. My grandmother's sexual history, bristling with infant mortality in the usual style of her period, was robust and decisive: three tall, handsome sons grew up, and one attentive daughter. Her husband treated her kindly. She had money, many grandchildren, and religion to sustain her. White hair, glasses, soft skin, wrinkles, needlework—all the paraphernalia of motherliness were hers; yet it was a cold, grudging, disputatious old woman who sat all day in her sunroom making tapestries from a pattern, scanning religious periodicals, and setting her iron jaw against any infraction of her ways.

Combativeness was, I suppose, the dominant trait in my grandmother's nature. An aggressive churchgoer, she was quite without Christian feeling; the mercy of the Lord Jesus had never entered her heart. Her piety was an act of war against the Protestant ascendancy. The religious magazines on her table furnished her not with food for meditation but with fresh pretexts for anger; articles attacking birth control, divorce, mixed marriages, Darwin, and secular education were her favorite reading. The teachings of the Church did not interest her, except as they were a rebuke to others; "Honor thy father and thy mother," a commandment she was no longer called upon to practice, was the one most frequently on her lips. The extermination of Protestantism, rather than spiritual perfection, was the boon she prayed for. Her mind was preoccupied with conversion; the capture of a soul for God much diverted her fancy—it made one less Protestant in the world. Foreign missions, with their overtones of good will and social service, appealed to her less strongly; it was not a *harvest* of souls that my grandmother had in mind.

This pugnacity of my grandmother's did not confine itself to sectarian enthusiasm. There was the defense of her furniture and her house against the imagined encroachments of visitors. With her, this was not the gentle and tremulous protectiveness endemic in old ladies, who fear for the safety of their possessions with a truly touching anxiety, inferring the fragility of all things from the brittleness of their old bones and hearing the crash of mortality in the perilous tinkling of a tea cup. My grandmother's sentiment was more autocratic: she hated having her chairs sat in or her lawns stepped on or the water turned on in her basins, for no reason at all except pure officiousness; she even grudged the mailman his daily promenade up her sidewalk. Her home was a center of power, and she would not allow it to be derogated by easy or democratic usage. Under her jealous eye, its social properties had atrophied, and it functioned in the family structure simply as a political headquarters. Family conferences were held there, consultations with the doctor and the clergy; refractory children were brought there for a lecture or an interval of thought-taking; wills were read and loans negotiated and emissaries from the Protestant faction on state occasions received. The family had no friends, and entertaining was held to be a foolish and unnecessary courtesy as between blood relations. Holiday dinners fell, as a duty, on the lesser members of the organization: the daughters and daughters-in-law (converts from the false religion) offered up Baked Alaska on a platter, like the head of John the Baptist, while the old people sat enthroned at the table, and only their digestive processes acknowledged, with rumbling, enigmatic salvos, the festal day.

Yet on one terrible occasion my grandmother had kept open house. She had accommodated us all during those fatal weeks of the influenza epidemic, when no hospital beds were to be had and people went about with masks or stayed shut up in their houses, and the awful fear of contagion paralyzed all services and made each man an enemy to his neighbor. One by one, we had been carried off the train which had brought us from distant Puget Sound to make a new home in Minneapolis. Waving good-by in the Seattle depot, we had not known that we had carried the flu with us into our drawing rooms, along with the presents and the flowers, but, one after another, we had been struck down as the train proceeded eastward. We children did not understand whether the chattering of our teeth and Mama's lying torpid in the berth were not somehow a part of the trip (until then, serious illness, in our minds, had been associated with innovations—it had always brought home a new baby), and we began to be sure that it was all an adventure when we saw our father draw a revolver on the conductor who was trying to put us off the train at a small wooden station in the middle of the North Dakota prairie. On the platform at Minneapolis, there were stretchers, a wheel chair, redcaps, distraught officials, and, beyond them, in the crowd, my grandfather's rosy face, cigar, and cane, my grandmother's feathered hat, imparting an air of festivity to this strange and confused picture, making us children certain that our illness was the beginning of a delightful holiday.

We awoke to reality in the sewing room several weeks later, to an atmosphere of castor oil, rectal thermometers, cross nurses, and efficiency, and though we were shut out from the knowledge of what had happened so close to us, just out of our hearing—a scandal of the gravest character, a coming and going of priests and undertakers and coffins (Mama and Daddy, they assured us, had gone to get well in the hospital)—we became aware, even as we woke from our fevers, that everything, including ourselves, was different. We had shrunk, as it were, and faded, like the flannel pajamas we wore, which during these few weeks had grown, doubtless from the disinfectant they were washed in, wretchedly thin and shabby. The behavior of the people around us, abrupt, careless, and preoccupied, apprised us without any ceremony of our diminished importance. Our value had paled, and a new image of ourselves—the image, if we had guessed it, of the orphan—was already forming in our minds. We had not known we were spoiled, but now this word, entering our vocabulary for the first time, served to define the change for us and to herald the new order. Before we got sick, we were spoiled; that was what was the matter now, and everything we could not understand, everything unfamiliar and displeasing, took on a certain plausibility when related to this fresh concept. We had not known what it was to have trays dumped summarily on our beds and no sugar and cream for our cereal, to take medicine in a gulp because someone could not be bothered to wait for us, to have our arms jerked into our sleeves and a comb ripped through our hair, to be bathed impatiently, to be told to sit up or lie down quick and no nonsense about it, to find our questions unanswered and our requests unheeded, to lie for hours alone and wait for the doctor's visit, but this, so it seemed, was an oversight in our training, and my grandmother and her household applied themselves with a will to remedying the deficiency.

Their motives were, no doubt, good; it was time indeed that we learned that the world was no longer our oyster. The happy life we had had—the May baskets and the valentines, the picnics in the yard, and the elaborate snowman—was a poor preparation, in truth, for the future that now opened up to us. Our new instructors could hardly be blamed for a certain impatience with our parents, who had been so lacking in foresight. It was to everyone's interest, decidedly, that we should

forget the past—the quicker, the better—and a steady dis-
paragement of our habits ("Tea and chocolate, can you imagine, and all those frosted cakes—no wonder poor Tess was
always after the doctor") and praise that was rigorously comparative ("You have absolutely no idea of the improvement
in those children") flattered the feelings of the speakers and
prepared us to accept a loss that was, in any case, irreparable.
Like all children, we wished to conform, and the notion that
our former ways had been somehow ridiculous and unsuitable
made the memory of them falter a little, like a child's recita-
tion to strangers. We no longer demanded our due, and the
wish to see our parents insensibly weakened. Soon we ceased
to speak of it, and thus, without tears or tantrums, we came to
know they were dead.

Why no one, least of all our grandmother, to whose reper-
tory the subject seems so congenial, took the trouble to tell us,
it is impossible now to know. It is easy to imagine her "breaking" the news to those of us who were old enough to listen in
one of those official interviews in which her nature periodi-
cally tumefied, becoming heavy and turgid, like her porten-
tous bosom, like peonies, her favorite flower, or like the dress-
maker's dummy, that bombastic image of herself that, half
swathed in a sheet for decorum's sake, lent a museumlike solemnity to the sewing room and aroused our first sexual curiosity. The mind's ear frames her sentences, but in reality she did
not speak, whether from a hygienic motive (keep the mind ignorant and the bowels open), or from a mistaken kindness, it is
difficult to guess. Perhaps really she feared our tears, which
might rain on her like reproaches, since the family policy at
the time was predicated on the axiom of our virtual insen-
tience, an assumption that allowed them to proceed with us as
if with pieces of furniture. Without explanations or coddling,
as soon as they could safely get up, my three brothers were dis-
patched to the other house; they were much too young to
"feel" it, I heard the grownups murmur, and would never
know the difference "if Myers and Margaret were careful." In

my case, however, a doubt must have been experienced. I was six—old enough to "remember"—and this entitled me, in the family's eyes, to greater consideration, as if this memory of mine were a lawyer who represented me in court. In deference, therefore, to my age and my supposed powers of criticism and comparison, I was kept on for a time, to roam palely about my grandmother's living rooms, a dangling, transitional creature, a frog becoming a tadpole, while my brothers, poor little polyps, were already well embedded in the structure of the new life. I did not wonder what had become of them. I believe I thought they were dead, but their fate did not greatly concern me; my heart had grown numb. I considered myself clever to have guessed the truth about my parents, like a child who proudly discovers that there is no Santa Claus, but I would not speak of that knowledge or even react to it privately, for I wished to have nothing to do with it; I would not co-operate in this loss. Those weeks in my grandmother's house come back to me very obscurely, surrounded by blackness, like a mourning card: the dark well of the staircase, where I seem to have been endlessly loitering, waiting to see Mama when she would come home from the hospital, and then simply loitering with no purpose whatever; the winter-dim first-grade classroom of the strange academy I was sent to; the drab treatment room of the doctor's office, where every Saturday I screamed and begged on a table while electric shocks were sent through me, for what purpose I cannot conjecture. But this preferential treatment could not be accorded me forever; it was time that I found my niche. "There is someone here to see you"—the maid met me one afternoon with this announcement and a half-curious, half-knowledgeable smile. My heart bounded; I felt almost sick (who else, after all, could it be?), and she had to push me forward. But the man and woman surveying me in the sun parlor with my grandmother were strangers, two unprepossessing middle-aged people—a great-aunt and her husband, so it seemed—to whom I was now commanded to give a hand and a smile, for, as my grandmother remarked, Myers and Margaret had come to take me home that very afternoon to live with them, and I must not make a bad impression.

Once the new household was running, our parents' death was officially conceded and sentiment given its due. Concrete references to the lost ones, to their beauty, gaiety, and good manners, were naturally not welcomed by our guardians, who possessed none of these qualities themselves, but the veneration of our parents' *memory* was considered an admirable exercise. Our evening prayers were lengthened to include one for our parents' souls, and we were thought to make a pretty picture, all four of us in our pajamas with feet in them, kneeling in a neat line, our hands clasped before us, reciting the prayer for the dead. "Eternal rest grant unto them, oh Lord, and let the perpetual light shine upon them," our thin little voices cried, but this remembrancing, so pleasurable to our guardians, was only a chore to us. We connected it with lights out, washing, all the bedtime coercions, and particularly with the adhesive tape that, to prevent mouth-breathing, was clapped upon our lips the moment the prayer was finished, sealing us up for the night, and that was removed, very painfully, with the help of ether, in the morning. It embarrassed us to be reminded of our parents by these persons who had superseded them and who seemed to evoke their wraiths in an almost proprietary manner, as though death, the great leveler, had brought them within their province. In the same spirit, we were taken to the cemetery to view our parents' graves; this, in fact, being free of charge, was a regular Sunday pastime with us, which we grew to hate as we did all recreation enforced by our guardians—department-store demonstrations, band concerts, parades, trips to the Old Soldiers' Home, to the Botanical Gardens, to Minnehaha Park, where we watched other children ride on the ponies, to the Zoo, to the water tower—diversions that cost nothing, involved long streetcar trips or endless walking or waiting, and that had the peculiarly fatigued, dusty, proletarianized character of American municipal entertainment. The two mounds that now were our parents associated themselves in our minds with Civil War cannon balls and monuments to the doughboy dead; we contemplated them stolidly, waiting for a sensation, but these twin grass beds, with their junior-executive headstones, elicited nothing whatever; tired of this interminable staring, we would beg to be allowed to go play in some collateral mausoleum, where the dead at least were buried in drawers and offered some stimulus to fancy.

For my grandmother, the recollection of the dead became a mode of civility that she thought proper to exercise toward us whenever, for any reason, one of us came to stay at her house. The reason was almost always the same. We (that is, my brother Kevin or I) had run away from home. Independently of each other, this oldest of my brothers and I had evolved an identical project—to get ourselves placed in an orphan asylum. We had noticed the heightening of interest that mention of our parentless condition seemed always to produce in strangers, and this led us to interpret the word "asylum" in the old Greek sense and to look on a certain red brick building, seen once from a streetcar near the Mississippi River, as a haven of security. So, from time to time, when our lives became too painful, one of us would set forth, determined to find the red brick building and to press what we imagined was our legal claim to its protection. But sometimes we lost our way, and sometimes our courage, and after spending a day hanging about the streets peering into strange yards, trying to assess the kindheartedness of the owner (for we also thought of adoption), or a cold night hiding in a church confessional box or behind some statuary in the Art Institute, we would be brought by the police, by some well-meaning householder, or simply by fear and hunger, to my grandmother's door. There we would be silently received, and a family conclave would be summoned. We would be put to sleep in the sewing room for a night, or sometimes more, until our feelings had subsided and we could be sent back, grateful, at any rate, for the promise that no reprisals would be taken and that the life we had run away from would go on "as if nothing had happened."

Since we were usually running away to escape some anticipated punishment, these flights at least gained us something, but in spite of the taunts of our guardians, who congratulated us bitterly on our "cleverness," we ourselves could not feel that we came home in triumph as long as we came home at all. The cramps and dreads of those long nights made a harrowing impression on us. Our failure to run away successfully put us, so we thought, at the absolute mercy of our guardians; our last weapon was gone, for it was plain to be seen that they could always bring us back and we never understood why they did not take advantage of this situation to thrash us, as they used to put it, within an inch of our lives. What intervened to save us, we could not guess—a miracle, perhaps; we were not acquainted with any *human* motive that would prompt Omnipotence to desist. We did not suspect that these escapes brought consternation to the family circle, which had acted, so it conceived, only in our best interests, and now saw itself in danger of unmerited obloquy. What would be the Protestant reaction if something still more dreadful were to happen? Child suicides were not unknown, and quiet, asthmatic little Kevin had been caught with matches under the house. The family would not acknowledge error, but it conceded a certain mismanagement on Myers' and Margaret's part. Clearly, we might become altogether intractable if our homecoming on these occasions were not mitigated with leniency. Consequently, my grandmother kept us in a kind of neutral detention. She declined to be aware of our grievance and offered no words of comfort, but the comforts of her household acted upon us soothingly, like an automatic mother's hand. We ate and drank contentedly; with all her harsh views, my grandmother was a practical woman and would not have thought it worthwhile to unsettle her whole schedule, teach her cook to make a lumpy mush and watery boiled potatoes, and market for turnips and parsnips and all the other vegetables we hated, in order to approximate the conditions she considered suitable for our characters. Humble pie could be costly, especially when cooked to order.

Doubtless she did not guess how delightful these visits seemed to us once the fear of punishment had abated. Her knowledge of our own way of living was luxuriously remote. She did not visit our ménage or inquire into its practices, and though hypersensitive to a squint or a dental irregularity (for she was liberal indeed with glasses and braces for the teeth, disfiguring appliances that remained the sole token of our bourgeois origin and set us off from our parochial-school mates like the caste marks of some primitive tribe), she appeared not to notice the darns and patches of our clothing, our raw hands and scarecrow arms, our silence and our elderly faces. She imagined us as surrounded by certain playthings she had once bestowed on us—a sandbox, a wooden swing, a wagon, an ambulance, a toy fire engine. In my grandmother's consciousness, these objects remained always in pristine condition; years after the sand had spilled out of it and the roof had rotted away, she continued to ask tenderly after our lovely sand pile and to manifest displeasure if we declined to join in its praises. Like many egoistic people (I have noticed this trait in myself), she was capable of making a handsome outlay, but the act affected her so powerfully that her generosity was still lively in her memory when its practical effects had long vanished. In the case of a brown beaver hat, which she watched me wear for four years, she was clearly blinded to its matted nap, its shapeless brim, and ragged ribbon by the vision of the price tag it had worn when new. Yet, however her mind embroidered the bare tapestry of our lives, she could not fail to perceive that we felt, during these short stays with her, *some* difference between the two establishments, and to take our wonder and pleasure as a compliment to herself.

She smiled on us quite kindly when we exclaimed over the food and the nice, warm bathrooms, with their rugs and electric heaters. What funny little creatures, to be so impressed

by things that were, after all, only the ordinary amenities of
life! Seeing us content in her house, her emulative spirit
warmed slowly to our admiration: she compared herself to our
guardians, and though for expedient reasons she could not afford to deprecate them ("You children have been very un-
grateful for all Myers and Margaret have done for you"), a
sense of her own finer magnanimity disposed her subtly in our
favor. In the flush of these emotions, a tenderness sprang up
between us. She seemed half reluctant to part with whichever
of us she had in her custody, almost as if she were experiencing a genuine pang of conscience. "Try and be good," she
would advise us when the moment for leave-taking came,
"and don't provoke your aunt and uncle. We might have made
different arrangements if there had been only one of you to
consider." These manifestations of concern, these tacit admis-
sions of our true situation, did not make us, as one might have
thought, bitter against our grandparents, for whom ignorance
of the facts might have served as a justification, but, on the
contrary, filled us with love for them and even a kind of sympathy—our sufferings were less terrible if someone acknowledged their existence, if someone were suffering for us, for
whom we, in our turn, could suffer, and thereby absolve of
guilt.

During these respites, the recollection of our parents formed
a bond between us and our grandmother that deepened our
mutual regard. Unlike our guardians or the whispering ladies
who sometimes came to call on us, inspired, it seemed, by a
pornographic curiosity as to the exact details of our feelings
("Do you suppose they remember their parents?" "Do they
ever *say* anything?"), our grandmother was quite uninter-
ested in arousing an emotion of grief in us. "She doesn't feel it
at all," I used to hear her confide, of me, to visitors, but contentedly, without censure, as if I had been a spayed cat that,
in her superior foresight, she had had "attended to." For my
grandmother, the death of my parents had become, in retro-

spect, an eventful occasion upon which she looked back with pleasure and a certain self-satisfaction. Whenever we stayed with her, we were allowed, as a special treat, to look into the rooms they had died in, for the fact that, as she phrased it, "they died in separate rooms" had for her a significance both romantic and somehow self-gratulatory, as though the separation in death of two who had loved each other in life were beautiful in itself and also reflected credit on the chatelaine of the house, who had been able to furnish two master bedrooms for the emergency. The housekeeping details of the tragedy, in fact, were to her of paramount interest. "I turned my house into a hospital," she used to say, particularly when visitors were present. "Nurses were as scarce as hen's teeth, and *high*— you can hardly imagine what those girls were charging an hour." The trays and the special cooking, the laundry and the disinfectants recalled themselves fondly to her thoughts, like items on the menu of some long-ago ball-supper, the memory of which recurred to her with a strong, possessive nostalgia.

My parents had, it seemed, by dying on her premises, become in a lively sense her property, and she dispensed them to us now, little by little, with a genuine sense of bounty, just as, later on, when I returned to her a grown-up young lady, she conceded me a diamond lavaliere of my mother's as if the trinket were an inheritance to which she had the prior claim. But her generosity with her memories appeared to us, as children, an act of the greatest indulgence. We begged her for more of these mortuary reminiscences as we might have begged for candy, and since ordinarily we not only had no candy but were permitted no friendships, no movies, and little reading beyond what our teachers prescribed for us, and were kept in quarantine, like carriers of social contagion, among the rhubarb plants of our neglected yard, these memories doled out by our grandmother became our secret treasures; we never spoke of them to each other but hoarded them, each against the rest, in the miserly fastnesses of our hearts. We returned, therefore, from our grandparents' house replenished in all our faculties;

these crumbs from the rich man's table were a banquet indeed to us. We did not even mind going back to our guardians, for we now felt superior to them, and besides, as we well knew, we had no choice. It was only by accepting our situation as a just and unalterable arrangement that we could be allowed to transcend it and feel ourselves united to our grandparents in a love that was the more miraculous for breeding no practical results.

In this manner, our household was kept together, and my grandparents were spared the necessity of arriving at a fresh decision about it. Naturally, from time to time a new scandal would break out (for our guardians did not grow kinder in response to being run away from), yet we had come, at bottom, to despair of making any real change in our circumstances, and ran away hopelessly, merely to postpone punishment. And when, after five years, our Protestant grandfather, informed at last of the facts, intervened to save us, his indignation at the family surprised us nearly as much as his action. We thought it only natural that grandparents should know and do nothing, for did not God in the mansions of Heaven look down upon human suffering and allow it to take its course?

1. How do the descriptive details that McCarthy provides at the beginning of the selection about the sewing room help you to understand her situation in her family?

2. In what ways are you made aware of a difference between McCarthy's sense of her situation when she experienced it as a child and her adult view of it while writing about it? Does she discuss the difference explicitly? Does she suggest the difference in the style of her writing?

3. How does McCarthy describe her grandmother? Look at the long list of details in the fourth, sixth, and seventh paragraphs. Do they emphasize one or two traits of the grandmother or a variety of her qualities?

4. Choose two or three moments in McCarthy's account that you find amusing and discuss how she creates a sense of the comic possibilities of the situation. Since McCarthy is usually

*recalling painful childhood experiences, what is the function
of the comedy?*

5. *McCarthy has written that this selection "is not really concerned with individuals. It is primarily an angry indictment
of privilege for its treatment of the underprivileged, a single,
breathless, voluble speech on the subject of human indiffer-
ence." Do you think she made you aware of these intentions
when you read the selection? Was her method of characterization different from that of other writers in this chapter because
she was not "concerned with individuals"?*

∾ James Thurber ∾

(1894-1961)

James Thurber was born and brought up in Columbus, Ohio. Thurber worked as a newspaperman for various papers until he finally joined the staff of The New Yorker *magazine in 1927. From that time on, the bulk of Thurber's work— sketches, reminiscences, cartoons, short stories, and essays— were written for the magazine, and they established him as one of America's great humorists. His portrait of Doc Mar- lowe comes from* Let Your Mind Alone *(1937), a collection of his magazine pieces from the middle Nineteen Thirties.*

DOC MARLOWE

I was too young to be other than awed and puzzled by Doc Marlowe when I knew him. I was only sixteen when he died. He was sixty-seven. There was that vast difference in our ages and there was a vaster difference in our backgrounds. Doc Marlowe was a medicine-show man. He had been a lot of other things, too: a circus man, the proprietor of a concession at Coney Island, a saloon-keeper; but in his fifties he had trav- eled around with a tent-show troupe made up of a Mexican named Chickalilli, who threw knives, and a man called Pro- fessor Jones, who played the banjo. Doc Marlowe would come out after the entertainment and harangue the crowd and sell bottles of medicine for all kinds of ailments. I found out all this about him gradually, toward the last, and after he died.

From James Thurber: *Let Your Mind Alone*. Published by Harper & Row. Copy- right © 1937 by James Thurber, copyright © 1965 by Helen W. Thurber and Rosemary Thurber Sauers. Originally printed in *The New Yorker*. Reprinted by permission of Mrs. James Thurber.

When I first knew him, he represented the Wild West to me, and there was nobody I admired so much.

I met Doc Marlowe at old Mrs. Willoughby's rooming house. She had been a nurse in our family, and I used to go and visit her over week-ends sometimes, for I was very fond of her. I was about eleven years old then. Doc Marlowe wore scarred leather leggings, a bright-colored bead vest that he said he got from the Indians, and a ten-gallon hat with kitchen matches stuck in the band, all the way around. He was about six feet four inches tall, with big shoulders, and a long, drooping mustache. He let his hair grow long, like General Custer's. He had a wonderful collection of Indian relics and six-shooters, and he used to tell me stories of his adventures in the Far West. His favorite expressions were "Hay, boy!" and "Hay, boy-gie!," which he used the way some people now use "Hot dog!" or "Doggone!" He told me once that he had killed an Indian chief named Yellow Hand in a tomahawk duel on horseback. I thought he was the greatest man I had ever seen. It wasn't until he died and his son came on from New Jersey for the funeral that I found out he had never been in the Far West in his life. He had been born in Brooklyn.

Doc Marlowe had given up the road when I knew him, but he still dealt in what he called "medicines." His stock in trade was a liniment that he had called Snake Oil when he traveled around. He changed the name to Blackhawk Liniment when he settled in Columbus. Doc didn't always sell enough of it to pay for his bed and board, and old Mrs. Willoughby would sometimes have to "trust" him for weeks at a time. She didn't mind, because his liniment had taken a bad kink out of her right limb that had bothered her for thirty years. I used to see people whom Doc had massaged with Blackhawk Liniment move arms and legs that they hadn't been able to move before he "treated" them. His patients were day laborers, wives of streetcar conductors, and people like that. Sometimes they would shout and weep after Doc had massaged them, and several got up and walked around who hadn't been able to walk before. One man hadn't turned his head to either side for seven years before Doc soused him with Blackhawk. In half an hour he could move his head as easily as I could move mine. "Glory be to God!" he shouted. "It's the secret qualities in the ointment, my friend," Doc Marlowe told him, suavely. He always called the liniment ointment.

News of his miracles got around by word of mouth among the poorer classes of town—he was not able to reach the better people (the "tony folks," he called them)—but there was never a big enough sale to give Doc a steady income. For one thing, people thought there was more magic in Doc's touch than in his liniment, and, for another, the ingredients of Blackhawk cost so much that his profits were not very great. I know, because I used to go to the wholesale chemical company once in a while for him and buy his supplies. Everything that went into the liniment was standard and expensive (and well-known, not secret). A man at the company told me he didn't see how Doc could make much money on it at thirty-five cents a bottle. But even when he was very low in funds Doc never cut out any of the ingredients or substituted cheaper ones. Mrs. Willoughby had suggested it to him once, she told me, when she was helping him "put up a batch," and he had got mad. "He puts a heap of store by that liniment being right up to the mark," she said.

Doc added to his small earnings, I discovered, by money he made gambling. He used to win quite a few dollars on Saturday nights at Freck's saloon, playing poker with the market-men and the railroaders who dropped in there. It wasn't for several years that I found out Doc cheated. I had never heard about marked cards until he told me about them and showed me his. It was one rainy afternoon, after he had played seven-up with Mrs. Willoughby and old Mr. Peiffer, another roomer of hers. They had played for small stakes (Doc wouldn't play cards unless there was some money up, and Mrs. Willoughby wouldn't play if very much was up). Only twenty or thirty cents had changed hands in the end. Doc had won it all. I remember my astonishment and indignation when it dawned on me that Doc had used the marked cards in playing the old lady and the old man. "You didn't cheat *them*, did you?" I asked him. "Jimmy, my boy," he told me, "the man that calls the turn wins the money." His eyes twinkled and he seemed to enjoy my anger. I was outraged, but I was helpless. I knew I could never tell Mrs. Willoughby about how Doc had cheated her at seven-up. I liked her, but I liked him, too. Once he had given me a whole dollar to buy fireworks with on the Fourth of July.

I remember once, when I was staying at Mrs. Willoughby's, Doc Marlowe was roused out of bed in the middle of the night by a poor woman who was frantic because her little girl was sick. This woman had had the sciatica driven out of her by his liniment, she reminded Doc. He placed her then. She had never been able to pay him a cent for his liniment or his "treatments," and he had given her a great many. He got up and dressed, and went over to her house. The child had colic, I suppose. Doc couldn't have had any idea what was the matter, but he sopped on liniment; he sopped on a whole bottle. When he came back home, two hours later, he said he had "relieved the distress." The little girl had gone to sleep and was all right the next day, whether on account of Doc Marlowe or in spite of him I don't know. "I want to thank you, Doctor," said the mother, tremulously, when she called on him that afternoon. He gave her another bottle of liniment, and he didn't charge her for it or for his "professional call." He used to massage, and give liniment to, a lot of sufferers who were too poor to pay. Mrs. Willoughby told him once that he was too generous and too easily taken in. Doc laughed—and winked at me, with the twinkle in his eye that he had had when he told me how he had cheated the old lady at cards.

Once I went for a walk with him out Town Street on a Saturday afternoon. It was a warm day, and after a while I said I wanted a soda. Well, he said, he didn't care if he took something himself. We went into a drugstore, and I ordered a choc-

olate soda and he had a lemon phosphate. When we had finished, he said, "Jimmy, my son, I'll match you to see who pays
for the drinks." He handed me a quarter and he told me to toss
the quarter and he would call the turn. He called heads and
won. I paid for the drinks. It left me with a dime.

I was fifteen when Doc got out his pamphlets, as he called
them. He had eased the misery of the wife of a small-time
printer and the grateful man had given him a special price on
two thousand advertising pamphlets. There was very little in
them about Blackhawk Liniment. They were mostly about
Doc himself and his "Life in the Far West." He had gone out
to Franklin Park one day with a photographer—another of his
numerous friends—and there the photographer took dozens of
pictures of Doc, a lariat in one hand, a six-shooter in the other.
I had gone along. When the pamphlets came out, there were
the pictures of Doc, peering around trees, crouching behind
bushes, whirling the lariat, aiming the gun. "Dr. H. M. Marlowe Hunting Indians" was one of the captions. "Dr. H. M.
Marlowe after Hoss-Thieves" was another one. He was very
proud of the pamphlets and always had a sheaf with him. He
would pass them out to people on the street.

Two years before he died Doc got hold of an ancient,
wheezy Cadillac somewhere. He aimed to start traveling
around again, he said, but he never did, because the old automobile was so worn out it wouldn't hold up for more than a
mile or so. It was about this time that a man named Hardman
and his wife came to stay at Mrs. Willoughby's. They were
farm people from around Lancaster who had sold their place.
They got to like Doc because he was so jolly, they said, and
they enjoyed his stories. He treated Mrs. Hardman for an old
complaint in the small of her back and wouldn't take any
money for it. They thought he was a fine gentleman. Then
there came a day when they announced that they were going
to St. Louis, where they had a son. They talked some of settling
in St. Louis. Doc Marlowe told them they ought to buy a nice
auto cheap and drive out, instead of going by train—it
wouldn't cost much and they could see the country, give them-

selves a treat. Now, he knew where they could pick up just such a car.

Of course, he finally sold them the decrepit Cadillac—it had been stored away somewhere in the back of a garage whose owner kept it there for nothing because Doc had relieved his mother of a distress in the groins, as Doc explained it. I don't know just how the garage man doctored up the car, but he did. It actually chugged along pretty steadily when Doc took the Hardmans out for a trial spin. He told them he hated to part with it, but he finally let them have it for a hundred dollars. I knew, of course, and so did Doc, that it couldn't last many miles.

Doc got a letter from the Hardmans in St. Louis ten days later. They had had to abandon the old junk pile in West Jefferson, some fifteen miles out of Columbus. Doc read the letter aloud to me, peering over his glasses, his eyes twinkling, every now and then punctuating the lines with "Hay, boy!" and "Hay, boy-gie!" "I just want you to know, Dr. Marlowe," he read, "what I think of low-life swindlers like you [Hay, boy!] and that it will be a long day before I put my trust in a two-faced lyer and imposture again [Hay, boy-gie!]. The garrage man in W. Jefferson told us your old rattle-trap had been doctored up just to fool us. It was a low down dirty trick as no swine would play on a white man [Hay, boy!]." Far from being disturbed by the letter, Doc Marlowe was plainly amused. He took off his glasses, after he finished it and laughed, his hand to his brow and his eyes closed. I was pretty mad, because I had liked the Hardmans, and because they had liked him. Doc Marlowe put the letter carefully back into its envelope and tucked it away in his inside coat pocket, as if it were something precious. Then he picked up a pack of cards and began to lay out a solitaire hand. "Want to set in a little seven-up game, Jimmy?" he asked me. I was furious. "Not with a cheater like you!" I shouted, and stamped out of the room, slamming the door. I could hear him chuckling to himself behind me.

The last time I saw Doc Marlowe was just a few days before

he died. I didn't know anything about death, but I knew that he was dying when I saw him. His voice was very faint and his face was drawn; they told me he had a lot of pain. When I got ready to leave the room, he asked me to bring him a tin box that was on his bureau. I got it and handed it to him. He poked around in it for a while with unsteady fingers and finally found what he wanted. He handed it to me. It was a quarter, or rather it looked like a quarter, but it had heads on both sides. "Never let the other fella call the turn, Jimmy, my boy," said Doc, with a shadow of his old twinkle and the echo of his old chuckle. I still have the two-headed quarter. For a long time I didn't like to think about it, or about Doc Marlowe, but I do now.

1. Why do you think Thurber wants to write about Doc Marlowe?

2. Thurber frequently tells you of particular phrases that Doc Marlowe used. What is his point in drawing your attention to Marlowe's language?

3. Thurber tells of Marlowe cheating an old lady at cards in one paragraph and then of his helping someone in the middle of the night at no charge in the next paragraph. What is his purpose in putting these two stories together? What sense of Marlowe's character does it give you?

4. How does Thurber's story of Doc Marlowe and the Hardmans fit into this portrait?

5. What does the last line of the sketch mean? How does it help to express Thurber's attitude? Do you see a difference between his interest in Doc Marlowe as a youngster and his interest now?

∽ Lillian Hellman ∽

(1907-   )

Lillian Hellman was born and brought up in New Orleans and educated at New York University and Columbia University. Her career as a playwright began with the New York success of The Children's Hour *(1934). Her dramas have received many awards, and such plays as* The Little Foxes *(1940),* Watch On The Rhine *(1941), and* Toys In The Attic *(1960) have been great popular successes, both on Broadway and in later film versions. She has written two autobiographical volumes,* An Unfinished Woman *(1969) and* Pentimento *(1973), both filled with portraits of the memorable people in her life. In this selection, she writes of her relationship with Dashiell Hammett, the creator of such classic works of detective fiction as* The Maltese Falcon *and* The Thin Man.

DASHIELL HAMMETT

For years we made jokes about the day I would write about him. In the early years, I would say, "Tell me more about the girl in San Francisco. The silly one who lived across the hall in Pine Street."

And he would laugh and say, "She lived across the hall in Pine Street and was silly."

"Tell more than that. How much did you like her and how—?"

He would yawn. "Finish your drink and go to sleep."

But days later, maybe even that night, if I was on the find-out kick, and I was, most of the years, I would say, "O.K., be stubborn about the girls. So tell me about your grandmother and what you looked like as a baby."

"I was a very fat baby. My grandmother went to the movies every afternoon. She was very fond of a movie star called Wallace Reid and I've told you all this before."

I would say I wanted to get everything straight for the days after his death when I would write his biography and he would say that I was not to bother writing his biography because it would turn out to be the history of Lillian Hellman with an occasional reference to a friend called Hammett.

The day of his death came on January 10, 1961. I will never write that biography because I cannot write about my closest, my most beloved friend. And maybe, too, because all those questions through all the thirty-one on and off years, and the sometime answers, got muddled, and life changed for both of us and the questions and answers became one in the end, flowing together from the days when I was young to the days when I was middle-aged. And so this will be no attempt at a biography of Samuel Dashiell Hammett, born in St. Mary's County, Maryland, on May 27, 1894. Nor will it be a critical appraisal of his work. In 1966 I edited and published a collection of his stories. There was a day when I thought all of them very good. But all of them are not good, though most of them, I think, are very good. It is only right to say immediately that by publishing them at all I did what Hammett did not want to do: he turned down all offers to republish the stories, although I never knew the reason and never asked. I did know, from what he said about "Tulip," the unfinished novel that I included in the book, that he meant to start a new literary life and maybe didn't want the old work to get in the way. But sometimes I think he was just too ill to care, too worn out to listen to plans or read contracts. The fact of breathing, just breathing, took up all the days and nights.

In the First World War, in camp, influenza led to tuberculosis and Hammett was to spend years after in army hospitals.

He came out of the Second World War with emphysema, but how he ever got into the Second World War at the age of forty-eight still bewilders me. He telephoned me the day the army accepted him to say it was the happiest day of his life, and before I could finish saying it wasn't the happiest day of mine and what about the old scars on his lungs, he laughed and hung up. His death was caused by cancer of the lungs, discovered only two months before he died. It was not operable—I doubt that he would have agreed to an operation even if it had been—and so I decided not to tell him about the cancer. The doctor said that when the pain came, it would come in the right chest and arm, but that the pain might never come. The doctor was wrong: only a few hours after he told me, the pain did come. Hammett had had self-diagnosed rheumatism in the right arm and had always said that was why he had given up hunting. On the day I heard about the cancer, he said his gun shoulder hurt him again, would I rub it for him. I remember sitting behind him, rubbing the shoulder and hoping he would always think it was rheumatism and remember only the autumn hunting days. But the pain never came again, or if it did he never mentioned it, or maybe death was so close that the shoulder pain faded into other pains.

He did not wish to die and I like to think he didn't know he was dying. But I keep from myself even now the possible meaning of a night, very late, a short time before his death. I came into his room, and for the only time in the years I knew him there were tears in his eyes and the book was lying unread. I sat down beside him and waited a long time before I could say, "Do you want to talk about it?"

He said, almost with anger, "No. My only chance is not to talk about it."

And he never did. He had patience, courage, dignity in those last, awful months. It was as if all that makes a man's life had come together to prove itself: suffering was a private matter and there was to be no invasion of it. He would seldom even ask for anything he needed, and so the most we did—my secretary and Helen, who were devoted to him, as most women always had been—was to carry up the meals he barely touched, the books he now could hardly read, the afternoon coffee, and the martini that I insisted upon before the dinner that wasn't eaten.

One night of that last year, a bad night, I said, "Have another martini. It will make you feel better."

"No," he said, "I don't want it."

I said, "O.K., but I bet you never thought I'd urge you to have another drink."

He laughed for the first time that day. "Nope. And I never thought I'd turn it down."

Because on the night we had first met he was getting over a five-day drunk and he was to drink very heavily for the next eighteen years, and then one day, warned by a doctor, he said he would never have another drink and he kept his word except for the last year of the one martini, and that was my idea.

We met when I was twenty-four years old and he was thirty-six in a restaurant in Hollywood. The five-day drunk had left the wonderful face looking rumpled, and the very tall thin figure was tired and sagged. We talked of T. S. Eliot, although I no longer remember what we said, and then went and sat in his car and talked at each other and over each other until it was daylight. We were to meet again a few weeks later and, after that, on and sometimes off again for the rest of his life and thirty years of mine.

Thirty years is a long time, I guess, and yet as I come now to write about them the memories skip about and make no pattern and I know only certain of them are to be trusted. I know about that first meeting and the next, and there are many other pictures and sounds, but they are out of order and out of time, and I don't seem to want to put them into place. (I could have done a research job, I have on other people, but I didn't want to do one on Hammett, or to be a bookkeeper of my own life.) I don't want modesty for either of us, but I ask myself now if it can mean much to anybody but me that my second

318

sharpest memory is of a day when we were living on a small island off the coast of Connecticut. It was six years after we had first met: six full, happy, unhappy years during which I had, with help from Hammett, written *The Children's Hour*, which was a success, and *Days to Come*, which was not. I was returning from the mainland in a catboat filled with marketing and Hammett had come down to the dock to tie me up. He had been sick that summer—the first of the sicknesses—and he was even thinner than usual. The white hair, the white pants, the white shirt made a straight, flat surface in the late sun. I thought: Maybe that's the handsomest sight I ever saw, that line of a man, the knife for a nose, and the sheet went out of my hand and the wind went out of the sail. Hammett laughed as I struggled to get back the sail. I don't know why, but I yelled angrily, "So you're a Dostoevsky sinner-saint. So you are." The laughter stopped, and when I finally came in to the dock we didn't speak as we carried up the packages and didn't speak through dinner.

Later that night, he said, "What did you say that for? What does it mean?"

I said I didn't know why I had said it and I didn't know what it meant.

Years later, when his life had changed, I did know what I had meant that day: I had seen the sinner—whatever is a sinner—and sensed the change before it came. When I told him that, Hammett said he didn't know what I was talking about, it was all too religious for him. But he did know what I was talking about and he was pleased.

But the fat, loose, wild years were over by the time we talked that way. When I first met Dash he had written four of the five novels and was the hottest thing in Hollywood and New York. It is not remarkable to be the hottest thing in either city—the hottest kid changes for each winter season—but in his case it was of extra interest to those who collect people that the ex-detective who had bad cuts on his legs and an indentation in his head from being scrappy with criminals was gentle in manner, well educated, elegant to look at, born of early settlers, was eccentric, witty, and spent so much money on women that they would have liked him even if he had been none of the good things. But as the years passed from 1930 to 1948, he wrote only one novel and a few short stories. By 1945, the drinking was no longer gay, the drinking bouts were longer and the moods darker. I was there off and on for most of those years, but in 1948 I didn't want to see the drinking anymore. I hadn't seen or spoken to Hammett for two months until the day when his devoted cleaning lady called to say she thought I had better come down to his apartment. I said I wouldn't, and then I did. She and I dressed a man who could barely lift an arm or a leg and brought him to my house, and that night I watched delirium tremens, although I didn't know what I was watching until the doctor told me the next day at the hospital. The doctor was an old friend. He said, "I'm going to tell Hammett that if he goes on drinking he'll be dead in a few months. It's my duty to say it, but it won't do any good." In a few minutes he came out of Dash's room and said, "I told him. Dash said O.K., he'd go on the wagon forever, but he can't and he won't."

But he could and he did. Five or six years later, I told Hammett that the doctor had said he wouldn't stay on the wagon.

Dash looked puzzled. "But I gave my word that day."

I said, "Have you always kept your word?"

"Most of the time," he said, "maybe because I've so seldom given it."

He had made up honor early in his life and stuck with his rules, fierce in the protection of them. In 1951 he went to jail because he and two other trustees of the bail bond fund of the Civil Rights Congress refused to reveal the names of the contributors to the fund. The truth was that Hammett had never been in the office of the Congress, did not know the name of a single contributor.

The night before he was to appear in court, I said, "Why don't you say that you don't know the names?"

"No," he said, "I can't say that."

"Why?"

"I don't know why. I guess it has something to do with keeping my word, but I don't want to talk about that. Nothing much will happen, although I think we'll go to jail for a while, but you're not to worry because"—and then suddenly I couldn't understand him because the voice had dropped and the words were coming in a most untypical nervous rush. I said I couldn't hear him, and he raised his voice and dropped his head. "I hate this damn kind of talk, but maybe I better tell you that if it were more than jail, if it were my life, I would give it for what I think democracy is, and I don't let cops or judges tell me what I think democracy is." Then he went home to bed, and the next day he went to jail.

1. Near the beginning of this selection, Hellman says that she is not writing a biography of Hammett or a critical appraisal of his work. How would you describe what she has accomplished here?

2. Why do you think Hellman begins her account with a brief dialogue between herself and Hammett? What are they talking about and how is it important to this piece?

3. In the paragraph beginning "Thirty years is a very long time . . ." Hellman denies following any particular order in writing about her relationship with Hammett. What kind of sequence or shape do you think the selection does have?

4. What sense of Hellman herself do you get from her recollections? Does she reveal herself in the things she admires about Hammett? In her conversations with him?

∽ George Orwell ∽

(1903-1950)

See the biographical note on page 61. The following selection is from Orwell's first book, Down and Out in Paris and London *(1933), an autobiographical account of his times of privation in those two cities while he was trying to get a start as a writer. Occasionally Orwell would take to the road in England; the following selection is Orwell's characterization of one of the tramps with whom he traveled.*

[PADDY THE TRAMP]

Paddy was my mate for about the next fortnight, and, as he was the first tramp I had known at all well, I want to give an account of him. I believe that he was a typical tramp and there are tens of thousands in England like him.

He was a tallish man, aged about thirty-five, with fair hair going grizzled and watery blue eyes. His features were good, but his cheeks had lanked and had that greyish, dirty in the grain look that comes of a bread and margarine diet. He was dressed, rather better than most tramps, in a tweed shooting-jacket and a pair of old evening trousers with the braid still on them. Evidently the braid figured in his mind as a lingering scrap of respectability, and he took care to sew it on again when it came loose. He was careful of his appearance altogether, and carried a razor and bootbrush that he would not sell, though he had sold his "papers" and even his pocket-knife long since. Nevertheless, one would have known him for a tramp a hundred yards away. There was something in his drifting style of walk, and the way he had of hunching his shoulders forward, essentially abject. Seeing him walk, you felt instinctively that he would sooner take a blow than give one.

He had been brought up in Ireland, served two years in the war, and then worked in a metal polish factory, where he had lost his job two years earlier. He was horribly ashamed of being a tramp, but he had picked up all a tramp's ways. He browsed the pavements unceasingly, never missing a cigarette end, or even an empty cigarette packet, as he used the tissue paper for rolling cigarettes. On our way into Edbury he saw a newspaper parcel on the pavement, pounced on it, and found that it contained two mutton sandwiches, rather frayed at the edges; these he insisted on my sharing. He never passed an automatic machine without giving a tug at the handle, for he said that sometimes they are out of order and will eject pennies if you tug at them. He had no stomach for crime, however. When we were in the outskirts of Romton, Paddy noticed a bottle of milk on a doorstep, evidently left there by mistake. He stopped, eyeing the bottle hungrily.

"Christ!" he said, "dere's good food goin' to waste. Somebody could knock dat bottle off, eh? Knock it off easy."

I saw that he was thinking of "knocking it off" himself. He looked up and down the street; it was a quiet residential street and there was nobody in sight. Paddy's sickly, chap-fallen face yearned over the milk. Then he turned away, saying gloomily:

"Best leave it. It don't do a man no good to steal. T'ank God, I ain't never stolen nothin' yet."

It was funk, bred of hunger, that kept him virtuous. With only two or three sound meals in his belly, he would have found courage to steal the milk.

He had two subjects of conversation, the shame and comedown of being a tramp, and the best way of getting a free meal. As we drifted through the streets he would keep up a monologue in this style, in a whimpering, self-pitying Irish voice:

"It's hell bein' on de road, eh? It breaks yer heart goin' into dem bloody spikes. But what's a man to do else, eh? I ain't had a good meat meal for about two months, an' me boots is getting bad, an'—Christ! How'd it be if we was to try for a cup o' tay at one o' dem convents on de way to Edbury? Most times dey're good for a cup o' tay. Ah, what'd a man do widout religion, eh? I've took cups o' tay from de convents, an' de Baptists, an' de Church of England, an' all sorts. I'm a Catholic meself. Dat's to say, I ain't been to confession for about seventeen year, but still I got me religious feelin's, y'understand. An' dem convents is always good for a cup o' tay . . ." etc. etc. He would keep this up all day, almost without stopping.

His ignorance was limitless and appalling. He once asked me, for instance, whether Napoleon lived before Jesus Christ or after. Another time, when I was looking into a bookshop window, he grew very perturbed because one of the books was called *Of the Imitation of Christ*. He took this for blasphemy. "What de hell do dey want to go imitatin' of *Him* for?" he demanded angrily. He could read, but he had a kind of loathing for books. On our way from Romton to Edbury I went into a public library, and, though Paddy did not want to read, I suggested that he should come in and rest his legs. But he preferred to wait on the pavement. "No," he said, "de sight of all dat bloody print makes me sick."

Like most tramps, he was passionately mean about matches. He had a box of matches when I met him, but I never saw him strike one, and he used to lecture me for extravagance when I struck mine. His method was to cadge a light from strangers, sometimes going without a smoke for half an hour rather than strike a match.

Self-pity was the clue to his character. The thought of his bad luck never seemed to leave him for an instant. He would break long silences to exclaim, apropos of nothing, "It's hell when yer clo'es begin to go up de spout, eh?" or "Dat tay in de spike ain't tay, it's piss," as though there was nothing else in the world to think about. And he had a low, worm-like envy of anyone who was better off—not of the rich, for they were beyond his social horizon, but of men in work. He pined for work as an artist pines to be famous. If he saw an old man working he would say bitterly, "Look at dat old —— keepin' able-bodied men out o' work"; or if it was a boy, "It's dem young devils what's takin' de bread out of our mouths." And all foreigners to him were "dem bloody dagoes"—for, according to his theory, foreigners were responsible for unemployment.

He looked at women with a mixture of longing and hatred. Young, pretty women were too much above him to enter into his ideas, but his mouth watered at prostitutes. A couple of scarlet-lipped old creatures would go past; Paddy's face would flush pale pink, and he would turn and stare hungrily after the women. "Tarts!" he would murmur, like a boy at a sweetshop window. He told me once that he had not had to do with a woman for two years—since he had lost his job, that is—and he had forgotten that one could aim higher than prostitutes. He had the regular character of a tramp—abject, envious, a jackal's character.

Nevertheless, he was a good fellow, generous by nature and capable of sharing his last crust with a friend; indeed he did literally share his last crust with me more than once. He was probably capable of work too, if he had been well fed for a few months. But two years of bread and margarine had lowered his standards hopelessly. He had lived on this filthy imitation of food till his own mind and body were compounded of inferior stuff. It was malnutrition and not any native vice that had destroyed his manhood.

1. Orwell says that he wants to tell us about a "typical" tramp. How does his interest in a type of person make his account different from those of other writers in this chapter who want to emphasize a particular person?

2. In what ways does Orwell's narrative make you aware that he is quite different from Paddy and that he himself is not a tramp?

3. How is Paddy characterized by what he actually says? How would you explain the relation between Paddy's remarks and Orwell's comments on those remarks?

4. Does Orwell's portrait of Paddy have any social purpose? Is he suggesting anything about the economic or social conditions that create unemployment or is he primarily interested in Paddy as a picturesque character?

5. As in "Marrakech" (see   p. 236), Orwell is interested here in writing about people who have very little status in their society. Do you see similarities in Orwell's methods in the two selections? In his attitudes?

Possibilities for Writing

1. Choose a person you would find interesting to write about and make a list, as long as you can, of qualities, actions, gestures, physical characteristics, habits, interests, possessions, etc., that you associate with the person. Then write a character sketch based on some of the material on your list. In class, discuss how you used the list: what items you selected and why, what order you used them in and why.

2. Sometimes a single incident can confirm or enlarge our sense of the personality and character of someone we know well. Write a character sketch based on such an incident, in which you make clear how the incident communicated so much about this other person. You might compare your method of presenting an incident with that of Joan Baez, who uses this technique in discussing her father.

3. Write a character sketch of someone you have known for some time and have seen frequently (a close friend or a relative, perhaps). Then write a sketch of someone who impresses or interests you, but whom you have met only once or twice or whom you have only read about and seen on television. In class, compare your two characterizations and discuss what you, as a writer, have done differently in each piece.

4. Write an essay discussing how James Thurber makes you aware that as a young boy he thought differently about Doc

Marlowe than he does now. What attracts the young Thurber to Marlowe? In what ways does he have difficulty understanding Marlowe's behavior? What explains the change in feelings that Thurber mentions in the last sentence of the sketch?

5. Write an essay comparing what Yeats found memorable about his grandfather with what N. Scott Momaday found memorable about his grandmother. What special kind of dignity or authority is associated with each grandparent? What feelings does each writer express about his grandparent? Which writer is more interested in conveying a child's point of view?

CHAPTER SIX

~~~~~~

PERSPECTIVES
ON
EXPERIENCE

Introduction: Generalization and Abstraction

As every self-portrait in this anthology makes clear, the pur-
pose of autobiography is not simply to create a record of our
lives, but to create a meaningful record. We have seen that the
act of remembering and putting memories on paper is inseparable from a process of conscious and unconscious selection in
which we choose to include some things because they are rele-
vant or meaningful and to exclude others. The same process of
selection that governs what we perceive and what we remember also applies to the language we use to convey such perceptions and memories—our words inevitably involve us in
creating and revealing meanings. The sum of these selections
becomes a point of view, a particular way of seeing meanings
in the world and expressing them in words.

We have also discovered that a further way of creating
meaning is through our ability to generalize. We are never
content to exist simply as custodians of the separate moments
of our past; we want to organize our experiences, grouping
them so that we can see pattern and relationship and can make
sense of them at last. In the preceding chapter we discussed
how generalizations could substitute for or serve as the culmi-
nation of a number of separate perceptions, binding those perceptions together into a characterization. Now it is necessary
to make a further distinction between two complementary
methods of enlarging upon a single moment of experience.
One method—generalization—carries us beyond that single

moment by placing its elements in broader or more general categories. We can gain some sense of how generalization works if we look at four related sentences, introduced here to illustrate stages of generalization. The first refers to a single specific event: (1) "On Tuesday John tried to impress Nancy by taking her to the most expensive restaurant in New York." The second sentence still focuses on John, but now includes many actions of a type similar to the specific event mentioned in the first sentence: (2) "John always tries to impress women by taking them to expensive places." The third sentence generalizes further by placing John himself in a larger category: (3) "American men show their interest in women by spending money on them." The fourth sentence goes furthest of all, since it claims to apply to all men universally: (4) "All men believe that their bank account has sex appeal."

As we have seen, these four sentences follow an ascending order of generalization. Sentence 2 generalizes in a very limited way, since it refers to only one person and to only one facet of his behavior. Because of its limited scope, such a statement is often called a low-level generalization; Frank O'Connor relied on generalizations of this type in his characterization of his father (Ch. 5). High-level generalizations take in a wider spectrum of human agents and their actions; at their most inclusive, as in sentence 4, general statements do not include any qualifying context. As the level of generalization increases, the statements made need more careful support if they are to be convincing. We might accept sentence 2 as representing a fairly familiar kind of male chauvinism, but we would probably be skeptical of the accuracy of sentence 3, without some careful qualification. Sentence 4 is clearly too broad to be persuasive and, like most extreme generalizations, tells us much more about the values of the writer than it does about the subject matter. Taken together the sentences show how every writer needs to be aware of the degree to which he is generalizing and of the degree to which he needs to support each generalization.

The second method of enlarging an individual moment of experience is abstraction. Abstraction separates a quality or characteristic from the concrete instances that embody it. John's behavior toward Nancy, in our earlier example, could be summarized by the abstraction "extravagant" or "self-promoting," words which are broader in their reference than the specific action by John that they describe. Another writer (John himself, perhaps) might use other abstractions, such as "generous" or "discriminating," to summarize the qualities that define John's behavior. Abstractions, like generalizations, are forceful markers of the writer's values and point of view. For this reason, a writer must be careful to use such language with precision, knowing not only how widely it applies but also what kind of judgments it reveals.

The reason that generalization and abstraction are important concepts for the autobiographer is that they enable him to form explicit patterns from the specific memories of his earlier life. One of the great attractions of our personal past for us as writers is that it is both familiar and finished; we know it but are not enveloped in it, as we are in the changing and uncertain condition of our present life. Since we possess a degree of detachment toward our past, we often want to make some explicit interpretation of our experience. To do that we need to introduce abstractions and larger generalizations and introduce them with some frequency. In other words, there may be times when we want to convey the special savor of some moment in our lives as only we could have experienced it, concretely and particularly, but there may be other times when we want to represent our experience as a member of some class or group—as a student, say, or as an adolescent, or as an American. We have already seen how Frank O'Connor made generalizations that were limited because they applied only to his father. But O'Connor might have written of these same memories and seen them within a pattern that would apply to many other people as well as to his father. For example, he might use his memories to comment on drinking among Irish working-class men or to illustrate the effects that an alcoholic parent has on the lives of the rest of the family. As "my father" becomes included in words that refer to larger categories, the writer moves to some higher level of generalization (Irish working class men or alcoholic parents).

THE PURPOSES OF GENERALIZATION

When we generalize about ourselves we invariably demonstrate a degree of detachment about our own lives. If we convert one of O'Connor's descriptions of his father to the first person ("I was a naturally melancholy man; though I was always pleased when people called, I rarely called on anybody myself"), we can see that using limited generalizations about oneself creates a necessary separation between the writer and the person who is being written about. Such generalizations remind us that autobiography is indeed about another person: ourselves as we were at some past moment. From our vantage point in the present we can see that past moment and place it as something significant in our understanding of who we are.

Even though generalizations and abstractions about ourselves cost us some degree of intimacy and spontaneity in autobiography, we use them because we wish to show that we understand the meaning of our own lives. Not only do we want to determine the shape of our lives by deciding what memories we will include, but we also want to demonstrate that we have thought out our experiences and connected them with other times and other places in our lives. Any autobiographer generalizes to some extent about his own past because he recognizes that his authority as a writer depends on convincing his reader that he is presenting a considered account of what has happened to him.

The other reason most writers try to generalize from their personal experience is to place themselves in some broad category with which their audience can associate. When James Baldwin writes about living through the winter in a tiny Swiss village, an experience which very few of his readers could ever have shared, he sees his situation as that of a black American in an uncomprehending environment. His experience becomes that of a black man facing the non-African world and his anguish and rage become the feelings endured by anyone alien and misunderstood. Generalization is Baldwin's way of transforming an autobiographical experience that might initially seem to us quite limited and specialized into something that touches on the concerns of our quite different lives. By generalizing in the way that he does, Baldwin's account can awaken the interest of a great range of potential readers—not just American blacks, or whites anxious for a better understanding of racial relations, but anyone concerned by the issue of how human beings treat whatever they think of as alien to their own culture. When a writer like Baldwin generalizes about some aspect of his past, he is simply trying to insist that his life does have relevance for other people whose lives may be quite different from his own. Generalization is one vehicle by which the writer can identify himself with some area of shared human concern.

At the same time, however, a writer who places too much emphasis on generalizations about his life or fails to support them is in danger of obscuring whatever is uniquely interesting about himself and becoming too much of a representative man. We are all familiar with the kind of person who is always identifying himself with some vast general class: "As a believer in the democratic system, I would like to say . . ." or "My experience has taught me that man must and will prevail." Such statements usually strike us as pompous and empty, concealing rather than revealing any kind of personal vision. Some writers think of these windy examples when they imagine themselves generalizing about their lives, and they sensibly want to avoid that kind of meaningless assertion. As a result, many writers see higher-level generalizations as a prerogative of the very old and feel that only an autobiographer safely retired from participation in the world's activities can make general pronouncements without embarrassment. They would recognize the eloquence of Edmund Wilson's "Epilogue" in this chapter, but would judge its dignity and force inimitable, because it is so dependent upon the weight of Wilson's age and experience.

It is true that "conclusions" and "reflections" do seem most appropriate from someone whose lengthy and varied life justifies a large view of the human condition, but a much younger writer has a perfect right to generalize from his experience, so long as he is careful to make his experiences create a proper context for his generalizations. The point becomes clearer when we return to the Baldwin essay, published when he was twenty-nine years old. Here is a characteristic passage: "The rage of the disesteemed is personally fruitless, but it is also absolutely inevitable; this rage, so generally discounted, so little understood even among the people whose daily bread it is, is one of the things that makes history." Baldwin is using very large generalizations indeed—"the disesteemed," "history"—but we cannot judge them simply by their inclusiveness and wonder what a twenty-nine-year-old can know about "history." We have to see whether such large statements float unattached in the essay or whether they seem to be bound up with the particulars of the personal experience that Baldwin is presenting. The issue is not whether the generalization is valid, but whether it is apt, whether it fits the specific circumstances the writer has included and is a suitable response to them. Furthermore, the level of generalization the writer uses must be maintained with some consistency. We are probably willing to accept Baldwin's large statement about history for two reasons: first, he has managed to show how daily incidents in his life in the village provoke the generalization; second, he has established himself from the beginning of his essay as someone who reflects broadly on his experience. His life in the village makes him think of his generally isolated state among white people, and makes him speculate on his relation to the whole tradition of white European culture—Dante, Shakespeare, Michelangelo—so his comment on "history" follows appropriately enough from these other reflections.

The way in which a young writer can assign meaning to particular experiences by generalizing from them is reflected with a somewhat different emphasis in the selection by Joyce Maynard. She is only nineteen when she writes about her past, but she defines herself as a representative member of a generation growing up in a particular culture at a particular time. Perhaps she is too insistent too soon about her own representativeness—everything in her account quickly becomes converted to "we" and "our"—but her generalizations are such that she is always able to call for support from the concrete details of things she has seen and felt and done. For example, when she makes the point that her generation was the first to take technology for granted, she then continues, "What was a space shot to us, except an hour cut from social studies to gather before a TV in the gym as Cape Canaveral counted down?" Maynard is therefore able to interpret her experiences for us in a frame that neither suppresses the actual qualities of her life nor inflates them with an unnatural burden of significance.

Baldwin and Maynard demonstrate that a writer of any age or circumstances can convincingly generalize from his or her experience as long as the generalization keeps some mooring in the world of the tangible and the specific. Because of the necessary interdependence of the particular and the general, the concrete and the abstract, writing about ourselves effectively does not entail a step-by-step mastery, first of narration, then of description, and so on, until we finally succeed in producing a sentence or a paragraph of vast generalization. Although the chapters in this book necessarily follow a sequence, the goal in writing is the integration of all the skills that have been discussed. Ideally, each writer should try to strike some congenial balance in which he is able to reproduce past experience vividly, and at the same time take advantage of his distance from that past moment to explain it more fully. There may be occasions when he emphasizes narrative flow or descriptive accuracy to the exclusion of anything else, but usually he will also need abstraction and generalization to show how particular experiences contribute to the meaning of his autobiography.

AUTOBIOGRAPHY AND OTHER FORMS OF WRITING

Personal experience, furthermore, can give substance to other kinds of writing besides formal autobiography. A writer can often make autobiographical material serve a valuable but subordinate role within the framework of a general argument about an issue or an idea. Jessica Mitford, for example, is not primarily interested in being autobiographical in the excerpt from *Kind and Unusual Punishment*. Instead, she wishes to draw upon personal memories to support and clarify her statements about the penal system in America. As a result, her account is not consistently an account of personal experience: often she is describing prison procedures which she will never have to undergo, or interviewing prisoners in order to document aspects of prison life she will never see. Mitford's distinctive purposes do not make this selection different in kind from others in the chapter, but they do create a special emphasis, one which makes the reader more aware of a life being used for illustrative purposes. Her recollections make us conscious of the degradation of the lives of inmates in a typical "detention center," and of the failures and inequities of the system she describes, rather than making us see her own life in a more vivid or comprehensible way.

Mitford's general views have undoubtedly been influenced by events in her personal past, but many times a writer needs to discuss matters that have little or nothing to do with his own life. In these circumstances, generalization and abstraction provide him with a way to write about ideas and issues that do not derive directly from his own experience. Such conceptual language enables him to write about capital punishment although he has never been inside a prison or about divorce although he has never signed a marriage license. However, when a writer turns away from the concrete details provided by personal experience, he cannot simply assert his general views without specific support; he must find other forms of documentation or illustration to validate his statements. On some occasions a writer will combine personal and impersonal evidence to establish his authority, as V. S. Pritchett gracefully introduces historical data about other autobiographers along with his recollections of the frustrations involved in writing his own autobiography. On other occasions, including a good number of writing situations in college, a writer will wish to establish a viewpoint of unquestioned objectivity and will eliminate any reference to personal experience or personal feelings, using as evidence only the work of published authorities and being careful to balance the comments of several such authorities when introducing a controversial issue. This is not cowardice, only an appropriate choice for the writer when his purpose makes him wish to have his readers trust his detachment.

Clearly, then, we will not find ourselves being autobiographical in everything we write, but we will always be making use of the skills we can learn especially well through writing about ourselves. Autobiography makes us narrate our experiences, describe our environments, characterize our friends, explain our behavior, analyze our feelings and motives, argue for our beliefs, and summarize our accomplishments—in short, it may at any given moment call upon us to adopt one or another of the techniques any good writer has to master. Simultaneously, autobiography gives each of us the chance to root our language first and foremost in our own self-awareness, and from this source fashion a personal voice in our writing, one that should survive as identifiably ours even when we turn to more impersonal topics. We should therefore value autobiography highly because it endows us with two gifts that all writers cherish: the freedom to choose among diverse ways of presenting our subject and the opportunity to speak for it with unchallenged authority.

∽ Joyce Maynard ∽

(1953-   )

*Joyce Maynard grew up in Durham, New Hampshire, where
her father taught at the state university. She wrote her autobiography,* Looking Back *(1972), while still an undergraduate
at Yale. She describes the turbulent experiences of the 1960s
as a member of the generation most immediately influenced
by the events and the style of the period.*

[GROWING UP IN THE SIXTIES]

To my friend Hanna, at five, I am a grown-up. I do not feel
like one—at nineteen, I'm at the midway point between the
kindergartner and her mother, and I belong to neither generation—but I can vote, and drink in New York, and marry without parental consent in Mississippi, and get a life sentence, not
reform school, if I shoot someone premeditatedly. Walking
with Hanna in New York and keeping to the inside, as the
guidebooks tell me, so that doorway muggers lunging out will
get not her but me, I'm suddenly aware that, of the two of us,
I am the adult, the one whose life means less, because I've
lived more of it already; I've moved from my position as protected child to child protector; I am the holder of a smaller
hand where, just ten years ago, *my* hand was held through
streets whose danger lay not in the alleys but in the roads
themselves, the speeding cars, roaring motorcycles. I have left
childhood, and though I longed to leave it, when being young
meant finishing your milk and missing "Twilight Zone" on

TV because it came on too late, now that it's gone I'm uneasy. Not fear of death yet (I'm still young enough to feel immortal) or worry over wrinkles and gray hair, but a sense that the fun is over before it began, that I'm old before my time—why isn't someone holding *my* hand still, protecting *me* from the dangers of the city, guiding me home?

I remember kneeling on the seat of a subway car, never bothering to count the stops or peer through all those shopping bags and knees to read the signs, because *she* would know when to get off, she'd take my hand; I remember looking out the window to see the sparks fly, underpants exposed to all the rush-hour travelers and never worrying that they could see, while all around me, mothers had to cross their legs or keep their knees together. And later, driving home, leaning against my mother's shoulder while her back tensed on the seat and her eyes stared out at the yellow lines, it was so nice to know I was responsible for nothing more than brushing my teeth when we got home, and not even that, if we got home late enough.

Hanna doesn't look where we're going, never bothers to make sure she can find her way home again, because she knows I will take care of those things, and though I feel I am too young to be so old in anybody's eyes, it's just a feeling, not a fact. When it rains, she gets the plastic rain hat, and when the ball of ice cream on her cone falls off, I give her mine. But if Hanna uses my ice cream and my hat, my knowledge of the subways and my hand, well, I use Hanna too: she's my excuse to ride the Ferris wheel, to shop for dolls. And when the circus comes to town—Ringling Brothers, no less—and I take her, everything evens up. Walking to Madison Square Garden, stepping over sidewalk lines and dodging muggers, she is my escort more than I am hers.

I think of one time in particular.

There we sat, in our too-well-cushioned seats, Hanna in her navy blue socks and flower barrettes, I beside her, holding the overpriced miniature flashlight she had shamed me into buying (because everyone else in our row had one), earnestly obeying the ringmaster's instructions to wave it when the lights went out—frantically, a beacon in the night—because Hanna's hands were too full of other circus-going apparatus: a celluloid doll whose arm already hung loose, the Cracker Jack she wanted for the prize inside, the Jujubes that she swallowed dutifully like pills. We all seemed a little sad, Hanna and me and all the other flashlight wavers who surrounded us, like people I'd see in a movie and feel sorry for—the grown-ups, the ticket buyers, because the admission fee hadn't really bought us into youngness again, even the little kids, because most of them had barely had it to begin with. We grew up old, Hanna even more than I. We are cynics who see the trap door in the magic show, the pillow stuffing in Salvation Army Santa Clauses, the camera tricks in TV commercials ("That isn't really a genie's hand coming out of the washing machine," Hanna tells me, "it's just an actor with gloves on.") So at the circus, there was a certain lack of wonder in the crowd, a calm, shrugging atmosphere of "So what else is new?" She leaned back on her padded seat, my four-year-old, watching me twirl her flashlight for her ("Keep up with those flashlights, kids," the ringmaster had said), chewing her hot dog, anticipating pratfalls, toughly, smartly, sadly, wisely, agedly unenthralled, more wrapped up in the cotton candy than in the Greatest Show on Earth. Above us, a man danced on a tightrope while, below, poodles stood on their heads and elephants balanced, two-legged, over the spangled bodies of trusting circus girls, and horses leapt through flaming hoops and jugglers handled more balls than I could count and never dropped one.

Perhaps it was that we had too much to look at and so weren't awed by any one thing. But even more, it was that we had seen greater spectacles, unmoved, that our whole world was a visual glut, a ten-ring circus even Ringling Brothers couldn't compete with. A man stuck his head into a tiger's mouth and I pointed it out, with more amazement than I really felt, to my cool, unfazed friend, and when she failed to look (I, irritated now—"these seats cost money . . .") turned her head for her, forced her to take the sight in. The tiger could have bitten the tamer's head off, I think, swallowed him whole and turned into a monkey and she wouldn't have blinked. We watched what must have been two dozen clowns pile out of a Volkswagen without Hanna's knowing what the point of all that was. It isn't just the knowledge that they emerge from a trap door in the sawdust that keeps Hanna from looking up, either. Even if she didn't know the trick involved, she wouldn't care.

I don't think I'm reading too much into it when I say that, at five, she has already developed a sense of the absurd—the kind of unblinking world-weariness that usually comes only to disillusioned middle-aged men and eighty-year-old rocking-chair sitters. I sometimes forget that Hanna is just five, not eighty; that she believes she will grow up to be a ballerina and tells me that someday she'll marry a prince; that she is afraid of the dark, she isn't big enough for a two-wheeler; her face clouds over in the sad parts of a Shirley Temple movie and lights up at the orange roof of a Howard Johnson's. Maybe I'm projecting on Hanna the feelings I have about my own childhood and growing up when I say that she seems, sometimes, to be so jaded. I think not, though. I watch her watching the monkeys dance and, sensing my eyes on her, and for my benefit, not from real mirth, she laughs a TV-actress laugh. She throws her head back (a shampoo ad) and smiles a toothpaste commercial smile so that baby teeth show—sex appeal?—and says, for my benefit, "This is lots of fun, isn't it?" the way people who aren't enjoying themselves much, but feel they should be, try to convince themselves they are.

What all this has to do with growing up old—Hanna and me, five and nineteen, watching the circus—is that Hanna has already begun her aging and I, once having aged, am trying to return. We're different generations, of course, but—though Hanna doesn't know what Vietnam is, or marijuana—we've both been touched by the sixties or, at least, its aftermath. I've grown up old, and I mention Hanna because she seems to have been born that way, almost, as if each generation tarnishes the innocence of the next. In 1957 I was four going on twenty, sometimes; Hanna at the circus borders on middle age . . . I feel the circle—childhood and senility—closing in.

A word like *disillusioned* doesn't apply to a five-year-old's generation or—though they call my generation "disillusioned" all the time—to mine. I grew up without many illusions to begin with, in a time when fairy tales were thought to be unhealthy (one teacher told my mother that), when fantasy existed mostly in the form of Mr. Clean and Speedy Alka-Seltzer. We were sensible, realistic, literal-minded, unromantic, socially conscious and politically minded, whether we read the papers (whether we could even read, in fact) or not. The Kennedys were our fairy-tale heroes, integration and outer space and The Bomb the dramas of our first school years. It was not a time when we could separate our own lives from the outside world. The idea then was *not* to protect the children—"expose" them, that was the term, and surely there's some sense, at least, in that—but it was carried too far with us. We were dragged through the mud of Relevance and Grim Reality, and now we have a certain tough, I've-been-there attitude. Not that we really know it all, but we often think we do. Few things shock or surprise us, little jolts our stubborn sureness that our way is right or rattles our early formed and often ill-founded, opinionated conclusions. We imagine hypocrisy in a politician's speeches. We play at vulnerability—honesty, openness, the sensitivity-group concept of *trust*, but what we're truly closer to is venerability. I think of the sixteen-year-old McGovern worker who tells me she was an idealistic socialist when she was young, and of the whole new breed, just surfacing, of drug users who have come full circle and, at twenty, given up dope (before some of us have begun, even).

All of which adds to this aged, weary quality I'm talking about. Oh yes, I know we are the Pepsi Generation. I know what they all say about our "youthful exuberance"—our music, our clothes, our freedom and energy and go-power. And it's true that, physically, we're strong and energetic, and that we dance and surf and ride around on motorbikes and stay up all night while the parents shake their heads and say "Oh, to be young again . . ." What sticks in my head, though, is another image. I hear low, barely audible speech, words, breathed out as if by some supreme and nearly superhuman effort, I see limp gestures and sedentary figures. Kids sitting listening to music, sitting rapping, just sitting. Or sleeping—that, most of all. Staying up late, but sleeping in later. We're tired, often more from boredom than exertion, old without being wise, worldly not from seeing the world but from watching it on television.

Every generation thinks it's special—my grandparents because they remember horses and buggies, my parents because of the Depression. The over-thirties are special because they knew the Red Scare and Korea, bobby socks and beatniks. My older sister is special because she belonged to the first generation of teen-agers (before that, people in their teens were *adolescents*), when being a teen-ager was still fun. And I am caught in the middle. Mine is the generation of unfulfilled expectations. "When you're older," my mother promised, "you can wear lipstick." But when the time came, of course, lipstick wasn't being worn. "When we're big, we'll dance like that," my friends and I whispered, watching Chubby Checker twist on "American Bandstand." But we inherited no dance steps; ours was a limp, formless shrug to watered-down music that rarely made the feet tap. "Just wait till we can vote," I said, bursting with ten-year-old fervor, ready to fast, freeze, march and die for peace and freedom as Joan Baez, barefoot, sang, "We Shall Overcome." Well, now we can vote, and we're old enough to attend rallies and knock on doors and wave placards, and suddenly it doesn't seem to matter any more. My generation is special because of what we missed rather than what we got, because in a certain sense we are the first and the last. The first to take technology for granted. (What was a space shot to us,

346

except an hour cut from social studies to gather before a TV in the gym as Cape Canaveral counted down?) The first to grow up with TV. My sister was eight when we got our set, so to her it seemed magic and always somewhat foreign. She had known books already and would never really replace them. But for me, the TV set was like the kitchen sink and the telephone, a fact of life.

We inherited a previous generation's hand-me-downs and took in the seams, turned up the hems, to make our new fashions. We took drugs from the college kids and made them a high school commonplace. We got the Beatles, but not those lovable look-alikes in matching suits with barber cuts and songs that made you want to cry. They came to us like a bad joke—aged, bearded, discordant. And we inherited the Vietnam war just after the crest of the wave—too late to burn draft cards and too early not to be drafted. The boys of 1953—my year—will be the last to go.

So where are we now? Generalizing is dangerous. Call us the apathetic generation and we will become that. Say times are changing, nobody cares about prom queens and getting into the college of his choice any more—say that (because it sounds good, it indicates a trend, gives a symmetry to history) and you make a movement and a unit out of a generation unified only in its common fragmentation. We tend to stay in packs, of course—at rock concerts and protest marches, but not so much because we are a real group as because we are, for all our talk of "individuality" and "doing one's thing," conformists who break traditions, as a rule, only in the traditional ways.

Still, we haven't all emerged the same because our lives were lived in high school corridors and drive-in hamburger joints as well as in the pages of *Time* and *Life* and the images on the TV screen. National and personal memory blur so that, for me, November 22, 1963, was a birthday party that had to be called off and Armstrong's moon walk was my first full can of beer. But memory—shared or unique—is, I think, a clue to why we are where we are now. Like overanxious patients in analysis, we treasure the traumas of our childhood. Ours was more traumatic than most. The Kennedy assassination has become our myth: talk to us for an evening or two—about movies or summer jobs or the weather—and the subject will come up ("where were *you* when you heard . . ."), as if having lived through Jackie and the red roses, John-John's salute and Oswald's on-camera murder justifies our disenchantment. If you want to know who we are now—if you wonder whether ten years from now we will end up just like all those other generations that thought they were special—with 2.2 kids and a house in Connecticut—if that's what you're wondering, look to the past because, whether we should blame it or not, we do.

1. What general point does Maynard wish to illustrate by telling you of her afternoon at the circus? How do the details of what happened support and clarify her general point? In what ways would her account have been different if her main purpose had been to describe a circus performance?

2. What other generalizations about her generation does Maynard make in this selection? What methods does she use to support the generalizations and make you see her point more clearly?

3. At what points does Maynard refer to "I" (herself and her own experiences) and at what points to "we" (all the people of her generation)? When and how does she move back and forth between "I" and "we"?

4. Why does Maynard, who wants to write about her generation, also say that "Generalization is dangerous"? Does her way of telling her story make her overgeneralize or not?

5. What aspects of this selection help to convince you that this is a young person writing about the experiences of her peers, not an adult observing a younger generation? Are there qualities in Maynard's style of writing that make her sound youthful?

∽ Edmund Wilson ∽

(1895-1972)

Edmund Wilson was educated at Princeton and established himself in the 1920s as a journalist and critic whose book reviews showed a remarkable ability to recognize young writers of special talent. For several decades, his essays served as a means of introducing and explaining modern literature to a wider public. Wilson had many interests and wrote about most of them, so that his books delve into such subjects as the background of the Russian Revolution, the literature of the American Civil War period, the condition of the American Indian, and the authenticity of the Dead Sea Scrolls. Wilson's broad familiarity with many cultures (he traveled widely and was interested in ethnology and anthropology) helps to explain the breadth and inclusiveness of his Epilogue in Upstate *(1971).*

EPILOGUE, 1970

What I have written above shows the gradual but steady expiration of the world of New York State as I knew it in my childhood and the modifications that its life has undergone. It is true that Lowville and Boonville have changed less—unless perhaps Charlottesville, Virginia—than any other part of this country that I knew when I was a child. But, as has been seen, it has reflected all the changes that, to a greater degree, have been taking place in the life of the country as a whole. I do not mean to deplore all these changes. Anyone who still takes seriously the American democratic ideal of opportunity for everybody to prosper according to his best abilities and to enjoy such advantages as he can understand ought not to complain of the many cars, the "mobile homes," of the movies and television sets, of the grills for outdoor cooking. None of these things seems to me attractive, but I probably have no right to be contemptuous about them or to blame them entirely on the people who manufacture and advertize them. If people want them, why should they not have them? Don't young people live better in trailers than they did in old-fashioned frame houses, which were often so ill-built and dreary. I remember that in Red Bank, New Jersey, a typical bourgeois suburb, the general possession of motor cars and of comfortable modern houses immensely cheered and brightened that suburban life. We were only four miles from the ocean, but nobody could get there to swim unless the family had a carriage or, later, an automobile, which at that time was expensive and required a driver. Few people habitually rode bicycles. But presently a trolley was installed, which ran between Red Bank and Seabright. And now everybody owns a car, and in summer one can go to the beach every day. Our old house in Red Bank stood not far from a kind of suburban slum, unsightly and supposed to be something of a den of immorality. My mother's new house that she bought after my father's death, more convenient and much lighter than our gloomy old place, stood in a new street called Buena Vista, and all along it were a class of people that in the past could never have lived so well. On the opposite side of the street from us was the family of a bank clerk, whose wife was pretty and well dressed and whose equally attractive daughter was a great friend of my daughter's. It is true that, when I walked along this street, the radio could be heard from every house and all were playing the same program, so that, no matter how far one walked, the continuity was never interrupted. The implications of this uniformity did not at that time escape me; but I generally approved of what was going on. This, for the people of the United States, was an improvement in their condition. Today in upstate Lewis County there

EDMUND WILSON

is a whole community of trailers among the trees of a little
woodland behind and across the road from the great mansion
and mowed grounds of Constable Hall. Constable Hall is now
a museum, and the big houses of the well-to-do professional
men and dairy owners and merchants have now either been
turned into funeral homes or are inhabited by several families.
To what other uses could these places be put? And the people
who ride in cars, though they are frequently killed or injured
in accidents, have no longer such constricted lives. The old
way of living up here threw them back on their own capacity
for instructing and amusing themselves: reading, playing the
piano, sentimental songs, charades, as well as making pies,
jams and breadstuffs and quilting and embroidery and the
other household arts. But they often, even in the bigger towns,
did not see very much of the world. Our old trips in carriages
to Carthage and Rome now seem so slow as almost to be comic.
I am able to go to Rome now as often as I like to have dinner
and see a movie. I have described the quality of the dinners—
though Rome has still, dating from 1908, an excellent Italian
restaurant; but at worst they are better than the savorless meat
and the vegetables in what we called "birds' bathtubs" of the
local hotels where we used to have to eat in the course of our
longer journeys. And even the worst of the movies are better
than the rare melodramas that occasionally made us laugh in
Boonville.

Of course there used to be a much greater difference between the "educated" and the "uneducated." Lowville Academy was once a great local center of schooling to which students came from miles around. The "Ivy League" colleges
were places of training for what were called "the learned pro-
fessions": law, medicine, the pulpit, certain kinds of science
and the academic career. Today every young American enjoys
the inalienable right to enroll at a state university and, as soon
as he pleases, drop out. Negro and white children both may go
all the way through primary school without ever learning to
read. An "education guidance" man I know, who can certainly

351

not in his work or his life be accused of being undemocratic, has told me that he has come to the conclusion that it is useless to try to educate a good many of the children beyond a necessary minimum. The problem of preventing the abler and more brilliant students from being retarded by the incapacity of the duller ones has sometimes been dealt with in the colleges by having special courses and classes for the former. I do not know enough about the present system to offer predictions or suggestions. I suppose that such vocational schools as the one I have described above must represent a new attempt to deal with the partially educable. It is a kind of successor to and substitute for the old apprentice system. There are in any case now relatively few examples of young people ambitious of meeting, outside the fields of technology, the higher standards of competence and culture.

My reaction to all the things that I disapprove and dislike is that of a member of a once privileged class which is being eliminated all over the world and has very little means any longer of asserting its superior "values." In this, the situation in the United States is not now very different from that in many other parts of the world—including the Soviet Union, except that in the latter the old educated and travelled and comfortable groups were less numerous and more quickly and completely suppressed. But our groups of well-to-do landowners and merchants and able professional men who made the American Revolution have now largely been reduced to the Nixons and Agnews of the present administration, who are hardly superior to the mediocrities that preside over the Soviet Union. It was thought by Veblen and others, that the technocrats would take over as a ruling class, and this to some extent has taken place. I cannot foresee the future, but can only go on with my old occupations.

. . .

But this passing of such splendors as New York State could pretend to has made me feel not only the transience of all forms of life in America, but at my age the constant flow and perishable character, rather than the constant renewal and hope, of everything on the earth. Greece and Rome and classical France left behind them much more durable monuments than our old mansions gone to ruin and our broken-off fragments of old canals; but the aeons of time required for the mammalian plantigrades of the human race to achieve what we can now see to be a very moderate and partial degree of civilization has been coming to discourage and bore me. I look at the creatures on the street and think, well, we have begun to walk upright and our toes, now more or less impractical, are shrinking like the toes of elephants' feet. We have now arrived at a skill of uttering and writing sounds that can convey rather special meanings. But our problems of future development are still absolutely appalling. I do not have any chance, and feel that I should not have the patience, to wait through the countless millennia that would get us past our ages of blind quarreling and of our blindness in sexual selection that makes so much trouble for the children we breed. How much longer must it be before the inhabitants of Russia, ignorant and easily led, spread over such enormous spaces and with so little hunger for information that at the time of the last war there were people to be found in Siberia who not only did not know that there was a war but even that there had been a revolution—how long will it be before such people can organize a modern democracy and cease to attempt to exterminate their original and creative countrymen? I speak of a modern democracy, but how long will it be, for that matter, before the United States can organize a livable society which is free from the even more modern tyranny of bureaucracy? Democracy is actually one of those vague words which are supposed to command approval without giving us a chance to take stock of what our "democracy" consists of. Can I even be sure that, in the language I use, I am formulating these issues correctly? Will these terms not seem very crude to a remotely distant future?—that future I cannot wait for. And where do we get the standards by which we judge our earthly conditions and which are bound to be subject to continual change? When I think of these struggles and transformations to come, I am almost ready to call it a day, at this time of my waning powers, for my own more or less well-meaning efforts. After all, are not my literary activities, like new roads and vocational schools, clumsy gestures in the interest of ends that can only be reached—and what then?—in the course of innumerable centuries that are now entirely unimaginable? As one grows weaker, one becomes more helpless, more lazy, and also more indifferent. Will the Soviet Union last? a Soviet citizen has just demanded. Will General Electric and General Motors— are they "Capitalism," "Democracy"?—last longer than Hyde Hall, which, even in Republican America, was supposed to be still representing Feudalism? We have spent no one knows how many million years, as have the black widow spider, the hammerhead shark, the deadly amanita and the leaf-nosed bat, building up or assembling or creating—we do not even know how to put it—what we call our bodies and brains, our consciousness. Only now are we beginning a little to understand how these organs and members work. The process of finding out more is going to be very tedious. At least, that is how I feel toward the end of a fairly long life that has left me with the feeling—illusion?—that I have seen or sampled many kinds of experience, that I know what this planet is, what its climates in different places and at different seasons are, what its flora and fauna are, what both its more primitive men and more mechanized men are like—so that, not expecting any real novelty, I have no longer any curiosity beyond such as the satisfaction of which will keep me mildly amused while my faculties are gradually decaying. My young vision of New York State now hardly exists, though I do not think, as I did last year, that I shall sell my old place here. In spite of the encroachments of the highways and the element of impoverished ambitionless inhabitants, I have still, I think, just enough money to keep the old place going, and I am still as comfortable here as I can hope to be anywhere. That the old life is passing away, that all around me are anarchy and what seems to me stupidity, does not move me much any more. I have learned to read the papers calmly and not to hate the fools I read about. As long as my health holds out, I shall have to go on living, and I am glad to have had some share in some of the better aspects of the life of this planet and of northern New York.

1. Wilson wrote this epilogue when he was in his seventies. How do his age and experience influence the shape or the method of this selection?

2. When Wilson discusses the changes he has seen in his lifetime, what specific subjects does he focus on and why? What is his attitude toward these changes?

3. Do you notice any differences in Wilson's generalizations in the first and second sections of this selection? Do the generalizations differ in scope? Are there shifts in what Wilson wants to discuss and in his feelings of optimism or pessimism?

4. What is Wilson's estimate of his own life? Does he judge it with pride or disappointment or in some other way? How are his attitudes toward himself related to his generalizations about the world he lives in?

5. How would you compare Wilson's perspective on his life with Maynard's on hers? Identify and explain as many specific differences as you can.

∾ E. B. White ∾

(1899-   )

*E. B. White was born in Mt. Vernon, New York, and became
a newspaper reporter after graduating from Cornell. In 1927,
he became a contributing editor to* The New Yorker, *beginning a lifelong association with the magazine. There he established his reputation as one of America's finest essayists and a
master of an exact and idiomatic American prose style. The
following selection, first published in* Harper's Magazine *in
1941, is taken from* One Man's Meat *(1941), one of several
collections of his essays.*

ONCE MORE TO THE LAKE

One summer, along about 1904, my father rented a camp on a
lake in Maine and took us all there for the month of August.
We all got ringworm from some kittens and had to rub Pond's
Extract on our arms and legs night and morning, and my
father rolled over in a canoe with all his clothes on; but outside
of that the vacation was a success and from then on none of us
ever thought there was any place in the world like that lake in
Maine. We returned summer after summer—always on August 1st for one month. I have since become a salt-water man,
but sometimes in summer there are days when the restlessness
of the tides and the fearful cold of the sea water and the inces-
sant wind which blows across the afternoon and into the evening make me wish for the placidity of a lake in the woods. A
few weeks ago this feeling got so strong I bought myself a

couple of bass hooks and a spinner and returned to the lake where we used to go, for a week's fishing and to revisit old haunts.

I took along my son, who had never had any fresh water up his nose and who had seen lily pads only from train windows. On the journey over to the lake I began to wonder what it would be like. I wondered how time would have marred this unique, this holy spot—the coves and streams, the hills that the sun set behind, the camps and the paths behind the camps. I was sure that the tarred road would have found it out and I wondered in what other ways it would be desolated. It is strange how much you can remember about places like that once you allow your mind to return into the grooves which lead back. You remember one thing, and that suddenly reminds you of another thing. I guess I remembered clearest of all the early mornings, when the lake was cool and motionless, remembered how the bedroom smelled of the lumber it was made of and of the wet woods whose scent entered through the screen. The partitions in the camp were thin and did not extend clear to the top of the rooms, and as I was always the first up I would dress softly so as not to wake the others, and sneak out into the sweet outdoors and start out in the canoe, keeping close along the shore in the long shadows of the pines. I remembered being very careful never to rub my paddle against the gunwale for fear of disturbing the stillness of the cathedral.

The lake had never been what you would call a wild lake. There were cottages sprinkled around the shores, and it was in farming country although the shores of the lake were quite heavily wooded. Some of the cottages were owned by nearby farmers, and you would live at the shore and eat your meals at the farmhouse. That's what our family did. But although it wasn't wild, it was a fairly large and undisturbed lake and there were places in it which, to a child at least, seemed infinitely remote and primeval.

I was right about the tar: it led to within half a mile of the shore. But when I got back there, with my boy, and we settled

into a camp near a farmhouse and into the kind of summertime I had known, I could tell that it was going to be pretty
much the same as it had been before—I knew it, lying in bed
the first morning, smelling the bedroom, and hearing the boy
sneak quietly out and go off along the shore in a boat. I began
to sustain the illusion that he was I, and therefore, by simple
transposition, that I was my father. This sensation persisted,
kept cropping up all the time we were there. It was not an entirely new feeling, but in this setting it grew much stronger. I
seemed to be living a dual existence. I would be in the middle
of some simple act, I would be picking up a bait box or laying
down a table fork, or I would be saying something, and suddenly it would be not I but my father who was saying the
words or making the gesture. It gave me a creepy sensation.

We went fishing the first morning. I felt the same damp
moss covering the worms in the bait can, and saw the dragonfly alight on the tip of my rod as it hovered a few inches from
the surface of the water. It was the arrival of this fly that convinced me beyond any doubt that everything was as it always
had been, that the years were a mirage and there had been no
years. The small waves were the same, chucking the rowboat
under the chin as we fished at anchor, and the boat was the
same boat, the same color green and the ribs broken in the
same places, and under the floor-boards the same fresh-water
leavings and débris—the dead helgramite, the wisps of moss,
the rusty discarded fish-hook, the dried blood from yesterday's
catch. We stared silently at the tips of our rods, at the dragon-
flies that came and went. I lowered the tip of mine into the
water, tentatively, pensively dislodging the fly, which darted
two feet away, poised, darted two feet back, and came to rest
again a little farther up the rod. There had been no years between the ducking of this dragonfly and the other one—the one
that was part of memory. I looked at the boy, who was silently
watching his fly, and it was my hands that held his rod, my
eyes watching. I felt dizzy and didn't know which rod I was
at the end of.

We caught two bass, hauling them in briskly as though they were mackerel, pulling them over the side of the boat in a businesslike manner without any landing net, and stunning them with a blow on the back of the head. When we got back for a swim before lunch, the lake was exactly where we had left it, the same number of inches from the dock, and there was only the merest suggestion of a breeze. This seemed an utterly enchanted sea, this lake you could leave to its own devices for a few hours and come back to, and find that it had not stirred, this constant and trustworthy body of water. In the shallows, the dark, water-soaked sticks and twigs, smooth and old, were undulating in clusters on the bottom against the clean ribbed sand, and the track of the mussel was plain. A school of minnows swam by, each minnow with its small individual shadow, doubling the attendance, so clear and sharp in the sunlight. Some of the other campers were in swimming, along the shore, one of them with a cake of soap, and the water felt thin and clear and unsubstantial. Over the years there had been this person with the cake of soap, this cultist, and here he was. There had been no years.

Up to the farmhouse to dinner through the teeming, dusty field, the road under our sneakers was only a two-track road. The middle track was missing, the one with the marks of the hooves and the splotches of dried, flaky manure. There had always been three tracks to choose from in choosing which track to walk in; now the choice was narrowed down to two. For a moment I missed terribly the middle alternative. But the way led past the tennis court, and something about the way it lay there in the sun reassured me; the tape had loosened along the back-line, the alleys were green with plantains and other weeds, and the net (installed in June and removed in September) sagged in the dry noon, and the whole place steamed with midday heat and hunger and emptiness. There was a choice of pie for dessert, and one was blueberry and one was apple, and the waitresses were the same country girls, there having been no passage of time, only the illusion of it as in a dropped curtain—the waitresses were still fifteen; their hair had been washed, that was the only difference—they had been to the movies and seen the pretty girls with the clean hair.

Summertime, oh summertime, pattern of life indelible, the fadeproof lake, the woods unshatterable, the pasture with the sweetfern and the juniper forever and ever, summer without end; this was the background, and the life along the shore was the design, the cottagers with their innocent and tranquil design, their tiny docks with the flagpole and the American flag floating against the white clouds in the blue sky, the little paths over the roots of the trees leading from camp to camp and the paths leading back to the outhouses and the can of lime for sprinkling, and at the souvenir counters at the store the miniature birch-bark canoes and the post cards that showed things looking a little better than they looked. This was the American family at play, escaping the city heat, wondering whether the newcomers in the camp at the head of the cove were "common" or "nice," wondering whether it was true that the people who drove up for Sunday dinner at the farmhouse were turned away because there wasn't enough chicken.

It seemed to me, as I kept remembering all this, that those times and those summers had been infinitely precious and worth saving. There had been jollity and peace and goodness. The arriving (at the beginning of August) had been so big a business in itself, at the railway station the farm wagon drawn up, the first smell of the pine-laden air, the first glimpse of the smiling farmer, and the great importance of the trunks and your father's enormous authority in such matters, and the feel of the wagon under you for the long ten-mile haul, and at the top of the last long hill catching the first view of the lake after eleven months of not seeing this cherished body of water. The shouts and cries of the other campers when they saw you, and the trunks to be unpacked, to give up their rich burden. (Arriving was less exciting nowadays, when you sneaked up in your car and parked it under a tree near the camp and took out the bags and in five minutes it was all over, no fuss, no loud wonderful fuss about trunks.)

Peace and goodness and jollity. The only thing that was wrong now, really, was the sound of the place, an unfamiliar nervous sound of the outboard motors. This was the note that jarred, the one thing that would sometimes break the illusion and set the years moving. In those other summertimes all motors were inboard; and when they were at a little distance, the noise they made was a sedative, an ingredient of summer sleep. They were one-cylinder and two-cylinder engines, and some were make-and-break and some were jump-spark, but they all made a sleepy sound across the lake. The one-lungers throbbed and fluttered, and the twin-cylinder ones purred and purred, and that was a quiet sound too. But now the campers all had outboards. In the daytime, in the hot mornings, these motors made a petulant, irritable sound; at night, in the still evening when the afterglow lit the water, they whined about one's ears like mosquitoes. My boy loved our rented outboard, and his great desire was to achieve singlehanded mastery over it, and authority, and he soon learned the trick of choking it a little (but not too much), and the adjustment of the needle valve. Watching him I would remember the things you could do with the old one-cylinder engine with the heavy flywheel, how you could have it eating out of your hand if you got really close to it spiritually. Motor boats in those days didn't have clutches, and you would make a landing by shutting off the motor at the proper time and coasting in with a dead rudder. But there was a way of reversing them, if you learned the trick, by cutting the switch and putting it on again exactly on the final dying revolution of the flywheel, so that it would kick back against compression and begin reversing. Approaching a dock in a strong following breeze, it was difficult to slow up sufficiently by the ordinary coasting method, and if a boy felt he had complete mastery over his motor, he was tempted to keep it running beyond its time and then reverse it a few feet from the dock. It took a cool nerve, because if you threw the switch a twentieth of a second too soon you would catch the flywheel when it still had speed enough to go up past center, and the boat would leap ahead, charging bull-fashion at the dock.

We had a good week at the camp. The bass were biting well and the sun shone endlessly, day after day. We would be tired at night and lie down in the accumulated heat of the little bedrooms after the long hot day and the breeze would stir almost imperceptibly outside and the smell of the swamp drift in through the rusty screens. Sleep would come easily and in the morning the red squirrel would be on the roof, tapping out his gay routine. I kept remembering everything, lying in bed in the mornings—the small steamboat that had a long rounded stern like the lip of a Ubangi, and how quietly she ran on the moonlight sails, when the older boys played their mandolins and the girls sang and we ate doughnuts dipped in sugar, and how sweet the music was on the water in the shining night, and what it had felt like to think about girls then. After breakfast we would go up to the store and the things were in the same place—the minnows in a bottle, the plugs and spinners disarranged and pawed over by the youngsters from the boys' camp, the fig newtons and the Beeman's gum. Outside, the road was tarred and cars stood in front of the store. Inside, all was just as it had always been, except there was more Coca Cola and not so much Moxie and root beer and birch beer and sarsaparilla. We would walk out with a bottle of pop apiece and sometimes the pop would backfire up our noses and hurt. We explored the streams, quietly, where the turtles slid off the sunny logs and dug their way into the soft bottom; and we lay on the town wharf and fed worms to the tame bass. Everywhere we went I had trouble making out which was I, the one walking at my side, the one walking in my pants.

One afternoon while we were there at that lake a thunderstorm came up. It was like the revival of an old melodrama that I had seen long ago with childish awe. The second-act climax of the drama of the electrical disturbance over a lake in America had not changed in any important respect. This was the big scene, still the big scene. The whole thing was so familiar, the first feeling of oppression and heat and a general air around camp of not wanting to go very far away. In mid-afternoon (it was all the same) a curious darkening of the sky, and a lull in everything that had made life tick; and then the way the boats suddenly swung the other way at their moorings with the coming of a breeze out of the new quarter, and the premonitory rumble. Then the kettle drum, then the snare, then the bass drum and cymbals, then crackling light against the dark, and the gods grinning and licking their chops in the hills. Afterward the calm, the rain steadily rustling in the calm lake, the return of light and hope and spirits, and the campers running out in joy and relief to go swimming in the rain, their bright cries perpetuating the deathless joke about how they were getting simply drenched, and the children screaming with delight at the new sensation of bathing in the rain, and the joke about getting drenched linking the generations in a strong indestructible chain. And the comedian who waded in carrying an umbrella.

When the others went swimming my son said he was going in too. He pulled his dripping trunks from the line where they had hung all through the shower, and wrung them out. Languidly, and with no thought of going in, I watched him, his hard little body, skinny and bare, saw him wince slightly as he pulled up around his vitals the small, soggy, icy garment. As he buckled the swollen belt suddenly my groin felt the chill of death.

1. What specific details help you to understand White's relation to the natural world? Why does White call the lake and its surroundings "this holy spot"? Does the rest of his account justify this phrase?
2. How would you describe White's attitude toward the past? What parallels does he find between past and present? What differences? Does he regard the past as better than the present,

worse, or simply different? What evidence can you show to support your judgment?

3. How does White make you see that the week that he and his son spent at the lake is important to him because he associates it with more general concerns? How does he make specific memories lead to these more general themes?

4. How effective do you find the concluding paragraph and why? What bearing does it have on White's sense of the relationship between himself and his son?

∽ Jessica Mitford ∽

(1917-   )

Born into a titled family in England, Jessica Mitford developed left-wing political sympathies and left England when she was nineteen to participate in the Spanish Civil War. She has lived in the United States since 1939. She did not begin writing until she was nearly forty, and her books reflect her strong interest in exposing injustice and corruption in various aspects of American life. Kind and Usual Punishment *(1973) is a highly critical study of the United States' penal system; in this selection Mitford reports on her experiences playing the role of a prisoner for just a few hours.*

WOMEN IN CAGES

Our domicile was a short and narrow corridor on one side of which are the cells, at the far end a dining room with television set. Women were standing in desultory knots in the corridor, sitting in their cells, or watching TV. The overall impression: a combination of college dorm (silly jokes, putdowns, occasional manifestations of friendliness), lunatic asylum (underlying sense of desolate futility), a scene from *The Threepenny Opera* (graffiti on the walls: "Welcome to the Whores' Paradise!"). I was struck by the number of little-girl faces, kids who except for their funny-looking clothes could be part of a high-school class, and by one or two sad, vacant old faces. The median age here is twenty-five.

As we entered, our names were called out, we were handed sheets and led to our assigned cells, tiny cubicles with two beds, a dresser, and a clothesline for hanging coats and dresses (the prison, like most, is fearfully overcrowded and now holds more than twice its intended capacity). My cellmate was a pleasant-faced black woman in her early thirties, named Della. She welcomed me like a good hostess, helped me make my bed, and apologized for the stale, dead smell compounded of people, food, and disinfectant that pervaded our quarters: "We used to have at least some breeze, but they've cut off the air. There's a new rule against opening the corridor window because they claim the inmates were letting down rope to haul up contraband brought by their boyfriends. Now, does that make any sense? With the officers watching you like a hawk every minute of the day and night?"

From Della I learned that, as I had suspected, we had been let off lightly at "Reception." The usual routine, she told me, includes a vaginal examination as part of the search for contraband and a Lysol spraying of the head. She had found the experience horrifying, totally degrading. Furthermore some of the guards "get their kicks" from scaring the neophyte inmate by horrendous hints of what to expect from the "bull-daggers" (prison slang for lesbians). Is there actually much homosexuality, I asked? A certain amount, but not as much as the administration seems to think. "They are really hipped on the subject," she said. "They have bed checks all hours of the night, they come around flashing their bright lights, it's hard to get any sleep."

Della had been in the section for unsentenced prisoners for nine weeks waiting for her trial. In all that time she never saw her court-appointed lawyer, and her letters to him were unanswered. She met him for the first and only time in court on the day of her trial, where he advised her to plead guilty: "But he never asked me anything about my case, said he didn't want to hear. Said if we tried to fight it, the judge would be hard on me. But I don't see how he could have been any harder—six months for one count of soliciting!"

We wandered out into the crowded corridor to join the others. Because of the visitors, Della told me, everyone was on good behavior: "We *scrubbed* this place, girl!" And clean, though dreary, it certainly was.

Our group was there to learn, so we started asking questions. The Maryland legislator inquired about recreation facilities. "Re-cre-ation!" an inmate hooted derisively. "Come here, girls, I'll show you." She led us to one of the barred windows, through which we could barely descry a small concrete quadrangle entirely hemmed in by the building. On fine days, she explained, the entire population is sometimes taken down there for an hour or so if the correctional officers have time. Vocational training programs? "There's eight old broken-down typewriters somewhere in the building. I don't know if anybody ever uses them, though. Or you can go down to group therapy, but who wants it? A bunch of us bullshitting about our deprived lives?"

We had been told the authorities had arranged for the visitors to sample various aspects of prison life, that some would spend the night in sickbay, others would be brought before a disciplinary committee, accused of breaking the rules. To fortify myself against the latter eventuality I asked for a copy of the prison rule book. "No inmate shall engage in loud or boisterous talk, laughter, whistling or other vocal expression," it said in part. "Talking is permitted at all times except in church and in school, but talking must be conducted in a normal voice except on the recreation fields." One of the prisoners, a vivacious young black woman, confided to me that she was due to be disciplined that day for laughing too loud but had been reprieved because of our visit: "It's a dumb thing anyway to be punished for laughing. When you come to think of it, sometimes it's sort of a release to laugh out loud."

As in hospitals, food is served at unexpected times. At four thirty we went into the dining room to collect our trays of dinner. The food wasn't bad, but like most institutional cooking it was dull and starchy with a touch of wilted green. We ate tuna casserole, Jell-O, a choice of weak coffee or a puce-colored synthetic fruit drink. One of the few white prisoners came and sat beside me, a romantic-looking blonde in her early twenties; she reminded me vaguely of prison movies I had seen. Convicted of possession of heroin, she described her first days in the Detention Center as absolute torture: "You come down cold-turkey, they're not equipped here to treat addicts." She proved to be a discriminating connoisseur of the nation's prisons, and twinkled quite merrily as she rated them for me, one-star, two-star, as in a motel guide. "This joint's by no means the worst, but it's not the best, either." Her goal is to be admitted into one of the treatment centers for narcotics addicts, but so far she has been blocked because they are all full up. She has no idea when, or if, there will ever be an opening for her. What does she do all day? "I work some in the kitchen, just to keep from going crazy. There *isn't* anything to do here." Housekeeping jobs, she explained, are available on our floor but not for the unsentenced women on the floor below: "In some ways they're punished worse than we are, although they haven't even been found guilty of anything." Pay ranges from $5 a month to a top of $13, the higher rate being awarded on the basis of performance and "attitude"; there is no compensation for working part of a month.

"Jessica . . . Mitford . . . to the third . . . floor." The voice over the intercom was tinny and disembodied. I started to the door of our corridor and was at once intercepted by a correctional officer. "No, no, you can't go down by yourself," she said, shocked, and, seizing my arm, led me to the elevator. "You're wanted by the disciplinary committee," she said severely. Lock, double-lock all the way, from our fourth-floor abode to the elevator and down. A third-floor guard took over and led me to the small office where I was to be tried.

My prosecutors, jury, and judges (for the disciplinary committee incorporates all three functions) were the prison psychologist and two correctional officers. They were trying to look suitably stern, to make it all as "real" as possible. One of the officers read off the charges: "At 17.05 hours, Officer Smith opened the door to your cell and found you locked in a passionate embrace with Maureen [the reporter from the Washington *Post*]. As you know, this is an extremely serious offense. What have you to say?"

What, indeed. I could of course deny all (insist she wasn't my type?), but, mindful of my assignment for the ACLU, I decided to go another route. What if I challenged the whole legality of this "trial"? I took a deep breath.

"First, I should like to draw your attention to the prison rule book." (The trio seemed surprised; the rule book, it seems, is not generally available to prisoners.) "I see you have infractions broken down into two categories: *crimes* such as assault, theft, possession of narcotics, and failure to obey *rules*—wasting food, vulgar conversation, not making one's bed. Homosexual acts between inmates are listed here as a crime. Before I plead guilty or not guilty to the charge. I should like to see a copy of the statute under which homosexuality between consenting females is a crime. I don't believe it is a crime in any jurisdiction. I'm already in here for one crime. If you find me guilty of another, it will go very hard with me when my case comes before the parole board."

My inquisitors exchanged uncertain looks. "It's not a *statute*, it's a rule," said one.

"But as you've listed it as a *crime*, I want a lawyer to represent me. I want to cross-examine the officer who accused me, and to call witnesses who'll verify that I was in the dining room watching TV at 17.05 hours."

Nonplussed, the chief correctional officer said she thought they should send for Mrs. Patricia Taylor, the director of the Detention Center. This was done, and I repeated my request.

"Jessica, you must realize we're only trying to help you," said Mrs. Taylor.

"Well, thanks a lot. But I should still like to assert my right to the same procedural safeguards that should apply to any citizen accused of crime."

"You don't understand, Jessica, you are in an institution

now, you're an inmate, you haven't a right to a trial. *We'll* decide who's telling the truth. Now, if Officer Smith hadn't seen that, why would she say she had?"

"But I say she's lying, I'm not guilty and I want a chance to prove it. Why don't you bring her down here so I can question her, and clear myself?"

"Jessica, do you realize what would happen to discipline if we permitted the inmates to cross-examine the officers?"

We went over this a few times; I had made my point, but since it was only a charade (and I knew Maureen was waiting for her turn before the disciplinary committee) I soon gave up, and was duly sentenced to "ten days in Adjustment."

What if the situation had been real, I kept thinking? Instead of making this well-reasoned little speech about my constitutional rights I would have been shouting furiously, perhaps in tears. And instead of listening and answering calmly, would not my captors have responded in kind—put me down as a troublemaker or psycho for asserting my rights, and treated me accordingly? Now I was beginning to "feel." The governessy young criminology student would be proud of me!

Accompanied by the chief correctional officer, who firmly gripped my arm (did she think I might try to escape?), I traversed several corridors and those eerie wails gradually came closer. The officer in charge of Adjustment took me over. Here the stripping of individuality is turned up a notch. I am given a gray cotton shift in place of the patterned dress from the bin. Bra, shoes, cigarettes, wristwatch, wedding ring, paperback books are confiscated. To her chagrin, the officer discovers that all eight solitary cells are occupied (which means that about one in ten of the inmates is locked up there). I will have to double up with a thief who was put in Adjustment for beating up other women. Not a terribly reassuring thought. The door giving onto the corridor of solitary cells is immensely thick, opened by my keeper with several huge keys. Now we hear the screams full force—not just from Viola, they seem to be coming from several cells. *"Let me out!"* *"I want out!"* Women are moaning, shrieking, pounding with their fists against their doors. This is "Adjustment"? To what are they being adjusted?

"You have company," the officer announces tersely to my cellmate, and she double-locks the door behind us. Mindful of my companion's alleged infraction I flash her a conciliatory smile, but she is pleased to see me, makes me welcome, we sit on the bed (sole furnishing except for an open toilet that flushes only from the outside) and talk.

The Thief's Tale was well larded with fantasy, or so it seemed to me. A tall, attractive black woman about thirty years old, she was essentially "state-raised": orphaned at the age of eight, in and out of trouble, in and out of juvenile detention (but mostly in) until her middle twenties. "I tried to go straight for a spell, but I don't really dig it. On welfare, with two little kids to raise—what kind of life is that?" She turned to pickpocketing, a discipline in which she had received much theoretical instruction during her many years in reformatories. "The best place is near the Americana Hotel in New York, that's where lots of businessmen hang out." She told me she could clear upward of $500 on a good night and that once she netted $14,000 from the wallet of an unsuspecting passerby. Yet, in view of her expanding needs, she found it slow going: "My boyfriend and I wanted to start a nightclub in Atlantic City, we figured on $100,000 to open it. So I told him leave it to me, I'd raise it." The quickest way, she decided, was to travel around the country from motel to motel cashing bad checks in amounts of $500 to $1,000. She had got up to $40,000 of the needed capital when the feds caught up with her.

Our corridor had all but quieted down after the guard left. Now the screams started up again, coming apparently from the cell directly opposite ours, a terrible outcry of rage and misery, shrieks and obscenities interspersed with deep, racking sobs. We peered through the tiny grill in our door and could dimly see movement behind the opposite grill, hands clawing, head wildly shaking. My cellmate shouted soothing words across the corridor: "Now, honey, hush up, won't you? If you be a good girl and stop all that noise, I'll speak to Mrs. Taylor, and I'll see that she lets you out of there. If I say to let you out, she'll do it."

"Who is she?" I asked.

"She's a juvenile, she's down here because she's too young to go upstairs."

"*Too young?* How old is she?"

"Seventeen."

Of course I didn't believe a word of it. Just another of her delusions, I thought, like the $14,000 wallet, the obliging motel managers who cash $1,000 checks for strangers, her role as confidante and adviser to Mrs. Taylor.

Soon—in an hour and a half, to be exact—my "ten days" were up. For further clarification I sought out Mrs. Taylor, a highly qualified black administrator with a long background in social work and Corrections. No longer an "inmate," I was formally ushered into her office, where we discussed what I had heard and seen that day.

First, as to the general prison scene, what are the women here being punished for? The great majority, about 85 percent, are in for a combination of prostitution and narcotics (as one inmate had told me, "They go together like salt and pepper; once you're hooked on the stuff, you have to hustle to support your habit"). Does Mrs. Taylor think prostitution is a crime? No, she believes many women are driven to it by circumstances outside their control. What about drug addiction? That's not a crime either, it's a sickness and should be treated as such.

Checking Mrs. Taylor's opinions against those of others in authority, from correctional officers to Mr. Kenneth Hardy, director of the department, I found unanimity on these points. *None* believed that prostitution and drug addiction are "crimes." Thus the patently crazy situation in which the keepers themselves, up and down the line, believe their mandate to imprison these women rests on a fundamentally unsound premise. But, they all point out, they are merely doing the job required of them by the courts, the legislature, the public: "We don't choose the inmates, we have to take whoever the judges send us."

In our discussion of the Adjustment setup, this sense of total irrationality deepened.

The case of Viola: she is a diagnosed schizophrenic, Mrs. Taylor explained. Because of a recent court decision, she cannot be transferred to a mental institution without a sanity hearing; but the courts are so clogged with cases that no date for such a hearing has been set. How long will she stay locked away in Adjustment? Nobody knows.

The screaming girl across the corridor? My cellmate was right after all, she really *is* only seventeen, she really *is* there because she is too young to go upstairs—in solitary because of a mistake of the Juvenile Court. Finding that she was incorrigible in the children's prison, the judge sentenced her to Women's Detention. But the law says that juvenile offenders may not mix with the adult prison population, so she was put in Adjustment. At first she was allowed "privileges"—mail, books, cigarettes. After several days of total solitude she set her mattress on fire (perhaps, Mrs. Taylor surmised, "to draw attention to herself?"). Consequently she is now considered a "disciplinary case" and all privileges have been withdrawn. How long will she have to stay there? For about three months, until she turns eighteen.

"Aren't you afraid she'll go completely insane by that time?"

"Well . . . there is that danger . . ."

Why, I wanted to know, is the inmate who is being punished for some infraction denied books, newspapers, games—*anything* that might make solitary confinement more tolerable?

"The idea is to remove her completely from the environment. You heard those women screaming in there. If we'd kept you in there for twenty-four hours, you would have been screaming, too."

"Then—is that your purpose, to destroy my self-control, to reduce me to a helpless, howling infant?"

"That's a risk we have to take," said Mrs. Taylor with a faint smile.

What of homosexuality, recognized by everyone in Corrections as an inevitable consequence of long-term segregation of the sexes? Having driven them to it, why punish for it? "Love affairs" between women inmates, born out of loneliness, longing for human affection, lack of male companionship—does Mrs. Taylor consider this sort of behavior criminal? "No, but if permitted it might lead to jealousy and fights. Besides, I am responsible for their morals while they are in here." *Their* morals? Yet Mrs. Taylor had something there, I thought. Is this not the essence of women's prisons, the punishment of unchaste, unwomanly behavior, a grotesque bow to long-outmoded nineteenth-century notions of feminine morality?

There is, Mrs. Taylor regretfully conceded, barely even the pretense of a useful trade or educational program for the women, most of whom she expects to see back again in her custody shortly after they are let out. They exit and reenter as through a revolving door, three quarters of those who are in now have been here before. Chances of getting a decent job when they leave, slim enough for ghetto women in any circumstances, are almost nonexistent for those with prison records, so inevitably they turn to their old ways when released.

This, then, is an American women's prison of the 1970's—and "not the worst," as my dinner companion said. A life of planned, unrelieved inactivity and boredom . . . no overt brutality but plenty of random, largely unintentional cruelty . . . a pervasive sense of helplessness and frustration engulfing not only the inmates but their keepers, themselves prisoners trapped in the weird complex of paradoxes that is the prison world.

And everyone passes the buck. The administrators protest they are merely carrying out the orders of the courts, in a setting they have inherited and are powerless to alter. The judges say they have no choice but to enforce the laws as given to them by the legislature. The lawmakers? With one eye on re-election they bow readily to mindless demands for ever "tougher measures" as a panacea for the nation's ills.

1. In what way does Mitford's narration of events make it clear that she is not an actual prisoner confined in the jail for months or years? In what ways does her account differ from what you might expect to hear from someone who had served time in prison?

2. What does Mitford gain by writing about her personal experience rather than discussing the problem of prisons in more general terms?

3. Discuss the portraits Mitford offers of the prisoners she meets. Compare them in detail with her characterizations of prison administrators and other official personnel.

4. Mitford is not really writing an autobiography; she uses her personal experience primarily to examine the subject of penal conditions. How does her purpose affect the way she talks about her experience? Is her method different from that used by other writers in this chapter?

5. At what points and in what ways does Mitford introduce more general observations about prison life and the penal system? What issues seem particularly important to her? How does she present these issues? Does she suggest solutions?

∽ James Baldwin ∽

(1924-   )

Raised in Harlem, James Baldwin was a Pentacostal preacher while still in his teens and then embarked on a literary career. He lived in near poverty in New York and Paris until his first novel was published in 1952. Since that time, Baldwin has written fiction and drama, as well as a series of essays exploring the tensions and bitterness felt by the black man in a world controlled by whites. Through his writing, lectures, and television appearances, Baldwin has played an important role, both as interpreter and prophet, in articulating a black point of view. This selection is taken from his first collection of essays, Notes of a Native Son *(1953).*

STRANGER IN THE VILLAGE

From all available evidence no black man had ever set foot in this tiny Swiss village before I came. I was told before arriving that I would probably be a "sight" for the village; I took this to mean that people of my complexion were rarely seen in Switzerland, and also that city people are always something of a "sight" outside of the city. It did not occur to me—possibly because I am an American—that there could be people anywhere who had never seen a Negro.

It is a fact that cannot be explained on the basis of the inaccessibility of the village. The village is very high, but it is only four hours from Milan and three hours from Lausanne. It is true that it is virtually unknown. Few people making plans for a holiday would elect to come here. On the other hand, the villagers are able, presumably, to come and go as they please—which they do: to another town at the foot of the mountain, with a population of approximately five thousand, the nearest place to see a movie or go to the bank. In the village there is no movie house, no bank, no library, no theater; very few radios, one jeep, one station wagon; and, at the moment, one typewriter, mine, an invention which the woman next door to me here had never seen. There are about six hundred people living here, all Catholic—I conclude this from the fact that the Catholic church is open all year round, whereas the Protestant chapel, set off on a hill a little removed from the village, is open only in the summertime when the tourists arrive. There are four or five hotels, all closed now, and four or five *bistros*, of which, however, only two do any business during the winter. These two do not do a great deal, for life in the village seems to end around nine or ten o'clock. There are a few stores, butcher, baker, *épicerie*, a hardware store, and a money-changer—who cannot change travelers' checks, but must send them down to the bank, an operation which takes two or three days. There is something called the *Ballet Haus*, closed in the winter and used for God knows what, certainly not ballet, during the summer. There seems to be only one schoolhouse in the village, and this for the quite young children; I suppose this to mean that their older brothers and sisters at some point descend from these mountains in order to complete their education—possibly, again, to the town just below. The landscape is absolutely forbidding, mountains towering on all four sides, ice and snow as far as the eye can reach. In this white wilderness, men and women and children move all day, carrying washing, wood, buckets of milk or water, sometimes skiing on Sunday afternoons. All week long boys and young men are to be seen shoveling snow off the rooftops, or dragging wood down from the forest in sleds.

The village's only real attraction, which explains the tourist season, is the hot spring water. A disquietingly high proportion of these tourists are cripples, or semicripples, who come year after year—from other parts of Switzerland, usually—to take the waters. This lends the village, at the height of the season, a rather terrifying air of sanctity, as though it were a lesser Lourdes. There is often something beautiful, there is always something awful, in the spectacle of a person who has lost one of his faculties, a faculty he never questioned until it was gone, and who struggles to recover it. Yet people remain people, on crutches or indeed on deathbeds; and wherever I passed, the first summer I was here, among the native villagers or among the lame, a wind passed with me—of astonishment, curiosity, amusement, and outrage. That first summer I stayed two weeks and never intended to return. But I did return in the winter, to work; the village offers, obviously, no distractions whatever and has the further advantage of being extremely cheap. Now it is winter again, a year later, and I am here again. Everyone in the village knows my name, though they scarcely ever use it, knows that I come from America—though, this, apparently, they will never really believe: black men come from Africa—and everyone knows that I am the friend of the son of a woman who was born here, and that I am staying in their chalet. But I remain as much a stranger today as I was the first day I arrived, and the children shout *Neger! Neger!* as I walk along the streets.

It must be admitted that in the beginning I was far too shocked to have any real reaction. In so far as I reacted at all, I reacted by trying to be pleasant—it being a great part of the American Negro's education (long before he goes to school) that he must make people "like" him. This smile-and-the-world-smiles-with-you routine worked about as well in this situation as it had in the situation for which it was designed, which is to say that it did not work at all. No one, after all, can be liked whose human weight and complexity cannot be, or has not been, admitted. My smile was simply another unheard-of phenomenon which allowed them to see my teeth—they did not, really, see my smile and I began to think that, should I take to snarling, no one would notice any difference. All of the physical characteristics of the Negro which had caused me, in America, a very different and almost forgotten pain were nothing less than miraculous—or infernal—in the eyes of the village people. Some thought my hair was the color of tar, that it had the texture of wire, or the texture of cotton. It was jocularly suggested that I might let it all grow long and make myself a winter coat. If I sat in the sun for more than five minutes some daring creature was certain to come along and gingerly put his fingers on my hair, as though he were afraid of an electric shock, or put his hand on my hand, astonished that the color did not rub off. In all of this, in which it must be conceded there was the charm of genuine wonder and in which there was certainly no element of intentional unkindness, there was yet no suggestion that I was human: I was simply a living wonder.

I knew that they did not mean to be unkind, and I know it now; it is necessary, nevertheless, for me to repeat this to myself each time that I walk out of the chalet. The children who shout *Neger!* have no way of knowing the echoes this sound raises in me. They are brimming with good humor and the more daring swell with pride when I stop to speak with them. Just the same, there are days when I cannot pause and smile, when I have no heart to play with them; when, indeed, I mutter sourly to myself, exactly as I muttered on the streets of a city these children have never seen, when I was no bigger than these children are now: *Your* mother *was a nigger*. Joyce is right about history being a nightmare—but it may be the nightmare from which no one *can* awaken. People are trapped in history and history is trapped in them.

There is a custom in the village—I am told it is repeated in many villages—of "buying" African natives for the purpose of converting them to Christianity. There stands in the church all year round a small box with a slot for money, decorated with a black figurine, and into this box the villagers drop their francs. During the *carnaval* which precedes Lent, two village children have their faces blackened—out of which bloodless darkness their blue eyes shine like ice—and fantastic horsehair wigs are placed on their blond heads; thus disguised, they solicit among the villagers for money for the missionaries in Africa. Between the box in the church and the blackened children, the village "bought" last year six or eight African natives. This was reported to me with pride by the wife of one of the *bistro* owners and I was careful to express astonishment and pleasure at the solicitude shown by the village for the souls of black folk. The *bistro* owner's wife beamed with a pleasure far more genuine than my own and seemed to feel that I might now breathe more easily concerning the souls of at least six of my kinsmen.

I tried not to think of these so lately baptized kinsmen, of the price paid for them, or the peculiar price they themselves would pay, and said nothing about my father, who having taken his own conversion too literally never, at bottom, forgave the white world (which he described as heathen) for having saddled him with a Christ in whom, to judge at least from their treatment of him, they themselves no longer believed. I thought of white men arriving for the first time in an African village, strangers there, as I am a stranger here, and tried to imagine the astounded populace touching their hair and marveling at the color of their skin. But there is a great difference between being the first white man to be seen by Africans and being the first black man to be seen by whites. The white man takes the astonishment as tribute, for he arrives to conquer and to convert the natives, whose inferiority in relation to himself is not even to be questioned; whereas I, without a thought of conquest, find myself among a people whose culture controls me, has even, in a sense, created me, people who have cost me more in anguish and rage than they will ever know, who yet do not even know of my existence. The astonishment with which I might have greeted them, should they have stumbled into my African village a few hundred years ago, might have rejoiced their hearts. But the astonishment with which they greet me today can only poison mine.

And this is so despite everything I may do to feel differently, despite my friendly conversations with the *bistro* owner's wife, despite their three-year-old son who has at last become my friend, despite the *saluts* and *bonsoirs* which I exchange with people as I walk, despite the fact that I know that no individual can be taken to task for what history is doing, or has done. I say that the culture of these people controls me—but they can scarcely be held responsible for European culture. America comes out of Europe, but these people have never seen America, nor have most of them seen more of Europe than the hamlet at the foot of their mountain. Yet they move with an authority which I shall never have; and they regard me, quite rightly, not only as a stranger in their village but as a suspect latecomer, bearing no credentials, to everything they have—however unconsciously—inherited.

For this village, even were it incomparably more remote and incredibly more primitive, is the West, the West onto which I have been so strangely grafted. These people cannot be, from the point of view of power, strangers anywhere in the world; they have made the modern world, in effect, even if they do not know it. The most illiterate among them is related, in a way that I am not, to Dante, Shakespeare, Michelangelo, Aeschylus, Da Vinci, Rembrandt, and Racine; the cathedral at Chartres says something to them which it cannot say to me, as indeed would New York's Empire State Building, should anyone here ever see it. Out of their hymns and dances come Beethoven and Bach. Go back a few centuries and they are in their full glory—but I am in Africa, watching the conquerors arrive.

The rage of the disesteemed is personally fruitless, but it is also absolutely inevitable; this rage, so generally discounted, so little understood even among the people whose daily bread it is, is one of the things that makes history. Rage can only with difficulty, and never entirely, be brought under the domination of the intelligence and is therefore not susceptible to any arguments whatever. This is a fact which ordinary representatives of the *Herrenvolk*, having never felt this rage and being unable to imagine it, quite fail to understand. Also, rage cannot be hidden, it can only be dissembled. This dissembling deludes the thoughtless, and strengthens rage and adds, to rage, contempt. There are, no doubt, as many ways of coping with the resulting complex of tensions as there are black men in the world, but no black man can hope ever to be entirely liberated from this internal warfare—rage, dissembling, and contempt having inevitably accompanied his first realization of the power of white men. What is crucial here is that, since white men represent in the black man's world so heavy a weight, white men have for black men a reality which is far from being reciprocal; and hence all black men have toward all white men an attitude which is designed, really, either to rob the white man of the jewel of his naïveté, or else to make it cost him dear.

The black man insists, by whatever means he finds at his disposal, that the white man cease to regard him as an exotic rarity and recognize him as a human being. This is a very charged and difficult moment, for there is a great deal of will power involved in the white man's naïveté. Most people are not naturally reflective any more than they are naturally malicious, and the white man prefers to keep the black man at a certain human remove because it is easier for him thus to preserve his simplicity and avoid being called to account for crimes committed by his forefathers, or his neighbors. He is inescapably aware, nevertheless, that he is in a better position in the world than black men are, nor can he quite put to death the suspicion that he is hated by black men therefore. He does not wish to be hated, neither does he wish to change places, and at this point in his uneasiness he can scarcely avoid having recourse to those legends which white men have created about black men, the most usual effect of which is that the white man finds himself enmeshed, so to speak, in his own language which describes hell, as well as the attributes which lead one to hell, as being as black as night.

Every legend, moreover, contains its residuum of truth, and the root function of language is to control the universe by describing it. It is of quite considerable significance that black men remain, in the imagination, and in overwhelming numbers in fact, beyond the disciplines of salvation; and this despite the fact that the West has been "buying" African natives for centuries. There is, I should hazard, an instantaneous necessity to be divorced from this so visibly unsaved stranger, in whose heart, moreover, one cannot guess what dreams of vengeance are being nourished; and, at the same time, there are few things on earth more attractive than the idea of the unspeakable liberty which is allowed the unredeemed. When, beneath the black mask, a human being begins to make himself felt one cannot escape a certain awful wonder as to what kind of human being it is. What one's imagination makes of other people is dictated, of course, by the laws of one's own personality and it is one of the ironies of black-white relations that, by means of what the white man imagines the black man to be, the black man is enabled to know who the white man is.

I have said, for example, that I am as much a stranger in this village today as I was the first summer I arrived, but this is not quite true. The villagers wonder less about the texture of my hair than they did then, and wonder rather more about me. And the fact that their wonder now exists on another level is reflected in their attitudes and in their eyes. There are the children who make those delightful, hilarious, sometimes astonishingly grave overtures of friendship in the unpredictable fashion of children; other children, having been taught that the devil is a black man, scream in genuine anguish as I approach. Some of the older women never pass without a friendly greeting, never pass, indeed, if it seems that they will be able to engage me in conversation; other women look down or look away or rather contemptuously smirk. Some of the men drink with me and suggest that I learn how to ski—

partly, I gather, because they cannot imagine what I would look like on skis—and want to know if I am married, and ask questions about my *métier*. But some of the men have accused *le sale nègre*—behind my back—of stealing wood and there is already in the eyes of some of them that peculiar, intent, paranoiac malevolence which one sometimes surprises in the eyes of American white men when, out walking with their Sunday girl, they see a Negro male approach.

There is a dreadful abyss between the streets of this village and the streets of the city in which I was born, between the children who shout *Neger!* today and those who shouted *Nigger!* yesterday—the abyss is experience, the American experience. The syllable hurled behind me today expresses, above all, wonder: I am a stranger here. But I am not a stranger in America and the same syllable riding on the American air expresses the war my presence has occasioned in the American soul.

For this village brings home to me this fact: that there was a day, and not really a very distant day, when Americans were scarcely Americans at all but discontented Europeans, facing a great unconquered continent and strolling, say, into a marketplace and seeing black men for the first time. The shock this spectacle afforded is suggested, surely, by the promptness with which they decided that these black men were not really men but cattle. It is true that the necessity on the part of the settlers of the New World of reconciling their moral assumptions with the fact—and the necessity—of slavery enhanced immensely the charm of this idea, and it is also true that this idea expresses, with a truly American bluntness, the attitude which to varying extents all masters have had toward all slaves.

But between all former slaves and slave-owners and the drama which begins for Americans over three hundred years ago at Jamestown, there are at least two differences to be observed. The American Negro slave could not suppose, for one thing, as slaves in past epochs had supposed and often done, that he would ever be able to wrest the power from his master's hands. This was a supposition which the modern era, which was to bring about such vast changes in the aims and dimensions of power, put to death; it only begins, in unprecedented fashion, and with dreadful implications, to be resurrected today. But even had this supposition persisted with undiminished force, the American Negro slave could not have used it to lend his condition dignity, for the reason that this supposition rests on another: that the slave in exile yet remains related to his past, has some means—if only in memory—of revering and sustaining the forms of his former life, is able, in short, to maintain his identity.

This was not the case with the American Negro slave. He is unique among the black men of the world in that his past was taken from him, almost literally, at one blow. One wonders what on earth the first slave found to say to the first dark child he bore. I am told that there are Haitians able to trace their ancestry back to African kings, but any American Negro wishing to go back so far will find his journey through time abruptly arrested by the signature on the bill of sale which served as the entrance paper for his ancestor. At the time—to say nothing of the circumstances—of the enslavement of the captive black man who was to become the American Negro, there was not the remotest possibility that he would ever take power from his master's hands. There was no reason to suppose that his situation would ever change, nor was there, shortly, anything to indicate that his situation had ever been different. It was his necessity, in the words of E. Franklin Frazier, to find a "motive for living under American culture or die." The identity of the American Negro comes out of this extreme situation, and the evolution of this identity was a source of the most intolerable anxiety in the minds and the lives of his masters.

For the history of the American Negro is unique also in this: that the question of his humanity, and of his rights therefore as a human being, became a burning one for several generations of Americans, so burning a question that it ultimately became one of those used to divide the nation. It is out of this argument that the venom of the epithet *Nigger!* is derived. It is an argument which Europe has never had, and hence Europe quite sincerely fails to understand how or why the argument arose in the first place, why its effects are so frequently disastrous and always so unpredictable, why it refuses until today to be entirely settled. Europe's black possessions remained—and do remain—in Europe's colonies, at which remove they represented no threat whatever to European identity. If they posed any problem at all for the European conscience, it was a problem which remained comfortingly abstract: in effect, the black man, *as a man*, did not exist for Europe. But in America, even as a slave, he was an inescapable part of the general social fabric and no American could escape having an attitude toward him. Americans attempt until today to make an abstraction of the Negro, but the very nature of these abstractions reveals the tremendous effects the presence of the Negro has had on the American character.

When one considers the history of the Negro in America it is of the greatest importance to recognize that the moral beliefs of a person, or a people, are never really as tenuous as life—which is not moral—very often causes them to appear; these create for them a frame of reference and a necessary hope, the hope being that when life has done its worst they will be enabled to rise above themselves and to triumph over life. Life would scarcely be bearable if this hope did not exist. Again, even when the worst has been said, to betray a belief is not by any means to have put oneself beyond its power; the betrayal of a belief is not the same thing as ceasing to believe. If this were not so there would be no moral standards in the world at all. Yet one must also recognize that morality is based on ideas and that all ideas are dangerous—dangerous because ideas can only lead to action and where the action leads no man can say. And dangerous in this respect: that confronted with the impossibility of remaining faithful to one's beliefs, and the equal impossibility of becoming free of them, one can be driven to the most inhuman excesses. The ideas on which American beliefs are based are not, though Americans often seem to think so, ideas which originated in America. They came out of Europe. And the establishment of democracy on the American continent was scarcely as radical a break with the past as was the necessity, which Americans faced, of broadening this concept to include black men.

This was, literally, a hard necessity. It was impossible, for one thing, for Americans to abandon their beliefs, not only because these beliefs alone seemed able to justify the sacrifices they had endured and the blood that they had spilled, but also because these beliefs afforded them their only bulwark against a moral chaos as absolute as the physical chaos of the continent it was their destiny to conquer. But in the situation in which Americans found themselves, these beliefs threatened an idea which, whether or not one likes to think so, is the very warp and woof of the heritage of the West, the idea of white supremacy.

Americans have made themselves notorious by the shrillness and the brutality with which they have insisted on this idea, but they did not invent it; and it has escaped the world's notice that those very excesses of which Americans have been guilty imply a certain, unprecedented uneasiness over the idea's life and power, if not, indeed, the idea's validity. The idea of white supremacy rests simply on the fact that white men are the creators of civilization (the present civilization, which is the only one that matters; all previous civilizations are simply "contributions" to our own) and are therefore civilization's guardians and defenders. Thus it was impossible for Americans to accept the black man as one of themselves, for to do so was to jeopardize their status as white men. But not so to accept him was to deny his human reality, his human weight and complexity, and the strain of denying the overwhelmingly undeniable forced Americans into rationalizations so fantastic that they approached the pathological.

At the root of the American Negro problem is the necessity of the American white man to find a way of living with the

Negro in order to be able to live with himself. And the history of this problem can be reduced to the means used by Americans—lynch law and law, segregation and legal acceptance, terrorization and concession—either to come to terms with this necessity, or to find a way around it, or (most usually) to find a way of doing both these things at once. The resulting spectacle, at once foolish and dreadful, led someone to make the quite accurate observation that "the Negro-in-America is a form of insanity which overtakes white men."

In this long battle, a battle by no means finished, the unforeseeable effects of which will be felt by many future generations, the white man's motive was the protection of his identity; the black man was motivated by the need to establish an identity. And despite the terrorization which the Negro in America endured and endures sporadically until today, despite the cruel and totally inescapable ambivalence of his status in his country, the battle for his identity has long ago been won. He is not a visitor to the West, but a citizen there, an American; as American as the Americans who despise him, the Americans who fear him, the Americans who love him— the Americans who became less than themselves, or rose to be greater than themselves by virtue of the fact that the challenge he represented was inescapable. He is perhaps the only black man in the world whose relationship to white men is more terrible, more subtle, and more meaningful than the relationship of bitter possessed to uncertain possessor. His survival depended, and his development depends, on his ability to turn his peculiar status in the Western world to his own advantage and, it may be, to the very great advantage of that world. It remains for him to fashion out of his experience that which will give him sustenance, and a voice.

The cathedral at Chartres, I have said, says something to the people of this village which it cannot say to me; but it is important to understand that this cathedral says something to me which it cannot say to them. Perhaps they are struck by the power of the spires, the glory of the windows; but they have known God, after all, longer than I have known him, and in a different way, and I am terrified by the slippery bottomless well to be found in the crypt, down which heretics were hurled to death, and by the obscene, inescapable gargoyles jutting out of the stone and seeming to say that God and the devil can never be divorced. I doubt that the villagers think of the devil when they face a cathedral because they have never been identified with the devil. But I must accept the status which myth, if nothing else, gives me in the West before I can hope to change the myth.

Yet, if the American Negro has arrived at his identity by virtue of the absoluteness of his estrangement from his past, American white men still nourish the illusion that there is some means of recovering the European innocence, of returning to a state in which black men do not exist. This is one of the greatest errors Americans can make. The identity they fought so hard to protect has, by virtue of that battle, undergone a change: Americans are as unlike any other white people in the world as it is possible to be. I do not think, for example, that it is too much to suggest that the American vision of the world—which allows so little reality, generally speaking, for any of the darker forces in human life, which tends until today to paint moral issues in glaring black and white—owes a great deal to the battle waged by Americans to maintain between themselves and black men a human separation which could not be bridged. It is only now beginning to be borne in on us—very faintly, it must be admitted, very slowly, and very much against our will—that this vision of the world is dangerously inaccurate, and perfectly useless. For it protects our moral high-mindedness at the terrible expense of weakening our grasp of reality. People who shut their eyes to reality simply invite their own destruction, and anyone who insists on remaining in a state of innocence long after that innocence is dead turns himself into a monster.

The time has come to realize that the interracial drama acted out on the American continent has not only created a new black man, it has created a new white man, too. No road whatever will lead Americans back to the simplicity of this

European village where white men still have the luxury of looking on me as a stranger. I am not, really, a stranger any longer for any American alive. One of the things that distinguishes Americans from other people is that no other people has ever been so deeply involved in the lives of black men, and vice versa. This fact faced, with all its implications, it can be seen that the history of the American Negro problem is not merely shameful, it is also something of an achievement. For even when the worst has been said, it must also be added that the perpetual challenge posed by this problem was always, somehow, perpetually met. It is precisely this black-white experience which may prove of indispensable value to us in the world we face today. This world is white no longer, and it will never be white again.

1. *Why does Baldwin give you so many descriptive details about the Swiss village at the beginning of his essay? Do they later help you to understand his own situation in the village? How do they contribute to his more general argument about the relationship between blacks and whites?*

2. *What significance does Baldwin find in the villagers' behavior toward him personally? In their collections for the African missions? Why does this experience in Switzerland rather than some American experience make him contemplate racial issues?*

3. *Once Baldwin has described the village, how much of the rest of the essay refers to his own experiences in the village? Where in the essay does he bring up these experiences and why?*

4. *How broadly does Baldwin attempt to generalize on the basis of his experience? How varied are the levels of generalization he introduces and how often does he clearly shift from one level to another?*

5. *What gives Baldwin his authority when he speaks so broadly of "people" or "white men" or "Negro Americans"? How does he make you pay attention to his generalizations and consider them seriously?*

∽ George Orwell ∽

(1903-1950)

See the biographical note on page 61. "Such, Such Were the Joys" was found among Orwell's papers after his death. It is based on his years (1911–1916) at St. Cyprian's (called Crossgates in the essay), a preparatory school where Orwell lived as a poor scholarship student among much wealthier classmates. Bingo and Sim, referred to in the essay, were the headmaster of the school and his wife; Orwell uses the nicknames they were given by the students. The selection here is the last of the six sections that comprise the essay.

SUCH, SUCH WERE THE JOYS

[CHILDREN AT SCHOOLS]

All this was thirty years ago and more. The question is: Does a child at school go through the same kind of experiences nowadays?

The only honest answer, I believe, is that we do not with certainty know. Of course it is obvious that the present-day *attitude* towards education is enormously more humane and sensible than that of the past. The snobbishness that was an integral part of my own education would be almost unthinkable today, because the society that nourished it is dead. I recall a conversation that must have taken place about a year before I left Crossgates. A Russian boy, large and fair-haired, a year older than myself, was questioning me.

"How much a-year has your father got?"

I told him what I thought it was, adding a few hundreds to make it sound better. The Russian boy, neat in his habits, produced a pencil and a small notebook and made a calculation.

"My father has over two hundred times as much money as yours," he announced with a sort of amused contempt.

That was in 1915. What happened to that money a couple of years later, I wonder? And still more I wonder, do conversations of that kind happen at preparatory schools now?

Clearly there has been a vast change of outlook, a general growth of "enlightenment," even among ordinary, unthinking middle-class people. Religious belief, for instance, has largely vanished, dragging other kinds of nonsense after it. I imagine that very few people nowadays would tell a child that if it masturbates it will end in the lunatic asylum. Beating, too, has become discredited, and has even been abandoned at many schools. Nor is the underfeeding of children looked on as a normal, almost meritorious act. No one now would openly set out to give his pupils as little food as they could do with, or tell them that it is healthy to get up from a meal as hungry as you sat down. The whole status of children has improved, partly because they have grown relatively less numerous. And the diffusion of even a little psychological knowledge has made it harder for parents and schoolteachers to indulge their aberrations in the name of discipline. Here is a case, not known to me personally, but known to someone I can vouch for, and happening within my own lifetime. A small girl, daughter of a clergyman, continued wetting her bed at an age when she should have grown out of it. In order to punish her for this dreadful deed, her father took her to a large garden party and there introduced her to the whole company as a little girl who wetted her bed: and to underline her wickedness he had previously painted her face black. I do not suggest that Bingo and Sim would actually have done a thing like this, but I doubt whether it would have much surprised them. After all, things do change. And yet—!

The question is not whether boys are still buckled into Eton collars on Sunday, or told that babies are dug up under gooseberry bushes. That kind of thing is at an end, admittedly. The real question is whether it is still normal for a school child to live for years amid irrational terrors and lunatic misunderstandings. And here one is up against the very great difficulty of knowing what a child really feels and thinks. A child which appears reasonably happy may actually be suffering horrors which it cannot or will not reveal. It lives in a sort of alien under-water world which we can only penetrate by memory or divination. Our chief clue is the fact that we were once children ourselves, and many people appear to forget the atmosphere of their own childhood almost entirely. Think for instance of the unnecessary torments that people will inflict by sending a child back to school with clothes of the wrong pattern, and refusing to see that this matters! Over things of this kind a child will sometimes utter a protest, but a great deal of the time its attitude is one of simple concealment. Not to expose your true feelings to an adult seems to be instinctive from the age of seven or eight onwards. Even the affection that one feels for a child, the desire to protect and cherish it, is a cause of misunderstanding. One can love a child, perhaps, more deeply than one can love another adult, but it is rash to assume that the child feels any love in return. Looking back on my own childhood, after the infant years were over, I do not believe that I ever felt love for any mature person, except my mother, and even her I did not trust, in the sense that shyness made me conceal most of my real feelings from her. Love, the spontaneous, unqualified emotion of love, was something I could only feel for people who were young. Towards people who were old—and remember that "old" to a child means over thirty, or even over twenty-five—I could feel reverence, respect, admiration or compunction, but I seemed cut off from them by a veil of fear and shyness mixed up with physical distaste. People are too ready to forget the child's *physical* shrinking from the adult. The enormous size of grownups, their ungainly, rigid bodies, their coarse wrinkled skins, their great relaxed eyelids, their yellow teeth, and the whiffs of musty clothes and beer and sweat and tobacco that disengage from them at every movement! Part of the reason for the ugliness of adults, in a child's eyes, is that the child is usually looking upwards, and few faces are at their best when seen from below. Besides, being fresh and unmarked itself, the child has impossibly high standards in the matter of skin and teeth and complexion. But the greatest barrier of all is the child's misconception about age. A child can hardly envisage life beyond thirty, and in judging people's ages it will make fantastic mistakes. It will think that a person of twenty-five is forty, that a person of forty is sixty-five, and so on. Thus, when I fell in love with Elsie I took her to be grown up. I met her again, when I was thirteen and she, I think, must have been twenty-three; she now seemed to me a middle-aged woman, somewhat past her best. And the child thinks of growing old as an almost obscene calamity, which for some mysterious reason will never happen to itself. All who have passed the age of thirty are joyless grotesques, endlessly fussing about things of no importance and staying alive without, so far as the child can see, having anything to live for. Only child life is real life. The schoolmaster who imagines he is loved and trusted by his boys is in fact mimicked and laughed at behind his back. An adult who does not seem dangerous nearly always seems ridiculous.

I base these generalisations on what I can recall of my own childhood outlook. Treacherous though memory is, it seems to me the chief means we have of discovering how a child's mind works. Only by resurrecting our own memories can we realise how incredibly distorted is the child's vision of the world. Consider this, for example. How would Crossgates appear to me now, if I could go back, at my present age, and see it as it was in 1915? What should I think of Bingo and Sim, those terrible, all-powerful monsters? I should see them as a couple of silly, shallow, ineffectual people, eagerly clambering up a social ladder which any thinking person could see to be on the point of collapse. I would be no more frightened of them than I would be frightened of a dormouse. Moreover, in those days they seemed to me fantastically old, whereas—though of this I am not certain—I imagine they must have been somewhat younger than I am now. And how would Johnny Hall appear, with his blacksmith's arms and his red, jeering face? Merely a scruffy little boy, barely distinguishable from hundreds of other scruffy little boys. The two sets of facts can lie side by side in my mind, because these happen to be my own memories. But it would be very difficult for me to see with the eyes of any other child, except by an effort of the imagination which might lead me completely astray. The child and the adult live in different worlds. If that is so, we cannot be certain that school, at any rate boarding school, is not still for many children as dreadful an experience as it used to be. Take away God, Latin, the cane, class distinctions and sexual taboos, and the fear, the hatred, the snobbery and the misunderstanding might still all be there. It will have been seen that my own main trouble was an utter lack of any sense of proportion or probability. This led me to accept outrages and believe absurdities, and to suffer torments over things which were in fact of no importance. It is not enough to say that I was "silly" and "ought to have known better." Look back into your own childhood and think of the nonsense you used to believe and the trivialities which could make you suffer. Of course my own case had its individual variations, but essentially it was that of countless other boys. The weakness of the child is that it starts with a blank sheet. It neither understands nor questions the society in which it lives, and because of its credulity other people can work upon it, infecting it with the sense of inferiority and the dread of offending against mysterious, terrible laws. It may be that everything that happened to me at Crossgates could happen in the most "enlightened" school, though perhaps in subtler forms. Of one thing, however, I do feel fairly sure, and that is that boarding schools are worse than day schools. A child has a better chance with the sanctuary of its home near at hand. And I think the characteristic faults of the English upper and middle classes may be partly due to the practice, general until recently, of sending children away from home as young as nine, eight or even seven.

I have never been back to Crossgates. In a way it is only within the last decade that I have really thought over my schooldays, vividly though their memory has haunted me. Nowadays, I believe, it would make very little impression on me to see the place again, if it still exists. And if I went inside and smelt again the inky, dusty smell of the big schoolroom, the rosiny smell of the chapel, the stagnant smell of the swimming bath and the cold reek of the lavatories, I think I should only feel what one invariably feels in revisiting any scene of childhood: How small everything has grown, and how terrible is the deterioration in myself!

1. This selection is the final section of a six-part essay based on Orwell's own experiences as a scholarship boy at an English preparatory school. How does Orwell's method make clear that he is concluding the essay?

2. What sort of perspective has the passage of thirty years given to Orwell as he writes about school? How does he organize the selection to reflect his mature experience?

3. Since Orwell's own schooling occurred so many years earlier, how is he able to make use of it as support for his present views of the school situation? When and how does he refer to his own experience for illustration?

4. How much of what Orwell sees as the difficulties children experience does he relate to flaws in schools, how much to the condition of childhood itself? Do you think Orwell's primary purpose here is to encourage educational reform?

∽ V. S. Pritchett ∽

(1900-   )

V. S. Pritchett typifies the English man of letters. He has written in virtually every form: novels, short stories, travel books, essays, literary criticism, and reminiscences. He has also been remarkably consistent as well as prolific, publishing a volume every year or two, each one showing the mark of a skillful and thoughtful writer. His autobiographical volumes, A Cab At the Door *(1968) and* Midnight Oil *(1971) are portraits of a genteel and eccentric English world that no longer exists.*

WRITING AN AUTOBIOGRAPHY

On the face of it, to write one's autobiography is the easiest and most grateful task in the world. No search for anti-hero or hero: he is you. No search for material, it is all there: your own life. No imagination is necessary; the question of structure—one of the most difficult problems in writing—is automatically solved by sticking to chronology, year after year. The first person singular seems to be the perfect camera-eye. Unless you suffer from a neurotic block, your childhood and early youth have long ago crystallized. This is the most vivid and certain part of your life.

So you set out. You write 20 pages and suddenly you stop. Why is it you are bewildered? Why do you have the sensation of being in a rowing boat in the middle of the ocean and having lost your oars? Who is this "I," you wonder, which of my many selves is writing? And what kind of autobiography did you mean to write? What is its theme? There is nothing to do but start again.

Let us suppose you are a famous statesman or general, a great bull fighter, opera singer, a surgeon or sportsman, or that you have been very close to the famous, a valet of the eminent. You have made your career; you have had adventures; you have known crowds of people. You will have kept notes, letters and diaries all your life. The public will expect that you reveal what you know and will hang upon your indiscretion. You will be writing your reminiscences or a memoir; you will not in the strict sense be writing your autobiography at all. Your truth will be a contribution to social history or anecdotage. Or suppose you have been the witness of a great event and put that down: the event and not yourself is the subject. You will be only a collection of enviable glimpses. What if you are a natural diarist—say, a Pepys or an Amiel—and inevitably reveal yourself? Does that make you an autobiographer? Rarely.

The born diarists are the snails of life: they are secretive and enclosed in their shells, and their whispering contributes either to history or—as in Amiel's case—to a case history. The pure autobiographer is concerned with shaping a past from the standpoint of a present that may be totally unlike it. That is why you tore up those 20 pages and paused to consider who your first-person singular is and what "truth" you intend to state.

For there is no absolute truth. You will be unable to tell all or you will be incapable of it. Or let us hope that you are, for one definition of a bore is that he is a man who tells you everything. The writer who has—and quotes—his diaries or preserved letters is in great danger here: this has been the bane of Victorian autobiography and is a continuing danger in America where keeping records has been enjoined almost as a historical obligation. The Boston memoir is the classic example.

Your difficulties with truth-telling arise from the fossilization of memory. Perhaps hypnosis could dissolve a trauma that has become sacred; but I cannot see what can be done about the fact that it is easier to remember things that happened 40 years ago than those that occurred in the last 10. Our lives are really a collection of adroit generalizations which enable us to push on from the present minute. The longer one lives, the less certain one is of who one is. So many people and events have swarmed in that the sense of a self—Gray's "pleasing anxious being"—who lives an hour, a day at a time and not in collections of years, is dispersed and even vulgarized. One begins to think there was no "I" after all.

And, in fact, the "I" is a relatively new invention. To start with, it is exclusively European in origin. Asia and Africa have no autobiographers. About seven years ago I read an excellent if severe book called "Design and Truth in Autobiography" by Roy Pascal, who pointed this out and added that in Europe there are no autobiographies in the classical period.

The genre can be said to have started with St. Augustine, but centuries passed before a Cellini, a Geronimo Cardano, a Saint Theresa appeared in the Renaissance. Unlike ourselves these writers are not recreating a past from the standpoint of the present; Cellini casting his statue, Saint Theresa in founding her convent, are proclaiming new selves in a new world and are conscious of themselves in the act. They differ from us in being very little conscious of their society as an overwhelming influence.

It is not until we reach the 18th and early 19th centuries that the confidence a man has in his society and his belief in the pleasure and interest of his private tastes and habits give him an avid concern with himself in relation to it. It is the age of the great autobiographers—of Rousseau, Gibbon, Franklin, Goethe and Casanova. Later, the strenuous effort towards self-realization among the new middle class, urged on also by the idea of the Romantic movement, gives us Harriet Martineau, John Stuart Mill, John Ruskin, even Henry Adams, and still later Wells and Beatrice Webb. Leonard Woolf's recent volumes are written as a valediction to a civilization determined on suicide.

In our own time, Mr. Pascal says, a writer like Koestler shows the self passing through historical calamity and asking why it was so chosen. One offers oneself as a sample of the historical process in one's own life time. And here, I wonder, if the present vogue of autobiography has not something dubious about it. Doesn't calamity really make nonsense of the distinctive individual; doesn't its stamp make us all alike?

What reason have I to believe that I have more than the common interest? I may be only a type. Am I dramatizing myself because I am lonely? The "I" in Cellini or Goethe, Newman and Henry James is a pronoun of pride; isn't it a badge of wistful desperation for us, the only thing left so that it has to "do" for everything we have lost? Fortunately for the autobiographer the social process still goes on even if it runs down, and the individual still asserts himself, but frantically now in the midst of it.

I have myself written an autobiography and can speak of the practical difficulties. I was forced to reject the official sounding family memoir. Unlike Bertrand Russell, I am not a great man or a public figure. I cannot draw on distinguished, public-spirited ancestors or famous family connections. I have visited Society, but, like most writers, only for a minute or two. That kind of life is no good to us. I have belonged to no celebrated set, and although I have met many celebrated people (for, as they say of London life, everyone knows everybody), I have not been very intimate with them. My most intimate meeting, I think, was with Georges Carpentier, the French boxer, who accidentally stepped back and trod hard on my toe on the Channel boat when I was off to France in my twenties. He walked away without saying a word.

As for my literary reminiscences or my reflections on literature in the past 45 years, they must wait. I am not fond of shop talk. But, being self-centered I could not resist writing about the unlikely background that made a writer of me. I confined myself to my prewriting years. At 21 they ended; after that, being a writer, I found myself being met by what I had already written.

After 21, unless one is a note-taker, a letter keeper or diarist —which I have rarely been—memory blurs, years and phases telescope. What about my inner life? I have not so far shown any talent for the confessional. That requires a certain temperament. In one sense all writing is a confession. But after 21, whether he is confessional or not, the autobiographer who writes intimately is in the difficulty that many people who were important to him are still alive. As a storyteller I have no consideration for people; nor should I have. But I cannot involve the living in my "truth" (though I have to admit that the discarded mistresses of great artists have not hesitated here).

The odd thing is that sitters will often tolerate a portrait done "warts and all" by a painter, but do not care for the same thing in print. They ring up their lawyers at once; and even praise offends, for one has not praised them for what they would like to be praised. From the autobiographer's point of view, people live far too long. Society asks too much of the "truthful" autobiographer when it obliges him to live on to his nineties before he can speak. By that time, as Somerset Maugham's nonagenarian revelations showed, one is apt to be vinegarish.

I can think of no vainglorious autobiography since Cellini, unless Frank Harris counts. There have been dedicated believers in imaginative lying like Ford Madox Ford. Goethe spoke of his "poetry" but also of his "truth." There have been exploiters of self-accusation like Rousseau. The three main difficulties of autobiography are one's self-pity, one's shames and one's self-justifications. It is also difficult to write exactly about chastity in a period like the present when it is regarded as ridiculous. Only the Turgenevs can write about early love; only the Pushkins can tell with a poet's brutality of how and why it ends. To feel is to tire. So much of love is love of love. It is also hard to record one's early opinions truthfully: one has forgotten their force. Self-pity is fairly easy to deal with now for we have been toughened. As for shame, one must not wallow. The youth you are ashamed of was, among other things, an engaging fellow; if he was a prig and pompous ass most of his contemporaries were pompous asses and prigs too. It was part of the general charm. The French who have an extreme regard for the solemnities of adolescence miss this romantic Anglo-Saxon worry. The real problem is how to avoid subtle and secretive self-justification, especially when one is recording discarded emotions or beliefs. Here one's standpoint of a present totally unlike the past is liable to bully or skillfully deceive.

Roy Pascal points out that Tolstoy's "A Confession" like other confessions of religious experience, has the fault of devaluing earlier experience, so that the unity of personality is broken. The sinner and the reformed sinner are, in fact, inseparable, and it is hard to admit this. We usually cover up by one or two eloquent but hollow passages. Schweitzer makes his development too logical. Henry Adams was attached to democratic ideas for longer than he admits in the "Education." We are so anxious to show that our blatant errors did not last a long time.

This common dilemma would vanish if we saw that it is normal for many of us to hold one belief or emotion and its opposite at the same time. And here it is hard to admit that one was swayed by snobbery, self-interest or the influence of persons now despised. It is hard not to convey that only the highest considerations really weighed with one. The phlegm and coolness of a Gibbon with his "I sighed as a lover but obeyed as a son" is beyond most of us. And it is dangerous even to be too good at candor; it may be nothing but vanity which was Valéry's criticism of Gide (Again I take this from Mr. Pascal): "To spin words to one's confessor is a serious matter: it will make him forget to absolve you."

For myself I had long ago recognized that, like my storytelling mother, I was an inventive person. I was one of those, I had to see, who invents himself and had not much capacity for

402

self-analysis or introspection except of the dreariest kind. I would be less interested in myself than the story I saw in other people: the most boring part of my autobiography described my early literary efforts. I could only be careless, so that my character, for good or ill, would become plain in what I said about others. I novelized and was, no doubt, inaccurate in this or that, but I told my truth. I never cease to be startled by the fantastic interior of most lives. I inherit a good ear and memory for what is spoken: I swear by the dialogue I have written.

My judgments are another matter. A more earnest, more detailed and documented narrative might have been more accurate. I think it would have been tedious. A tragic interpretation could have been made. Either would have been "true." I would find it impossible to continue the story of my life in the same vein. This suggests to me that where modern autobiography so often fails is that it tends to be written in the same key throughout.

1. Do you have the impression from this essay that Pritchett would be an interesting writer of autobiography himself? Why or why not?

2. To what extent does Pritchett make this essay autobiographical? In what ways does he enlarge upon his own experience to give a more general view of autobiography?

3. What use does Pritchett make of history in his essay? Does his discussion of the tradition of autobiography strike you as particularly scholarly? If not, how does he make you take his point of view seriously?

4. How does Pritchett organize his different observations about autobiography? Does the separation of the essay into two sections have some organizational basis that makes sense to you?

5. Summarize what you think Pritchett sees as the most important problems for the autobiographer. Can you identify selections in this collection that reflect one or another of these problems? Have you found any of these problems causing you difficulties in your own autobiographical writing?

Possibilities for Writing

1. Look back at some experience that covered an extended period of time in your life and is now over—for example, your senior year in high school, your last year in a high school club or on an athletic team, your summer job, a vacation trip you took that lasted several weeks. Write an essay in which you interpret and evaluate that experience, showing what it meant in the overall pattern of your life.

2. After you have read V. S. Pritchett's essay in this chapter, write your own essay on the subject of autobiography. Draw on the experience you have had during the semester to help you explain the special characteristics or the special difficulties of autobiographical writing.

3. Write an essay in which you use your personal experience as part of an argument for some specific social or institutional changes. For example, you could relate your own school experiences to some larger argument for changes that would make schools better or your own experiences as a driver to more general views of transportation problems.

4. Write an essay explaining whether Joyce Maynard convinces you that she speaks for her generation or not. Try to show as specifically as you can what you think her methods of establishing herself as a spokesman are and in what ways they succeed or fail.

5. Choose three of the Orwell essays in this anthology and show how they reveal themselves to be the work of a single writer. Concern yourself with Orwell's attitudes, his way of characterizing himself, and his way of presenting events and people.